ASSESSING AND MANAGING RISK IN PSYCHOLOGICAL PRACTICE:

An Individualized Approach

Bruce E. Bennett, PhD
American Psychological Association Insurance Trust

Patricia M. Bricklin, PhD
American Psychological Association Insurance Trust
Widener University

Eric Harris, JD, EdD
American Psychological Association Insurance Trust

Samuel Knapp, EdD
Pennsylvania Psychological Association

Leon VandeCreek, PhD
Wright State University

Jeffrey N. Younggren, PhD
American Psychological Association Insurance Trust

THE TRUST
Rockville, MD

Published by:
The Trust
111 Rockville Pike
Suite 900
Rockville, MD 20850

Printer: Automated Graphic Systems, Inc.
Cover design: Jeannie Chung
Page layout: Sean Kennedy

Library of Congress Cataloging-in-Publication Data
Assessing and Managing Risk in Psychological Practice:
An Individualized Approach/Bruce E. Bennett,
Patricia M. Bricklin, Eric Harris, Samuel Knapp,
Leon VandeCreek and Jeffrey N. Younggren

Includes bibliographical references and index.
ISBN 978-0-615-13416-1

PCN 2007902030

CONTENTS

ACKNOWLEDGMENTS

We thank the Massachusetts Psychological Association for allowing us to adapt portions of the following articles:

Harris, E. (2003, Winter). Resolving some areas of continuing confusion. *MassPsych: The Journal of the Massachusetts Psychological Association, 47,* 18–22, 29.

Harris, E. (2004, Spring/Summer). Some (relatively) simple risk management strategies. *Mass Psych: The Journal of the Massachusetts Psychological Association, 48,* 27–28.

We thank the Pennsylvania Psychological Association for allowing us to reprint portions of the following articles:

Knapp, S. (2003, August). Could the Titanic disaster have been avoided? Or promoting patient welfare through a systems approach. *The Pennsylvania Psychologist, 63,* 4, 18, 36.

Knapp, S. (2004, November). Well-being and professional development among psychologists. *The Pennsylvania Psychologist, 64,* 13, 17.

Knapp, S., & Baturin, R. (2003, March). Child custody and custody-related evaluations and interventions: What every psychologist should know. *The Pennsylvania Psychologist, 63,* 3–5.

Knapp, S., & Lemoncelli, J. (2005, October). Treating children in high-conflict families. *The Pennsylvania Psychologist, 65,* 4.

Knapp, S., Tepper, A., & Baturin, R. (2003, August). Practical considerations when responding to subpoenas and court orders. *The Pennsylvania Psychologist, 63,* 5, 16.

Mapes, B., & Knapp, S. (2005, December). Ethical and professional issues in assessing sexual offenders. *The Pennsylvania Psychologist, 65,* 3–4.

PREFACE

Practicing psychology is hard work. If you are the average psychologist, you are intelligent, hardworking, and committed to your profession. Yet you may find it difficult to do your best work in today's environment.

If you are the average psychologist who was licensed before 1990, you started your career in a practice environment in which managed care had minimal impact, and there was little risk of disciplinary action. You may not have had a separate ethics course in graduate school. Perhaps ethics was embedded in other courses or was something you were expected to pick up informally from your teachers and supervisors. You may have been shocked when you learned that one of your respected colleagues was accused of unethical behavior, disciplined by a licensing board, or removed from a managed care panel. You may have felt offended or anxious when you learned of the increase in legal risks when practicing psychology.

If you are the average psychologist who was licensed after 1990, you have practiced most of your career with managed care, may have had a separate graduate course in ethics, and have practiced in an environment in which legal risks are an acknowledged reality. In a sense, your career is easier because you did not know the autonomy and freedom enjoyed in the days before managed care. Nonetheless, you share the same professional hassles and stressors as your older colleagues. While we cannot make these hassles and stressors go away, we hope that this book will help you make some of them more manageable.

STRIVE FOR EXCELLENCE, NOT PERFECTION

You will make mistakes. In a litigious environment, psychologists may get the impression that they have to be perfect and cannot make any mistakes. That standard is unrealistic. You will make mistakes. Doing something that, in hindsight, was a mistake does not necessarily mean that you have been unethical or incompetent as long as you based your decision on generally acceptable clinical reasoning and knowledge. Our goal is to help you avoid making big mistakes and to minimize the frequency of smaller mistakes.

> You will make mistakes.
>
> You cannot help everyone.
>
> You will not know everything.
>
> You cannot go it alone.
>
> It is helpful to have a proper mix of confidence and humility.

You can't help everyone. But that doesn't mean that you can't help a lot of people. It does not make you incompetent or insensitive if you turn away a patient who requires services beyond your expertise or competence or who has treatment needs that exceed your resources. In fact, it is prudent to select patients with deliberation.

You won't know everything. Your training and experience should have been broad enough to enable you to assist the large majority of your patients. Also, it would be ideal if you knew enough to assist colleagues who seek your consultation on problematic cases on which you have special expertise. However, it is important that you know the limitations of your skills or your "personal skill inventory."

You cannot go it alone. You will have a much more difficult career and higher degree of risk if you try to go it alone. You will have no one around to tell you when you are about to make a mistake, when you are overestimating your competence in an area, when your skills are getting rusty, or when you have not kept up with advances in the field. Outliers risk becoming outlaws. (Remember, there are six authors of this book; none of us could have done as good a job if each of us had tried to write it alone.)

It is helpful to have a proper mix of confidence and humility. However, psychologists, by accepting their limitations and working together, can pool their resources, benefit from their collective wisdom, upgrade the quality of their services, help more people, and limit their risks. Psychologists are part of a long tradition of healers, motivated by compassion, grounded in science, and enriched by their profession's heritage. Ideally, this book is one small step in furthering that heritage.

When Sternberg explained why smart people do foolish things, he noted that they often make mistakes because they fail to recognize the limits of their own knowledge or fail to consider the interests of other people. Although intelligence and knowledge are important, Sternberg argued for the importance of wisdom or "the use of one's intelligence and creativity toward a common good through balancing one's interests, other people's interests and infusing moral and ethical values" (Sternberg, 2003, p. 5).

AN INDIVIDUALIZED NEW MODEL OF RISK MANAGEMENT

In this book, we present a new model for assessing and managing risk. We have been teaching ethics and risk management for years, as instructors in doctoral programs, teachers in continuing education programs, or consultants for individual psychologists on particular cases. We have helped many psychologists practice more ethically and safely. At the same time, our students, colleagues, workshop participants, and consultees have taught us much about how to present risk management principles and what to emphasize. Although the areas of risk and basic principles of risk management have stayed the same, our audiences have told us that they need to go beyond the basics and have requested that we go beyond the cookbook approach to ethics and risk management.

The earlier model of risk management focused on attacking denial or ignorance of risks, often by emphasizing the career-altering (or career-ending) consequences of a malpractice suit or disciplinary action. The earlier model also told you how the disciplinary systems worked and focused on the necessity of certain—almost universal—risk management strategies (e.g., consultation, documentation, and informed consent).

This new model assumes you have greater awareness of practice risks and a general familiarity with key risk management principles. We reiterate those risks and strategies throughout this book, but we go beyond them. We value your skills, acumen, and professional commitment. The new model encourages you to integrate your abilities, judgment, and dedication into your risk management strategies to improve the quality of patient care and reduce risks. We present two models (the risk management formula and Bloom's educational taxonomy) to illustrate how you can integrate risk management principles into your practice.

Under the old model, you needed to understand the basic concepts (such as consultation) and comprehend their purposes and when to apply them. Under the new model you are encouraged to integrate or synthesize the basic concepts into your overall system of patient management. The new model encourages you to think for yourself. We acknowledge that the minimum standards of professional conduct come from external resources such as professional codes of ethics, laws and regulations, and the mechanisms provided by disciplinary bodies. Nonetheless, the highest standards of professional conduct come from within. The three most important aspects of risk management are forethought (anticipation of problematic events), thought (mindfulness of relevant factors when resolving an immediate issue), and afterthought (learning from experience).

As a result, it is not appropriate for you to consider this book a manual that can present an absolute set of rules or give clear direction in every situation that arises. Instead, in this book, we describe a process or general format to help you consider and evaluate the factors that should guide your decisions. Of course, both the old and the new models appreciate that all psychologists must practice under a set of laws, regulations, and rules as determined by the American Psychological Association's "Ethical Principles of Psychologists and Code of Conduct" (APA Ethics Code; APA, 2002) or state and federal laws and regulations. We review the most salient of these laws in Section 3, chapters 2, 3, 4, 5, 6, 7, and 8.

USING THE RISK MANAGEMENT FORMULA TO DESCRIBE THE NEW MODEL

Throughout this book, we refer to the risk management formula (RM formula) as a heuristic to help you remember and think through the elements involved in assessing and reducing clinical, legal, and ethical risks. The basic RM formula is as follows:

$$\text{Clinical risk} = \frac{(P \times C \times D)}{TF}$$

In this formula, P = patient risk characteristics; C = context; D = disciplinary consequences; and TF = therapist factors.

The RM formula should help you remember facts and data that increase risks. However, the formula should do more, and ideally it can guide you in identifying ways that you can use your skills, judgment, and commitment in applying risk management procedures to reduce those risks. We describe and apply this RM formula in more detail in subsequent sections.

USING BLOOM'S TAXONOMY TO DESCRIBE THE NEW MODEL

The new model can be viewed according to an educational taxonomy based on the work of Bloom (1956). Educators have used Bloom's taxonomy for many years to describe the process and goals of education. According to Bloom, educational experiences can progress through six levels (knowledge, comprehension, application, analysis, synthesis, and evaluation). Thus, information goes from a basic memorization of facts to more complex levels, culminating in the application, analysis, and evaluation of information.

We apply Bloom's taxonomy to risk management and describe how psychologists can progress from basic levels in which they memorize risk management principles and ethical standards to higher levels in which they judiciously apply and integrate ethically based risk management principles into their day-to-day clinical decision making. The old model of risk management emphasized the lower three levels of Bloom's taxonomy (knowledge, comprehension, and application). The new model gives greater emphasis to the higher three levels (analysis, synthesis, and evaluation).

We begin by reviewing the format of Bloom's taxonomy before applying it directly to risk management. According to Bloom's Level 1, *knowledge* is remembering previously learned material such as specific facts. It represents the lowest level of learning. At the knowledge level, learners primarily read, take notes during lectures, or otherwise memorize information. For example, in the knowledge level of risk management, psychology learners (students, workshop participants, consultees, or readers) should be able to repeat the definition of risk management. (Risk management is the calculation of the probability of good or bad outcomes or consequences.)

In Level 2, *comprehension*, learners acquire the ability to grasp what the material means. It may mean translating material from one form to another or explaining or summarizing material. At the learning level, learners can demonstrate comprehension by explaining concepts to others. For example, at the comprehension level, learners can explain what risk management means.

Level 3, *application*, refers to the ability to use learned material in specific situations. The application level requires both knowledge and comprehension. At the application level, learners can apply the information to specific situations such as case vignettes, albeit at an elementary level.

Level 4, *analysis*, begins the level at which the new risk management model builds on previous models. Analysis refers to the ability to break down material into its components so that you can better understand its organization. Learning here requires an understanding of both the content and the structure or organization of information. For example, learners can apply, compare, or contrast the components of different risk management principles as they apply to specific cases.

Level 5, *synthesis*, refers to the ability to combine information to create meaningful structures. Learners can demonstrate synthetic ability when they are able to create a meaningful product or suggest helpful solutions to a problem. Whereas learners at the application level apply principles routinely and mechanically, learners at the synthesis level apply strategies based on overarching principles.

The last level, Level 6, *evaluation*, refers to the ability to judge the value of a given response. Learners demonstrate evaluative abilities by giving justifications or reasons for their decisions.

ORGANIZATION OF THE BOOK

This book is divided into three sections. In Section 1, we explain the types of professional risks, the disciplining processes of licensing boards and other disciplinary bodies, and basic information on incorporating ethical decision making into risk management decisions. In Section 2, we review three major facets of risk management: informed consent, documentation, and consultation. In Section 3, we review specific areas of professional liability, including competence, boundary violations, breaches of confidentiality, forensic work, psychological assessment, treating suicidal and other life-endangering patients, termination and abandonment, business issues, retirement and more. Throughout this book, we present and analyze case examples using the RM formula to illustrate risk management principles.

A FINAL NOTE

Ultimately risk management is a business decision in which you decide how much time and effort to put into implementing risk management principles into your professional practice (see Section 3, chap. 11, on insurance). We have tried to explain these risk management principles as clearly as possible. Whenever we thought it would be helpful, we added charts, illustrations, formulae, summary points, or memorable phrases to assist your learning.

If you have suggestions about how we might improve this book or the quality of teaching ethics and risk management in general, please e-mail us at RiskManagement@apait.org.

TAXONOMY OF RISK MANAGEMENT

Lower Levels

Knowledge: You have read the APA Ethics Code and are able to repeat and recognize many of the standards in the Code.

Comprehension: You can describe or summarize risk management to another psychologist (e.g., you are able to describe a potentially improper multiple relationship with a patient to another practitioner).

Application: In a given situation you can apply the relevant risk management principles (e.g., do not release confidential patient information without proper authorization).

Higher Levels

Analysis: You can separate risk management into general principles (such as informed consent, consultation, and documentation), compare and contrast their application, or categorize potential solutions.

Synthesis: You can incorporate risk management principles and the RM formula into your overall practice patterns. You can generalize them to novel situations and design or systematize risk management programs.

Evaluation: You can justify why you adopted certain risk management principles in your practice. You can compare different risk management strategies in specific situations and determine, evaluate, or infer their relative values.

It has been said that psychologists know more than they need to about how to do good in this world. That is, they tend to be "benefits oriented" and look for ways that they can help people. Although this is a commendable trait, it needs to be balanced with an appreciation that sometimes things do not go well, and sometimes things can go horribly wrong.

As much as we wish to be positive about the practice of psychology, bad events can and do occur. In this section, we describe one type of bad event (disciplinary actions from oversight bodies) that often occurs as a consequence of another type of bad event (patients being harmed or perceiving themselves to be harmed). It is an unfortunate reality that bad things happen to good psychologists. Highly competent psychologists may find themselves faced with a charge of ethical misconduct because they just happened to encounter the wrong patient under the wrong circumstances. However, by envisioning a worst-case scenario with a particular case, psychologists may be able to prevent themselves from experiencing that scenario. Fortunately, as we describe in more detail later, the acts that reduce the likelihood of disciplinary actions also decrease the likelihood of patients being harmed while at the same time increase the likelihood of patients being helped.

In this section, we review the elements that contribute to risk. Of course, one of the major factors that contributes to risk is your individual skills (we refer to them as individual therapist factors in the risk management [RM] formula that was introduced in the Preface), including the degree to which you can identify high-risk situations and follow the basic risk management elements (informed consent, documentation, and consultation) that we describe in detail in Section 2.

Risk is the calculation that a particular treatment, intervention, or service will lead to a good or bad outcome and that the outcome will have positive or negative consequences. This suggests that even good outcomes may have negative consequences and that bad outcomes do not always lead to negative consequences. Clearly, good outcomes are less likely to lead to negative consequences. Some risks are so remote that it does not make sense to expend energy to avoid them. Other risks are so serious that you should work hard to avoid them. Risk is a function of several factors that can be expressed in the RM formula,

$$\text{Clinical risk} = \frac{(P \times C \times D)}{TF}$$

In this formula, P = patient risk characteristics; C = context;
D = disciplinary consequences; and TF = therapist factors.

Clinical risk is determined by the interaction of all individual patient characteristics, the context of treatment, and individual therapist factors. Each of the elements of the formula is described in more detail below, although we give the most attention to individual therapist factors (your characteristics as a professional). Throughout this book we use this formula to analyze difficult patient management situations and recommend risk management solutions based on that analysis. Of course, this formula is heuristic. No formula can capture the dynamic and interactive nature of these factors. Nonetheless, we believe it will help you to conceptualize cases. We first review the factors in the RM formula and then present several examples in which the RM formula could be used.

PATIENT RISK CHARACTERISTICS

Psychologists who are involved in defending other psychologists in disciplinary proceedings have found certain characteristics overrepresented among patients who file complaints or lawsuits. High-risk patients include those who are diagnosed with serious personality disorders, have complex PTSD or dissociative identity disorders, report recovered memories of abuse, have been abused as children, present a serious risk to harm themselves or others, are wealthy, or are involved in lawsuits or other legal disputes. Sometimes these lawsuits reflect a litigious personality or a problem-solving set of behaviors that focuses on aggressive confrontations. In some instances, the stressors of the lawsuit may prompt such patients to display borderline-like behaviors. At other times, the mere presence of a lawsuit may require the psychologist to fulfill the role of the treating expert with a court. These categories are not mutually exclusive, of course, and a patient may be found in more than one.

Patients with serious personality disorders, such as borderline or narcissistic personality disorders, present special risks for psychologists. The specific diagnosis is less important than the presence of specific traits, such as a belief in one's entitlement to special treatment, a pattern of idealization and vilification of others, a pervasive inability to accept objective and constructive feedback, or the use of romantic seduction as a consistent strategy to express affection or closeness. More information on risk management techniques with high-risk patients appears throughout this book.

CONTEXTUAL RISK FACTORS

Context refers to the total circumstances under which you are seeing the patient, including the setting of the service (e.g., a solo practice, small group, or institution) and the type of service provided (e.g., treatment or evaluative services). Institutional treatment settings may reduce risks in so far as the institution may have clinical and legal resources greater than those generally available in solo or small group practices. However, an institutional setting, such as a hospital, may also have greater legal exposure in that it has a greater degree of perceived control over the behavior of the patient and practitioner.

Context also includes the type of service being requested by the client or patient. Some services, such as evaluations with financial or relationship consequences or treatment in the context of a highly conflicted divorce, involve increased legal risks. Other contexts that present greater risks include services delivered under supervision and services delivered when there is the potential or existence of a clinically contraindicated multiple relationship.

INDIVIDUAL THERAPIST FACTORS[1]

Psychologists can be more effective in calculating their risks if they accurately identify the individual factors that make up their "personal skill inventory" and accurately evaluate the *value* of the information they have in their "personal database." The phrase *personal skill inventory* refers to your knowledge, skills, past experiences, and emotional competencies. It is derived from your training, experiences, readings, study, consultation, and supervision. The phrase *personal database* refers to the fund of information you have about a particular diagnosis or area of professional practice. Your personal skill inventory should include the routine use of risk management strategies. (These are covered in more detail in Section 2.) Your personal database should include information about professional risks, including the characteristics of high-risk patients, contexts, and disciplinary consequences.

Psychologists can effectively use their personal skill inventory and personal database only if they understand them accurately. A continual danger is that your perceived personal skill inventory almost always will be greater than your actual skill inventory. You can reduce the gap between your perceived and actual skill inventories by ongoing contact and feedback with other mental health professionals. Psychologists who are professionally isolated risk becoming obsolete and developing gaps in their skill inventory and database without knowing it.

Psychologists who appreciate the limits of their personal skill inventory recognize that they cannot help all patients. Depending on the situation or the nature of the patient's needs, some patients are better served by institutions or agencies that provide a wider range of resources, such as 24-hour immediate response coverage, a multidisciplinary team with more resources (such as case managers), ready availability of psychiatric coverage, options for day treatment programming, and easy access to inpatient services. These institutions or agencies may be able to provide more control over the patient, and for some patients, that degree of temporary control may be clinically indicated. At a time when many psychologists face a decrease in income as a result of managed care, it may be difficult to turn away patients even if they have problems that are on the fringe of psychologists' areas of competence. The decision to take such patients needs to involve consideration of the risk that the patients may not be getting the

[1] Portions from "Well-Being and Professional Development Among Psychologists," by S. Knapp, 2004, November, *The Pennsylvania Psychologist, 64,* 13, 17. Copyright 2004 by Pennsylvania Psychological Association. Adapted with permission of the Pennsylvania Psychological Association.

care they need and of the professional risks to the psychologist.

Your personal skill inventory is augmented when you have a strong "system of protection," such as a consultation group, consultant, or other sources of high-quality feedback. Your personal skill inventory is diminished when external stressors distract your full attention from clinical tasks. For example, psychologists going through a painful and stressful divorce may find that their emotional energy for work is diminished, at least temporarily.

The quality of your individual skill inventory helps determine when you can take risks. Should you take that case that stretches the bounds of your expertise? Can you skip giving the additional test that you believe will add little additional clinical information to what you already have obtained? Should you use bartering as a method of payment with this patient? Should you become more confrontational or directive with this patient?

In each of the above examples of risk, you should at least give a clinical rationale for the action taken. If you have consulted appropriately and used appropriate risk management strategies, it may be quite safe and appropriate to follow your own judgment.

On the other hand, the patient-oriented risks described above differ substantially from "shortcuts" such as stretching your bounds of expertise because you have extraordinary financial strains (not because of the patient's clinical needs), becoming lax on your documentation, or failing to get consultation because of time pressures. None of the authors claim to be faultless paragons of virtue. All of us have had times, as a result of external circumstances, when we failed to complete the day's dictation or notes, delayed returning a phone call, or temporarily postponed a professional obligation. It is inevitable that external pressures will force all psychologists to prioritize at some point. However, those who take routine shortcuts engender greater risks of disciplinary actions and may be delivering less than adequate professional services. If you routinely take shortcuts, we encourage you to reassess your risks.

Shortcuts are especially problematic during expected and sometimes increased periods of personal or professional stress. During those times, you should make efforts to increase your use of risk management strategies. The life of a psychologist can be very rewarding, but it is also stressful. Knapp and Keller (2004a) found that the practice of psychology exposes psychologists to many adverse events including the possibility of a patient suicide, a patient harming another person, stalking, or harassing, to name a few. These adverse events can have a serious negative impact on the personality and emotional functioning of the psychologist. Working with individuals experiencing mental and emotional problems over a long time can and does lead to problems with burnout. In addition, the practice of psychology includes chronic stressors such as the negative affect of patients (e.g., extreme sadness and descriptions of trauma), resistance (e.g., missed appointments and denial), serious pathology (e.g., psychopathy and compulsiveness), and passive-aggressive behaviors. (Hellman, Morrison, & Abramowitz, 1986).

Of course, these all occur in the context of the personal stressors experienced by everyone. As much as you may want to separate your personal and private lives, it is impossible to do so completely. A bad day at home can spill over, even if minimally, to a less than optimal day at the office. Conversely, a bad day at the office can impact your personal and private life, creating a potential vicious circle of problems being transferred from home to office and office to home.

Personal and professional stressors increase during periods of life transitions, such as when moving or starting a new job. That is a time to be especially vigilant about potential risks or slips. Other personal life transitions may be anticipated, such as the decline in physical and mental skills as a result of aging, although many physical illnesses or injuries cannot be anticipated.

Fortunately, the life of a psychologist can be rewarding as well. Patients do improve, and they frequently express great appreciation for the help they have received. These accomplishments are rewarding. The goal is to maximize the rewards and minimize the stressors. Certainly, your cognitive and personal qualities are important, such as the ability to see humor in a difficult situation or to place setbacks in perspective. Coster and Schwebel (1997) found that well-being among psychologists was associated with high levels of self-awareness, self-monitoring, strong social relationships (from peers, spouses, friends, and others), and a balanced life. Optimistic perseverance is important as well. Dlugos and Friedlander (2001) found that passionately committed psychologists often approached obstacles in work as a challenge to be faced with persistence and creativity. Perhaps they experienced "flow" in their work. The passionately committed psychologists frequently solicited feedback on their work and sought diverse challenges or opportunities in their careers.

We are not Pollyannas about the work of professional psychologists, and we believe that frank discussions about the stresses of professional life are important. But recognition of these stressors should not diminish psychologists' fascination with the field of psychology as it continually increases in basic knowledge and application to human problems. "Be optimistic and be fully engaged in the field....be an active part of the field as it moves forward" (Paukert, 2005, p. 15).

A strong personal life helps to counterbalance professional demands. Coster and Schwebel (1997) found that well-functioning psychologists often took time for their personal and family lives. Mahoney (1997) found that the self-care habits of psychologists included engaging in a hobby, reading for pleasure, taking pleasure trips, attending movies or artistic events, or participating in physical exercise. It is a pleasant paradox that those psychologists who are most able to distance themselves from work and immerse themselves in family, friends, or avocations are most able to return to work with curiosity, vigor, and a sense of optimistic challenge.

Life management skills do not come automatically. Psychologists can manage their lives best when they create a supportive environment to help deal with stressors and transitions. The first step might be to reflect on the Golden Rule (do unto others as you would have them do unto you), which has been found in some form in all major world religions. In other words, if psychologists want to have a protective social network, it may be necessary to offer those same protections to others. Psychologists can display civic virtue. Join your local or state psychological association; serve on a committee; volunteer to do some work—even if it is low profile or unglamorous at times.

When psychologists see colleagues in need, they can offer to help them. They can offer to speak to a psychology class at the local university on a topic of interest to themselves and others.

DISCIPLINARY CONSEQUENCES

The institutions that regulate the practice of psychology can be divided into the proactive (before-the-fact) controls and the reactive (after-the-fact) controls (Knapp & VandeCreek, 2003). Proactive controls may reduce the likelihood of misconduct occurring and may increase the probability that psychologists will have the skills to benefit the public. For example, graduate programs help to ensure that their graduates have mastered the basic tools needed to be competent professionals. Licensing boards, through the licensing process, ensure that the graduates have had the required supervision and have mastered the body of knowledge unique to psychology. Professional associations and some professional liability insurance programs such as the American Psychological Association Insurance Trust (The Trust; 1-800-477-1200) provide consultation services to psychologists.[2] Professional associations may also have peer assistance programs that indirectly prevent acts of misconduct by helping distressed or disabled psychologists who are at a high risk for unethical conduct. Of course, none of the proactive controls can prevent all misconduct.

Reactive controls respond once misconduct has occurred. For example, licensing boards accept complaints against licensees who allegedly have violated the licensing law or its regulations; ethics committees of professional associations accept complaints against their members who allegedly have violated their ethics code; and malpractice courts accept complaints when patients appear to have been harmed by negligence. Less frequently used miscellaneous controls such as lawsuits based on breach of contract or criminal conduct are also available. Criminal laws are an external control to the extent that they are applicable to psychology, such as mandatory reporting laws of child abuse or laws prohibiting insurance fraud.

LICENSING BOARDS

Licensing boards are established at the state level. While their responsibilities vary somewhat from state to state, they are all established to protect the public, not to promote the welfare of psychologists. The license to practice a profession is a privilege established by the state; it is not a right (Bricklin, Bennett, & Carroll, 2003).

The members of the licensing board include psychologists and generally one or more public members. The members of the board are volunteers who receive very little compensation. Some of the public members have

---

[2] The Trust Advocate Program is intended to help individuals insured through the Trust sponsored Professional Liability program to avoid or reduce the risk of malpractice or disciplinary actions. The principle service is the availability of clinical and legal risk management consultation from an experienced attorney-psychologist.

considerable knowledge of the standards of the profession; others do not. It is expected that the public members will learn about the profession as they serve on the board over time.

Although licensing boards' procedures vary considerably from jurisdiction to jurisdiction, the following are common features. When a complaint is received, the case is handled by an investigator who reviews it and determines if it warrants investigation. In some jurisdictions, the licensing board can prosecute for events beyond those identified in the original complaint. For example, the complainant may accuse the psychologist of a boundary violation. In the investigation, however, the psychologist may be exonerated of that charge but be charged with inadequate record keeping, which was only discovered in the course of the investigation of the original charge. It is important to know the circumstances in your particular jurisdiction.

The standard used by the licensing board is whether the licensing law, its regulations, or other laws were violated. It is not necessary to prove that a patient was harmed. Many licensing boards adopt the American Psychological Association's "Ethical Principles of Psychologists and Code of Conduct" (APA Ethics Code; APA, 2002) or some variation of it. Consequently, the Ethics Code takes on legal importance beyond its adoption by APA. Other licensing boards might adopt the Association of State and Provincial Psychology Boards (ASPPB) Code of Conduct (2005), the association of all of the psychology licensing boards in the United States and Canada.

Because a licensing board action is an administrative rather than a criminal procedure, the respondent psychologist does not have the same due process rights as a criminal defendant. That is, the standards for the admission of evidence may be less stringent; hearsay evidence may be admissible and the standard of proof may be lower.

Licensing boards may issue disciplinary notices or even suspend or revoke a license if the misconduct is serious enough. Indeed, a license may be suspended prior to the completion of an investigation if the allegations are serious enough to warrant such action. Some licensing boards have the option of issuing educational letters that do not rise to the level of a disciplinary action. All adjudications are supposed to be reported to a national data bank managed by the ASPPB.

ETHICS COMMITTEES

The APA and many state, provincial, and territorial psychological associations (SPTAs) have ethics committees. These associations have jurisdiction only over members of their associations, not over all licensees.

Similar to licensing boards, ethics committees only enforce a standard of conduct; they do not determine whether a patient has been harmed. Ethics committees can issue disciplinary notices or remove an individual from the association. Some ethics committees have the option of issuing educational letters that do not rise to the level of a disciplinary action. Ethics committees may, under certain circumstances, report their findings to the state licensing board.

MALPRACTICE

Malpractice is a form of civil law whereby parties who are injured in a professional relationship may seek monetary compensation for their damages. The four essential ingredients of a malpractice case all begin with the letter *d*. There must be a *duty* between the professional and the client or patient; there must be *damage* to the client or patient; the professional must have *deviated* from acceptable (or minimal) professional norms of conduct; and there must be a *direct* link between the damage to the patient and the behavior of the professional (Simon, 1992).

Psychologists generally have a duty to the patient whom they are treating. When acting as a supervisor, the psychologist has a duty to the patient of the supervisee because the supervisee has no legal authority to provide treatment, except as an extension of the psychologist. Duties do not exist to third parties such as collateral contacts (e.g., persons who enter the therapy room only to facilitate the treatment of a patient or patients of psychologists who have consulted with another psychologist). However, in some states psychologists have duties to third parties who are readily identifiable victims of imminent danger by patients. In such situations, the duty is usually limited to warning or acting to protect that third party.

Malpractice actions are subject to a statute of limitations, which means that the lawsuit must be filed within a certain period of time. The exact length of the statute of limitations varies from state to state, but usually it is 2 or 3 years. Some states allow the statute of limitations to be waived for minors (until they reach the age of majority) or for adults under the discovery rule, which means that the "clock" does not start to run until the patients know or should have known that they were damaged by the negligence of the professional. Some states use the standard of contributory negligence, which means a court could rule that the acts of the psychologist substantially contributed to the harm, but the patient also bore some responsibility, and the damages could be limited according to the relative portion of the harm caused by the actions of the psychologist.

Whenever psychologists have professional relationships with patients, they incur the duty to use a reasonable standard of care. Although courts may vary in their exact definition of this term, generally it refers to the knowledge and skill ordinarily possessed by members of the profession in good standing. The APA Ethics Code does not use the term "reasonable standard of care," but it does use the modifier *"reasonable,"* which means

> the prevailing professional judgment of psychologists engaged in similar activities in similar circumstances, given the knowledge the psychologist had or should have had at the time. (APA Ethics Code, Introduction and Applicability)

The concept of the reasonable standard of care appears throughout this book.

Reading malpractice cases may help psychologists to appreciate the applicable standard of care. However, these cases must be read carefully. Often they are based on suits against hospitals or other institutions that have a high degree of control over the patients. Such cases have limited application to outpatient treatment where psychologists have far less control over the actions of their patients.

MALPRACTICE AND PATIENT FACTORS

Among physicians, data show that not all negligent conduct results in a lawsuit, and not all lawsuits involve negligent conduct. The presence of a malpractice suit has a low correlation with the actual occurrence of an adverse event (Burstin, Johnson, Lipsitz, & Brennan, 1993). The likelihood of a suit depends greatly on factors other than the objective harm to the patient or the degree to which the physician deviated from reasonable standards of care. Even after controlling for the severity of the medical injury, poor patients are much less likely to sue for malpractice than wealthy patients (Burstin et al., 1993).

Patient relationship factors appear to be highly important in whether physicians get sued for malpractice. Although psychologists do not have data on the correlation between relationship factors and malpractice for psychologists, the data from physicians may be instructive. Those primary care physicians who have fewer claims are more likely to use more orienting statements (explaining procedures to patients) and humor in their conversations and to use facilitating statements (statements that encourage patients to express their opinions or concerns; Levinson, Roter, Mullooly, Dull, & Frankel, 1997). When asked about their reasons for filing lawsuits, patients often reported that they felt that the physician had devalued their opinions, delivered information poorly, failed to understand their point of view, or tried to withhold information (Beckman, Markakis, Suchman, & Frankel, 1994; Levinson et al., 1997).

Of course, the practice of medicine is not identical to the practice of psychology. However, the findings suggest that you can reduce your risk of a malpractice suit if you spend more time on informed consent (orienting statements), try to involve patients in decision making throughout the therapeutic process, and listen respectfully to their perspectives, even when it may be clear that their perspective could well be part of the problem. These interpersonal skills should be part of your personal skill inventory and may be especially important when dealing with high-risk patients. Consistent with this interpretation is the finding from a survey of psychiatrists, effective listening was their most important therapeutic tool, surpassing all other diagnostic and intervention skills (Effective Listening Tops List, 2000).

TRENDS IN DISCIPLINARY ACTIONS

Over the last 10 years certain trends have emerged in regard to disciplinary actions by regulatory bodies. Ethics committees are adjudicating fewer cases. The APA, for example, has been disciplining fewer psychologists in recent years (in 2003, the Ethics Committee opened 25 matters against psychologists, as compared with 138 in 1995). The reasons for this decrease are not entirely clear. It may be, in part, because many complainants are filed with both APA and licensing boards, and APA frequently requires the licensing boards to finish their adjudications before starting its own. In addition, certain criteria must be met for APA to open a case even after a licensing board has taken disciplinary action. Also, part of the decrease may be because APA now allows psychologists who have been charged with an ethics complaint to resign instead of having to go through adjudication by the APA Ethics Committee. Finally, many ethics committees of SPTAs have discontinued adjudications and now focus only on education.[3]

While the incidence of malpractice for psychologists has been stable over the last 10 years, the risk of a licensing board complaint has increased substantially during this same time period. Unfortunately, even a letter of reprimand, the lowest form of disciplinary action from a licensing board, can have serious consequences for psychologists. It may result in the removal of the psychologist from a managed care panel or the loss of hospital privileges. The economic consequences, let alone the emotional consequences, can be substantial. Some licensing boards have become aware of the career-altering implications of these types of actions and have modified their procedures allowing them to have an opportunity to correct and guide the practice of psychologists without destroying their professional careers. In this, they have adopted a variety of "softer" administrative procedures that do not carry with them the professional stigma of letters of reprimand. However, these types of changes are not evident throughout the states.

Calculating the exact rate of disciplinary actions against psychologists is difficult. This is due to a number of factors including the fact that numbers taken from insurance pools are constantly changing; those who commit serious violations leave the provider pool, and new members join; people switch carriers, some practitioners retire from practice, and some leave the profession for other positions; and there are significant interrelater reliability problems in claims reporting and tracking by insurance claims managers across carriers. Regardless of the issues involved in reporting and tracking claims, approximately 1% of psychologists are subject to either a licensing board complaint or malpractice action each year. We know that risk varies on the basis of the nature of a practice. That is, those who do individual counseling logically have lower risk than forensic psychologists who do child custody evaluations. In addition, recent data show that the risk of board actions is substantially more than the risk of being sued for malpractice. The most recent data available indicate that practicing psychologists are four times more likely to be confronted by a board action than they are to be sued. In addition, research from ASPPB by Van Horne (2004) clearly demonstrates that there has been an increase in board actions against psychologists over the past years. Thus, it appears that some boards are becoming much more aggressive in disciplining and regulating the profession, a reality that forces psychologists practicing in the 21st century into a risk management mode that reduces the potential negative outcomes of this increased board oversight.

One must bear in mind that these figures are somewhat inaccurate and do not account for the possibility of multiple complaints (the same action resulting in both a malpractice suit and licensing board complaint) or that a few individuals will have several malpractice suits or licensing board complaints. As pointed out earlier, the data do not respect the reality that

---

[3] The authors wish to thank Dr. Stehpen Behnke, APA Ethics Director, for his help with this section.

not all areas of practice have the same risk. Nonetheless, the data make it clear that licensing board complaints are far more likely than malpractice suits, and that in the aggregate, psychologists would be wise to practice with an eye towards the possibility that sometime in a career they will have to deal with a legal action taken against them

TYPES OF COMPLAINTS

Categorizing complaints against psychologists with the reactive controls cannot be done with complete accuracy because the data are not collected in a standardized manner. For example, the data bank of ASPPB contains reports of individual licensing boards that, until recently, did not use a standard reporting system (Kirkland, Kirkland, & Reaves, 2004). Also, no uniform public reporting system or data set exists on criminal sanctions, institutional disciplinary actions, or other actions. Finally, sometimes the same action results in more than one disciplinary action. For example, the single act of failing to report suspected child abuse could result in both a misdemeanor finding and a disciplinary action by a licensing board.

According to data from the last 10 years of the APA Ethics Committee, the most common types of infractions addressed (except for being disciplined in another jurisdiction) were sexual relationships, nonsexual multiple relationships, insurance and fee problems, child custody, confidentiality, and practicing outside areas of competence. The most frequent types of complaints brought before the APA Ethics Committee are listed in Table 1.A.

TABLE 1.A
Most Common Types of Disciplinary Actions by APA Ethics Committee, 1994–2003 Cases with Multiple Categories

Category	No. of cases
Sexual misconduct (adult)	198
Nonsexual dual relationship	72
Insurance/fee problems	72
Child custody	65
Confidentiality	40
Outside competence	28
Inappropriate follow-up/ termination	20
Test misuse	20
Termination/supervision	21
False, fraudulent, or misleading advertising	17
Sexual misconduct (minor)	10
Inappropriate response to crisis	10

Note. Adapted from "Report of the Ethics Committee, 1995, 1996, 1997, 1998, 1999, 2000, 2001, 2002, 2003, 2004" by the American Psychological Association Ethics Committee, *American Psychologist*. Copyright 1994–2005 by the American Psychological Association. Adapted with permission.

According to the data from the ASPPB, the most common types of infractions reported to licensing boards are sexual relationships, unprofessional conduct (which according to ASPPB's classification included nonsexual multiple relationships), conviction of crimes, fraudulent acts, improper or inadequate record keeping, breach of confidentiality, inadequate or improper supervision, and impairment.

It is difficult to classify malpractice data precisely because plaintiffs' attorneys often take a "shot gun" approach and file multiple complaints even though many of the allegations may eventually be dropped from the suit. Nonetheless, despite these and other problems in categorizing the data,[4] according to the Trust, the most common types of actions that led to malpractice complaints were ineffective treatment or failure to consult or refer, 29%; failure to diagnose or improper diagnosis, 16%; child custody disputes, 10%; sexual intimacy, harassment, or misconduct, 9%; breach of confidentiality, 8%; suicide, 4%; and supervisory issues, 3%. Other less frequent allegations include conflict of interest, libel or slander, conflicts in reporting suspected sexual abuse, abandonment, repressed memory, and discrimination or harassment.

Despite the limitations of each of these individual data sets, certain common themes emerge. In order of frequency (from most to least common), sexual relationships, nonsexual multiple relationships, insurance and fee problems, participation in child custody cases, breaches of confidentiality, practicing outside of one's area of competence, test misuse, inadequate supervision, inappropriate follow-up or termination, inappropriate response to crises, and inadequate record keeping are the highest areas of risk.

EMOTIONAL CONSEQUENCES

Even for psychologists eventually found not guilty of an ethics violation, the very process of being investigated takes an emotional toll. In addition to the strain of the great expenditure of time and money, prosecuted psychologists often experience prolonged stress, social embarrassment, self-doubt, anxiety, and depression (Montgomery, Cupit, & Wimberly, 1999).

All of the authors have been involved in the disciplinary process at some level, either as board members, attorneys representing psychologists, expert witnesses, or consultants to individuals being investigated, sued, or prosecuted. In those roles, we have seen the pain that such proceedings reveal and cause for both the plaintiffs and the defendants. There is an unpleasant visceral quality to observing or participating in these proceedings that is hard to capture in words. We do not want to go through that process ourselves, and we do not want you to have to go through it either.

WHAT TO DO IF ACCUSED OF MISCONDUCT

If you receive notice that you are being sued or that a licensing board complaint has been filed against you, you should contact your professional liability insurance company immediately. Whether dealing with a malpractice suit or a complaint to a licensing board, do not attempt to resolve the

---

[4] In addition there is the ever-present interrelater reliability problem when various insurance adjusters allocate cases to a definite number of malpractice categories.

case yourself through negotiating with the person bringing the charges or anyone acting on behalf of that person. You must accept the fact that a former patient has now taken a hostile action against you and the matter has been turned over to other authorities that do not have your best interest as their focus. It is now an adversarial situation, and your tools as a therapist are ill suited to deal with this type of problem. Anything you say can be used against you. You risk making self-incriminating statements if you discuss the situation with anyone but your attorney or without the consent of your attorney. Your conversations with your attorney are privileged; your conversations with others are not. Do not alter or destroy records. Refer all communications from the plaintiff or the plaintiff's attorney to your attorney.

Unfortunately, some well-meaning psychologists have responded to formal complaints by calling the patient and trying to talk out the problems. Throughout this book we emphasize the clinical and risk management importance of listening, communicating, and negotiating with patients. Certainly during therapy it is clinically appropriate to deal with expressions of discontent seriously and to repair breaches in the therapeutic alliance. When clinically appropriate, sometimes psychologists show compassion and sensitivity by acknowledging an error in the application or timing of a specific technique.

However, after a complaint has been filed, the time for such communications with patients has ended. Naive psychologists may say things that could be used against them in future legal proceedings. For example, a psychologist may say to the person bringing the complaint, "I am sorry you feel this way," only to have the phrase repeated in court as an admission of guilt rather than as an apology.

Be patient. Complaints can take years to resolve. Although you will want, and probably deserve, a quick resolution, the legal wheels turn very slowly.

APPLYING THE RISK MANAGEMENT FORMULA

Throughout this book we make reference to the RM formula. The following examples illustrate how psychologists might apply the RM formula. At the macro level, we can reiterate the basic principles of risk management. However, at the micro level, only you, the psychologist, can evaluate your personal skill inventory and your personal database and determine how to proceed.

These examples are composites based on many similar situations faced by psychologists. Of course, the factors are interactive by necessity (e.g., your intervention may reduce the severity of patient risk characteristics) and dynamic (e.g., a patient with whom you can work well at one point in time might be impossible for you at another point in time). Nonetheless, the RM formula is a useful heuristic for evaluating risk.

$$\text{Clinical risk} = \frac{(P \times C \times D)}{TF}$$

In this formula, P = patient risk characteristics; C = context; D = disciplinary consequences; and TF = therapist factors.

> A psychologist was approached by the leaders of a religious denomination to evaluate an ordained minister who had a long pattern of disruptive behaviors including angry outbursts against parishioners for apparently innocuous behaviors that the minister interpreted as disrespectful. Efforts on the part of other ministers and lay leaders to encourage the minister to change were ineffective. Therefore, the denomination concluded that the complaints against the minister were serious and credible and they had to intervene formally. They wanted a recommendation as to whether they could develop a rehabilitation program for the minister, or if necessary, whether they needed to remove her from ordination. The psychologist used the RM formula to decide whether to take the case. (1.1)[5]

Patient risk factors. It was not possible for the psychologist to diagnose the client on the basis of the referral information, but there were suggestions of a possible personality disorder. The psychologist also considered the possibility that the client might be at a high risk to file a complaint.

Context risk factors. The context was to make a recommendation to a third party that could have serious implications for the minister's career. The psychologist knew that this was a high-risk context. In addition, the psychologist knew that adversarial contexts such as this often bring out problematic behaviors on the part of the individuals being evaluated. In Section 3, we review the implications of third-party assessments in more detail.

Individual therapist factors. The psychologist was very proficient in psychological testing and an excellent diagnostician, but she had never tested a member of the clergy suspected of impairment. Although she did not know the minister or any of the principals involved in the case personally, she was a member of the denomination and felt a responsibility to assist. Fortunately, this psychologist had done testing for third parties before and knew the basic informed consent, documentation, and risk management strategies that needed to be followed in such circumstances.

Disciplinary consequences. If the quality of the service fell below acceptable levels, there could be a malpractice suit or an allegation of misconduct before a licensing board or ethics committee.

Outcome. The psychologist appropriately recognized that this professional obligation would entail substantial risks in that she had never before evaluated an individual for a religious domination. She sought consultation from a colleague who had done such work before she made a decision about taking this case. Eventually she took this case but retained the services of her colleague as a consultant to guide her through this process. From a business perspective, she understood that the cost of the consultant would substantially reduce her income for taking this case, but she anticipated that if she did a good job, it could lead to other referrals in the future.

> An unmarried psychologist treated a patient for an adjustment disorder and terminated after four weeks with a successful outcome. The patient was a well-educated woman who was adjusting

---

[5] All of the examples are composites of cases and do not present information about an actual patient. Each example is followed by an identifying number in parentheses.

to the death of her husband. There appeared to be no serious pathology. The patient reported no previous mental health treatment. Approximately one year after the last session the ex-patient ran into the psychologist at the local pet store, and they started a conversation. The ex-patient invited the psychologist to attend a barbecue at her house. The psychologist used the RM formula to decide whether to attend the barbecue and invite the possibility of a more extended social relationship. (1.2)

Patient risk factors. Although the psychologist only saw the patient for a few weeks, she did not appear to have any of the serious personality disorders. The patient appeared mentally healthy and reported no background of previous mental health treatment.

Context risk factors. The treatment was brief and free of any complications. The bills were paid promptly without complaint, and there appeared to be little likelihood that the patient would need further treatment. The psychologist took no actions during treatment to suggest or invite the possibility of a posttermination relationship.

Disciplinary consequences. The APA Ethics Code permits consecutive multiple relationships as long as they

> *would not reasonably be expected to cause impairment or risk exploitation or harm.* (Standard 3.05a, Multiple Relationships)

Consequently, the psychologist needs to consider the possibility of exploitation or harm to the ex-patient. Although this vignette does not explicitly imply the possibility of a sexual relationship, Standard 10.08 (Sexual Intimacies With Former Therapy Clients/Patients) of the Ethics Code has specific prohibitions against sexual relationships with former patients for at least two years after termination. Even then, the burden is on the psychologist to demonstrate that the former patient would not be harmed by the relationship.

Individual therapist factors. The psychologist had been going through a difficult time as he recently moved to this town to take care of his aging mother who recently died. The psychologist had few friends in this new time and was anxious to establish a social network. He wondered if his interest in developing social relationships was blinding him to potential trouble spots.

Outcome. In this example, the patient and context factors suggest little clinical risk, but the therapist factors may be suspect. Consequently, the psychologist politely informed his ex-patient that he had previous plans that he might not be able to change (which was true) and that he would let her know later if he were able to attend. In the meantime, he sought consultation.

A psychologist was approached to provide therapy for children whose parents were undergoing a difficult, painful, and contentious divorce. The mother was a banker and the father was an attorney. The psychologist used the RM formula to help him decide whether to take the case. (1.3)

Patient risk factors. Both the parents had high-paying professional jobs. There was no special indication that either of the parents had significant personality disorders. However, this psychologist knew that the stress of custody litigation could sometimes cause parents to exhibit behaviors suggestive of personality disorders.

Context risk factors. As we discuss in Section 3, whenever treatment is provided in the context of a conflicted divorce or custody case, there is the danger that one or more of the parents may perceive the psychologist, rightly or wrongly, as aligning him- or herself with the other party. Parents in high-conflict divorces might not always present information accurately, may try to enlist the psychologist as an ally on their side, or may be using the therapy to obtain information that they can use against the other parent in the upcoming custody fight. Allegations of child abuse are common in high-conflict divorces, although the frequency of founded cases is lower under these circumstances.

Disciplinary consequences. In high-conflict divorces involving custody disputes, it is not uncommon for parents to file complaints against therapists, custody evaluators, or other parties if they believe it will strengthen their cases.

Individual therapist factors. The psychologist was a highly skilled child therapist and evaluator who had experience working with high-conflict families.

Outcome. The psychologist offered his service to the family under certain conditions. First, the court had to order the therapy (this was done to ensure that one parent would not use the threat of withdrawing consent as a means to influence the course of therapy in a counter-therapeutic manner). Second, the parents had to agree that they would not request the psychologist to communicate to either of their attorneys or to be otherwise involved in the custody dispute except for brief communications to any court-appointed custody evaluator. Third, payment had to be up-front for all sessions because the psychologist was aware that sometimes families will use nonpayment as a means to try to influence the course and content of psychotherapy. Fourth, the psychologist had the parents sign a consent form that he went over in detail, including information on the reporting of suspected child abuse, the possibility that a specialized consultant might be involved if one or more of the children presented problems that appeared outside of his area of expertise, and other conditions relevant to this type of case. He documented the informed consent process in detail.

A Detailed Ongoing Case Example With Discussion

Our final example in this section is a detailed case faced by a psychologist. We expand on this particular case example throughout the book.

You have been providing therapy to a difficult 26-year-old patient for the last 3 years. The insurance coverage has run out, and the patient is paying reduced fees. The treatment has had its ups and downs, some having to do with events in the life of the patient, but others having to do with what is going on in the therapeutic relationship. However, the patient is making progress as measured by improvement in ability to manage her own life. The alliance seems solid overall. There has been less progress in the underlying dynamics, particularly regarding relationships. However, under stress the patient tends to revert to dysfunctional thinking habits.

Then the patient misses sessions without adequate notice and bombards you with e-mails and telephone calls. She stops taking medications and falls behind in paying her bills. During these periods the risk of suicide gestures and attempts increases. About a year ago, in a similar situation, she made a suicide attempt of moderate lethality. There was a safety agreement in place at the time, and the patient did call you after she took the pills. Having been through this before, you are getting frustrated and having difficulty keeping those feelings out of the treatment.

Things in your professional and personal life are stressing you, including a reduction in income because of changes in managed care reimbursement. Your child is ready to go to college, and you are uncertain how you will pay for the expenses.

You believe you should move toward termination with the patient, but you are afraid that this will be a major setback for the patient and may precipitate a suicide attempt. The patient has no real support network. She has strained relationships with her parents who still try to intrude in her life and are angry about the limits set on them. The father is a dentist and the mother is a corporate attorney. You believe that if the patient succeeds in committing suicide, the parents may blame you.

The patient's primary care physician prescribes her medication, but he has limited his relationship with the patient to strict 15-minute appointments. You have urged the patient to find a psychiatrist, but this is difficult because of the policies of the managed care company. You care about the patient and identify with the difficult struggles she faces in her life. If you could set and enforce adequate limits, the treatment might be productive, but any attempt to do so now will probably fail.

A new dialectical behavior therapy program has started in town, but the patient has avoided all suggestions about adjunctive involvement in the group. As long as you are available, the patient will never seriously consider this program. If you terminate, it is predictable that the patient will respond with hostility. You believe that there is a real risk of a serious suicide attempt. The patient knows the system well enough to avoid involuntary hospitalizations until she has made a gesture or attempt. While you intend to offer adequate time to terminate, you are certain that the patient will not take advantage of the sessions and is likely to express her outrage through voice mails and e-mails. (1.4)

The psychologist appreciated the risks involved in this case but took steps to frame the context of treatment to increase the likelihood of therapeutic success. He also made ample use of the risk management strategies of informed consent, documentation, and consultation that we review in detail in Section 2.

Now let us consider this example using the RM formula.

Patient risk factors. There are many, but we start with the obvious. You have diagnosed the patient as having a borderline personality disorder. The patient manifests a disturbed relationship with you and with others in her life. The patient has threatened to harm herself. The facts that the parents have financial resources and that the mother is an attorney also increase the risk of a complaint or lawsuit.

Context risk factors. You are seeing the patient in a solo practice, and a primary care physician is monitoring the patient's medications. The patient is involved in no other mental health treatment activities. This is not the optimal setting of care. Ideally, she would have her medications prescribed and monitored by a psychiatrist or prescribing psychologist, and she would be treated as part of a larger system that has routine case consultation, 24-hour coverage, a day treatment program, or inpatient services if needed.

Disciplinary consequences. It is often a useful exercise to look at a worst-case scenario to identify the risks involved. If you terminate the patient and she harms herself through a suicide attempt or even is successful at committing suicide, you run the risk of a malpractice suit, a licensing board or an ethics complaint, or all three. If the patient has no family or relatives and no assets to pass along to heirs, these risks are minimized. Even if she does not harm herself, she still might be able to file a licensing board or ethics complaint. Perhaps she would argue that you violated the standards of the profession or the APA Ethics Code by your manner of terminating treatment. She might accuse you of abandonment. Even if you were eventually absolved of the charge of wrongful termination, the licensing board may find in the course of its investigation that you did not adequately document informed consent or committed some other violation unrelated to the initial complaint. As noted earlier, in some states, licensing boards have the option of amending their complaints to pursue the case against the psychologist.

Individual therapist factors. These include your emotional resources and the match between your knowledge, skills, experience, and strengths and the patient's needs. You will become better at making such matches if you have an accurate perception of your strengths and weaknesses.

Outcome. Of course in this situation, you need to ask yourself what is in the best interest of the patient and what are your obligations to the patient. Even though she may be angry with you, it may be in her best interest for you to stop therapy. In fact, in some situations, continued therapy with such patients may be clinically contraindicated.

However, you also need to protect yourself, your practice, and your good name in the community. It does no one any good to be the object of a frivolous or unfounded complaint. Our goal is to describe how, in this and other situations, you might reduce the risk of harm to both the patient and yourself.

Through forethought you can anticipate, prevent, or mitigate many problems. Through thought you can respond carefully and prudently when problems occur. By afterthought you can reflect back on what happened and modify future responses accordingly.

In the subsequent chapters we review this case in more detail and provide other cases that present risks for psychologists. We also review ways that you can reduce risks through the application of informed consent, consultation, documentation, and other risk management principles. Knowledge of the laws and rules governing the practice of psychology is essential. However, we also emphasize the use of ethical principles as guides to promoting patient welfare.

Seven Essential Points to Remember

1. Risk is a function of several factors, and the individual psychologist is the best judge as to whether a particular risk management action should be undertaken.

$$\text{Clinical risk} = \frac{P \times C \times D}{TF}$$

where P = patient risk characteristics; C = context;
D = disciplinary consequences; and TF = therapist factors.

2. Being ethical means more than just obeying the APA Ethics Code.

3. The most common disciplinary actions against psychologists are in the areas of sexual boundary violations, nonsexual boundary violations, child custody, treatment and abandonment, supervision, and inadequate diagnosis.

4. Licensing board complaints are more frequent than malpractice suits or ethics committee complaints.

5. Effective career management means giving sufficient attention to your emotional competence.

6. Effective career management includes embedding oneself into a supportive professional community such as the APA or a state or territorial psychological association. The first step in that process may be to invest oneself in helping one's colleagues, community, or profession. Remember the Golden Rule.

7. Any purported risk management actions that appear to harm patients or degrade the quality of care need to be reconsidered and consultation sought.

In this section we review the three key elements of risk management: informed consent, documentation, and consultation. It is important for psychologists to understand thoroughly what these concepts mean so that they can use them appropriately in real-life clinical situations. We have found that we can apply them best if we appreciate the moral principles on which they are based.

ETHICS AND RISK MANAGEMENT

As experienced psychologists know, being ethical is not the same as being legal (Bricklin, 2001). Handelsman, Knapp, and Gottlieb (2002) and Knapp and VandeCreek (2005) have used the term "positive ethics" to refer to ethics as a way to promote patient welfare, as opposed to the narrower view of ethics as a way to avoid disciplinary actions. Similarly, good risk management should involve more than just following the minimal legal requirements. Good risk management principles should help psychologists fulfill their highest ethical ideals.

The risk management principles you follow should be congruent with your general orientation toward your practice, and like other aspects of your practice, should be "consistent with your deepest values" (Pope & Vasquez, 2005, p. 3). Of course, we cannot deny the reality that disciplinary actions can occur in the practice of psychology. However, your risk management principles should not be driven by remote or irrational fears but motivated by your deepest values, such as desiring to serve others and to have a rewarding career.

Ethical principles are relevant to the discussion of risk management for at least two reasons. First, good risk management principles are based on ethical principles; false or bad risk management principles contradict ethical principles. The best risk management principle is to provide good services that facilitate patient healing and growth and avoid unnecessary anger and resentment when the results are less than favorable. Second, ethical principles help guide behavior in situations in which laws or disciplinary codes do not give direction.

ETHICAL GROUNDING OF RISK MANAGEMENT PRINCIPLES

Psychologists are more effective in applying risk management strategies when they understand the moral principles on which they are based.

Psychologists differ in their personal moral theories. However, many find that a principle-based frame of reference helps them to articulate their ethical values. Principle-based ethics, as applied to health care by Beauchamp and Childress (2001), was influential in framing the General (aspirational) Principles in the American Psychological Association's "Ethical Principles of Psychologists and Code of Conduct" (APA Ethics Code). We make references to the principle-based ethics as a foundation for risk management throughout this book, but more for illustrative purposes. We recognize that you may base your moral behavior on additional ethical theories such as feminism or perhaps on your religious traditions.

According to principle-based ethics, individuals are generally obligated to follow certain overarching moral principles. Different principle-based ethicists may phrase or categorize these ethical principles differently. Beauchamp and Childress (2001) have identified *beneficence* (working to promote patient welfare), *nonmaleficence* (avoiding patient harm), *justice,* and respect for patient *autonomy.* Kitchener (2000) also considered *fidelity* a key moral principle. Knapp and VandeCreek (2004) suggested *general beneficence* (obligations to society in general) as an additional principle, and the APA Ethics Code includes *integrity* as a separate principle.

When you are acting at the higher levels of Bloom's taxonomy (analysis, synthesis, and evaluation), you can more clearly identify the relationship of these moral principles to your clinical actions. You can incorporate these principles into your clinical practice, apply them in novel situations, appreciate nuanced applications depending on the context, and use them to clarify why you chose one particular action over another.

When practiced properly, risk management should help you better fulfill your professional roles and should promote good patient care. Any purported risk management principle that tells you to do something that appears to harm a patient or violates a moral principle needs to be reconsidered, and consultation should be sought. False risk management principles are likely to occur at the lower levels of Bloom's taxonomy when psychologists improperly apply risk management principles because they do not understand the overarching purpose. Table 2.A contains some false risk management principles that we have encountered in our presentations or consultations. These false principles contain absolute statements and appear to reflect a perception of a conflict between the interest of the psychologist and the welfare of the patient. For example, some psychologists perceive that they have increased their legal protection if they get a suicidal patient to sign a safety agreement. However, from a legal perspective, these safety agreements are meaningless. From a clinical perspective, these safety agreements may be clinically contraindicated if they are forced on a patient (e.g., they may not respect the patient's autonomy) or if they inhibit the productive relationship needed for effective treatment (e.g., they do not promote beneficence).

In some situations, the ethical application of risk management principles results in clear understanding of the treatment process (e.g., explain treatment and billing procedures to patients before therapy starts). In other situations, the risk management principles require the nuanced balancing of issues and strategies and an ethical decision-making process.

TABLE 2.A
False Risk Management Principles

1. Always get a suicidal patient to sign a safety contract.
2. Try not to keep records because they can be used against you if a complaint is filed.
3. Never keep detailed records when patients present a threat to harm themselves or others.
4. Informed consent obligations consist only of getting the signature of patients on an informed consent form.
5. Risk management is only concerned with protecting the psychologist from disciplinary actions.
6. Never self-disclose and never touch a patient.

ETHICAL DECISION MAKING

Neither the laws nor the APA Ethics Code can provide an answer to every situation that you will experience. Knapp and VandeCreek (2005) have identified four types of situations in which the disciplinary ethics codes do not give explicit direction. First, ethics codes in general, and specifically APA's, use qualifiers such as "reasonable" and "if appropriate," which indicate that you have to use your discretion in the application of that particular ethical principle. Second, the APA Ethics Code may be silent about how to act in an emerging area of practice. Third, the APA Ethics Code does not prescribe a specific course of action when institutional policies or laws conflict with the requirements of the Ethics Code or with each other. Instead the APA Ethics Code prescribes a general policy of asserting one's commitment to the Ethics Code while attempting to resolve the issues. However, it does not (nor could it) prescribe exactly how you are to demonstrate this commitment or how to resolve the issue and what to do if the issue is irresolvable. Finally, the APA Ethics Code does not describe your superogatory obligations (self-imposed obligations to go beyond the minimum standards of the profession). In those situations you need to look to moral or ethical principles or values to guide your behavior.

Generally, treatment occurs without any conflict in these principles. However, at times these principles may conflict, and you will have to weigh the moral principles and decide which one should be salient. For example, a psychologist cannot both respect the autonomy of a suicidal patient (and allow him or her to die) and promote beneficence (work for his or her well-being) at the same time. However, when one principle is used to trump another, the best solution is the one that maximizes adherence to a dominant ethical principle while minimizing harm to any competing ethical principle. For example, when deciding to place beneficence over respect for the autonomy of a suicidal patient, it is still desirable to give the patient as much control over treatment as possible, consistent with the goal of protecting his or her life.

THREE KEY RISK MANAGEMENT PRINCIPLES

As mentioned at the beginning of this section, the three key elements of risk management are *informed consent, documentation,* and *consultation.* It is important to understand thoroughly what these concepts mean so that you will be able to apply them appropriately in real-life clinical situations.

It may be helpful to view these risk management strategies as "poultices" or the mass of medications that physicians and healers in the past applied directly to a wound, sore, or lesion to promote healing. Psychologists who have worked in high-risk situations have witnessed and experienced the anger, hatred, and turmoil that can be generated in the context of providing services. For them, the metaphor of risk management strategies as poultices may appear especially appropriate.

These three key elements should be part of your forethought, thought, and afterthought processes. Think about them ahead of time and integrate them into your professional practice. Remember the moral reasons behind these risk management principles, and try to incorporate them into how you think about events as they unfold in therapy or assessment. Use these principles when you look back on your behavior, and try to learn from your failures and successes. They are especially important to use when the situation passes the "hair on the back of your neck test." As the potential for risk increases, the use of these poultices should increase.

You will apply these risk management principles better if you understand how they are linked to overarching ethical principles.

Informed consent should not be a rote legal exercise but an effort to promote patient autonomy by increasing patient participation in decision making. In addition, good informed consent procedures are linked to beneficence in so far as they have a secondary goal of improving patient adherence and investment in treatment. Tryon and Winograd (2001) reported that "patients who achieve better outcomes are those that are actively involved in the patient role, discussing concerns, feelings, and goals rather than resisting or passively receiving therapists' suggestions" (p. 388). Beahrs and Guthiel (2001) also argued that good informed consent procedures empower patients to gain information, ask questions, and use that knowledge to assist their recovery. Furthermore, informed consent procedures are linked to nonmaleficence in so far as they reduce the likelihood that misunderstandings of office policies or billing practices could harm the treatment relationship. While some states may have a narrow, specific definition of informed consent, ours is broader.

Documentation is related to the moral principles of beneficence and nonmaleficence. Documentation requirements are not just arbitrary rules created by oversight bodies but are designed for several reasons, including the promotion of patient welfare. Good documentation demonstrates that you used a reasonable standard of care in conceptualizing, planning, and implementing treatment. Documentation also ensures better communication with current and future treating professionals. It is especially important for accurate communication with other staff members when working in an institution or agency.

Consultation helps ensure competence, which is related to the moral principles of beneficence and nonmaleficence. All psychologists should have lifelong competence-enhancing strategies that include, among other things, continuing education and a system for quality feedback. While we assume that you have the basic skills in your *personal skill inventory* (and basic information in your *personal data base*) to treat your patients, all psychologists will encounter unexpected or unique twists and turns in treatment that require them to get professional consultations to ensure that a particular patient receives a reasonable level of care.

In summary, psychologists can use these risk management techniques to fulfill their highest aspirations as psychologists. The techniques that substantially reduce risks of disciplinary complaints also improve the quality of patient care.

It may be useful to view these risk management techniques from the standpoint of the risk management (RM) formula we introduced in the Preface and repeated in Section 1:

$$\text{Clinical risk} = \frac{(P \times C \times D)}{TF}$$

In this formula, P = patient risk characteristics; C = context; D = disciplinary consequences; and TF = therapist factors.

The key elements of risk management can have a positive impact on the factors in the RM formula. For example, informed consent will influence Patient Risk Characteristics (to the extent that it reduces unrealistic expectations and the potential for misunderstandings about the nature of treatment) and the Context of the treatment (by setting parameters, expectations, and procedures ahead of time). Documentation will strengthen the Individual Therapist Factors by demonstrating care in developing and implementing the treatment plan. Consultation will strengthen the Individual Therapist Factors by improving your *personal skill inventory* and *personal data base*. Of course, the factors in the formula are interactive so that a strengthened *personal skill inventory* may influence Patient Risk Characteristics, which influence Context of treatment, and so on.

The use of these risk management elements is especially important if you are taking therapeutic risks such as attempting a nontraditional treatment with a patient. Perhaps an intervention has an 80% chance of success and a 20% chance of harming the patient (and a 5% chance of resulting in a disciplinary complaint). In such situations it is especially important to increase usual risk management activities and to be scrupulous about the informed consent process, documentation, and consultation.

INFORMED CONSENT[1]

At the lower levels of Bloom's taxonomy, you are expected to fulfill the minimum legal requirements of getting informed consent. At the higher levels, you tailor the informed consent process to the unique circumstances of treatment, guided by an understanding of the overarching moral principles. You incorporate informed consent procedures throughout treatment, recognizing that it is an important tool in promoting patient autonomy and welfare. *Bloom's taxonomy of informed consent is shown in Table 2.B.*

---

[1] In this section we focus on informed consent, documentation, and consultation as risk management strategies. More information on the Health Insurance Portability and Accountability Act (HIPAA) Privacy Rule and its implications for informed consent and documentation are provided in Section 3, chapter 4, Privacy, Confidentiality, and Privileged Communications.

TABLE 2.B
Bloom's Taxonomy of Informed Consent

Knowledge: You know that you are required to get informed consent.
Comprehension: You can describe to others the minimum requirements of informed consent.
Application: You can go through an informed consent process as it applies to most routine patients.
Analysis: You can identify the components of informed consent, such as the abilities to listen, communicate, and negotiate. You can also tailor the process to the unique context of treatment or the unique needs of the patient and in a manner that motivates and involves patients in the therapy process.
Synthesis: You can incorporate the informed consent process into your overall treatment relationship, which is geared to improving patient welfare and increasing patient autonomy.
Evaluation: In any particular case, you can explain why the particular informed consent process you used helped further the treatment goals.

Competency to Give Informed Consent

According to the APA Ethics Code, informed consent requires that the person has the ability to give consent. The psychologist also gives the patient information relevant to the decision to participate, including informing him or her that his or her participation is voluntary and that he or she has the right to ask questions (Standard 3.10, Informed Consent). When patients are not legally capable of giving informed consent, psychologists seek to obtain their assent, or general agreement with treatment.

Competency to make informed decisions is not an all-or-none matter but is probably better described as falling along a continuum. The informed consent process becomes problematic when the competence of the party to give informed consent is in question, such as when treating older adults with declining mental abilities, patients who are neurologically impaired, adults with mental retardation, or those who are not fluent in the same language as the evaluator. Also, some patients may have the cognitive ability to understand the information under normal circumstances, but anxiety, pressure from family or peers, or other psychological factors may inhibit their ability to process that information or to act on it independently. Consequently, at times it may be necessary to take additional steps or extra time to help patients understand their treatment options.

Research on competence with persons with serious mental illnesses or mental retardation shows that alternative or complementary modes of communication (such as audiovisual aides, conversations with friends and caregivers, and extra time to ask questions) can help them to evaluate their options to participate in treatment (Fisher, 2002, Roberts, 2000). While such individuals might not understand the general nature of therapy through the traditional discussion between therapist and patient, they may reach a better understanding if the same information is given by friends or caregivers and they have time to ask additional questions.

Content of the Informed Consent Process

The minimum content of the informed consent process is established by governing authorities, such as the APA Ethics Code, state laws, or the Health Insurance Portability and Accountability Act (HIPAA, 1996) Privacy Rule, and by research on the informational preferences of patients or prospective patients. We give more detailed information on the HIPAA Privacy Rule in Section 3, chapter 4, Privacy, Confidentiality, and Privileged Communications. However, for our purposes here, the salient question is what would the average person want to know under the circumstances (use a "patient knows best" instead of a "doctor knows best" principle)? Patients enter therapy or other professional relationships with psychologists with implicit assumptions about what is or is not ethical and what should or should not occur. Although surveys show general congruence between the conceptions of what psychologists and prospective patients view as ethical, there are some differences that could impact the perception of what patients perceive to be unethical behavior.

Ironically, as a result of today's statutes and regulations, psychologists may have to give patients such a large amount of written material that not even the most sophisticated patients will be able to digest it, let alone understand how it applies to them (Harris, 2003). Consequently, psychologists should not rely on the documentation alone to ensure that patients understand the important features of treatment.

In the APA Ethics Code, special standards deal with informed consent for therapy, assessment, supervised services, and research. The Ethics Code requires that information be given on the limits of confidentiality, the nature of therapy, and fees (Standard 10.01, Informed Consent to Therapy). When psychologists provide couples or family therapy, they inform parties ahead of time about their roles (Standard 10.02, Therapy Involving Couples or Families). If therapy involves couples, families, or social units, it is important to determine as soon as possible who is the patient, who might be appropriate collateral contacts, and whether the interests of participants are in conflict (Standard 10.02, Therapy Involving Couples or Families). When psychologists provide group therapy, they describe the responsibilities and roles of parties ahead of time (Standard 10.03, Group Therapy). When psychologists provide court-ordered therapy, they inform recipients of the anticipated nature of services (Standard 3.10c, Informed Consent). Trainees must notify those they see of their supervised status and the name of the supervisor and contact information (Standard 10.01c, Informed Consent to Therapy).

State licensing boards may have additional informed consent requirements. Also, elements of informed consent are incorporated into HIPAA by way of the required Privacy Notice for covered entities (i.e., practitioners or agencies that transmit patient-protected health information electronically), which psychologists should give patients at the first session or as soon as feasible. (We provide more information on the Privacy Rule in Section 3, chap. 4, Privacy, Confidentiality, and Privileged Communications; however, we recommend that all psychologists act as if the Privacy Rule applied to them, even if they are not covered entities.)

Braaten and Handelsman (1997) surveyed current patients, former patients, and nonpatients and found that they all valued information about the therapy process (e.g., what techniques will be used, what techniques are inappropriate in therapy, risks of therapy, alternatives available, and extent and limits of confidentiality); procedural issues (e.g., how to contact the therapist in an emergency, how appointments are scheduled, and how long appointments last); and billing issues (e.g., how much therapy will cost). In addition, it may also be prudent to discuss third-party reimbursement issues, policies concerning payment and collection of overdue debts, policies concerning cancellation of appointments (e.g., if you charge for canceled appointments), and access to records.

Pomerantz and Grice (2001) found that undergraduates were more accepting of multiple relationships than professionals but less accepting of mental health professionals who do things that make the patients uncomfortable, such as securing payment or selectively accepting patients. This suggests that some patients may conceptualize therapy "with little acknowledgment of the therapists' rights or desires, particularly as they involve the 'business' of therapy" (p. 746). If so, then psychologists should be alert that some patients may interpret some of their business practices as unethical.

We suggest that you avoid emphasizing potential negative events if they are remote and unlikely. For example, it may not be necessary, unless required by law, to have an informed consent form that spends an inordinate amount of time discussing the impropriety of sexual contact between psychologists and patients. Such an emphasis may give the patient the impression that the psychologist is preoccupied with sex or has impulses that are difficult to control.

In addition, you may want to give more information to patients when providing specific treatment modalities. For example, when providing couples therapy, give information concerning potential roles and collateral contacts (Standard 10.02, Therapy Involving Couples or Families).

Psychologists also document informed consent (Standard 3.10d, Informed Consent). Often the patient's signature on an informed consent form fulfills this requirement. Psychologists who do not use informed consent forms should document the informed consent procedure in their notes. The APA Insurance Trust (the Trust) has a sample patient agreement form that covers the minimum information that should be given at the start of therapy.[2] Written forms are best when they are readable, straightforward, and use ordinary language. They should supplement, not replace, verbal communications. Below we discuss additional information that may be given or emphasized depending on the needs of particular patients.

Informed Consent as a Process

Traditionally, informed consent was viewed as a passive event that required giving patients information so that they could make an informed decision about whether to undergo treatment. The legal doctrine of informed consent derived from medical procedures such as surgery in which the patient was essentially a passive recipient of a procedure and one-time consent was sufficient. However, the process of psychotherapy differs substantially from surgery or other medical procedures. Although it is still necessary to give patients information, informed consent in psychotherapy is best viewed as an ongoing interactive process and not a one-time event. No

---

[2] You may obtain the form at www.apait.org and may download and modify it as necessary.

one can predict the course of therapy or what new information or events may emerge over time. Consequently, the informational needs of patients will vary over the course of therapy.

Remember that we identified the belief that informed consent only consists of getting a patient's signature as a false risk management principle. Informed consent should not be a one-way street but an opportunity for the psychologist to learn more about the unique needs and perspectives of the patient. Here, as in other professional services, the ability to listen and show empathy ("the capacity to understand what another person is experiencing from within the other person's framework"; Bellet & Maloney, 1991, p. 1831) is important.

Certainly, one of the salient tasks is to get general agreement on the goals of therapy. It may or may not be helpful to share the specific diagnosis with the patient. However, it is important to have general agreement on the focus of treatment using lay language. "Discussion of therapy goals aimed at achieving consensus should take place throughout therapy" (Tryon & Winograd, 2001, p. 388). A meaningful discussion of goals should strengthen the therapeutic alliance. Issues that enhance patient ownership and participation in treatment include an understanding of treatment options and risks and agreement on goals and processes of treatment.

At times patients may not be able to make informed treatment decisions immediately. The processes of preparing them for decision making may involve processes analogous to developing a scaffold or the titration process (in which bits of information are added and processed over time). If the patient responds poorly to the additional information, then more time should be taken before the effort for full information is undertaken again.

A psychologist received a referral of a patient who had recently suffered a severe physical trauma. The patient's first words on entering therapy were that he only came in to get the doctor off his back and was never going to return. The psychologist knew that fear of talking about traumatic events is common among trauma victims. Consequently, she said that she respected the patient's choice and went on to describe how therapy would proceed if the patient were to decide to return, including the fact that, in the treatment of trauma, the patient retains complete control over whether to, when, and how much to discuss the trauma. The patient left after 15 minutes without scheduling a follow-up appointment.

Later the patient rescheduled and asked more about specific treatments. The psychologist briefly described the processes of cognitive restructuring, relaxation, and adjunctive medications. In the first interview the anxiety of the patient rendered him incapable of receiving all the information that ordinarily would be given in the first session. However, the psychologist titrated the information by giving it over more than one session. (2.1)

The higher levels of informed consent (according to Bloom's taxonomy) tailor the process according to the overarching moral principles and the factors considered in the RM formula (e.g., patient characteristics, context, and therapist characteristics). If you are acting at the higher levels of Bloom's taxonomy, you will convey an attitude that encourages genuine patient participation. Prescribing a process and implementing it are two different things. The manner of implementing the informed consent process can be as important as the content itself. Your tone of voice, choice of words, and nonverbal communication should reflect that you really want the patient to ask questions and express concerns. If you view the informed consent process as an annoyance, then it will be hard not to convey this to your patients. If you view the informed consent process as an integral part of ensuring patient participation, then this is likely be conveyed to your patients as well.

Challenges to Informed Consent Recommendations

Some may argue that our emphasis on informed consent is misplaced because it requires spending an inordinate amount of time on remote issues that have little relevance to treatment. We view this matter differently. The informed consent process should focus on what the average person would want to know under the circumstances. This does not require spending valuable therapy time on issues with no relevance to the patient. However, our experience has been that, under some circumstances, such as when doing evaluations with consequences or when treating children in the context of a high-conflict divorce, there is a very real potential for misunderstandings. Furthermore, the high emotional arousal of patients at the beginning of treatment may prevent them from attending closely when important issues are first raised by the psychologist.

Informed Consent and the Risk Management Formula

It may be helpful to view informed consent from the perspective of the RM formula introduced in the Preface. As you may recall, that formula is as follows:

$$\text{Clinical risk} = \frac{(P \times C \times D)}{TF}$$

In this formula, P = patient risk characteristics; C = context;
D = disciplinary consequences; and TF = therapist factors.

Informed Consent and Patient Factors

In addition to the general information that you should give to every patient, you can give additional information based on unique circumstances. One of the salient characteristics is the diagnosis (or treatment needs) of the patient. For example, when treating patients with panic disorders, it may be desirable to describe to them some of the treatment options that could be effective. If the patient has already tried psychotherapy and had a poor treatment response, you may be able to comment about the type of psychotherapy received and how it compares to other forms of treatment for this particular disorder.

Other factors that may be discussed include the apparent interpersonal qualities of the patient.

A psychologist started treatment with a depressed patient with a comorbid dependent personality disorder. The psychologist wisely alerted the patient that he might feel frustrated at

> times because she would push him toward more independence than he might find comfortable. Also, the psychologist alerted him to the fact that his wish for approval might inhibit him from being honest with her about his satisfaction with treatment or the nature of his progress. (2.2)

At times it may be necessary to warn against iatrogenic problems with some patients.

> A psychologist had just started treating a patient with significant problems who announced after two sessions that she had elected to take a job out of state and would be moving in six weeks. The psychologist believed it would be clinically contraindicated to open up difficult issues, only to have therapy discontinue shortly thereafter. Prudently, he cautioned her about potential iatrogenic effects of continuing therapy only to have it interrupted in a few weeks. (2.3)

If indicated, it may also be desirable to discuss the impact of therapy on significant others.

> A psychologist started treatment with a woman who desired to become more assertive in her marriage. However, the psychologist became concerned that an increase in her assertiveness could jeopardize her fragile marriage. Awareness of this possibility led the psychologist to discuss with his patient ways to mitigate against those possible negative consequences, such as by including her husband in treatment. (2.4)

Another factor that may be relevant is the apparent need to include (or exclude) family members from treatment. This is especially important with adolescents and is discussed in detail in Section 3, chapter 3, Working With Couples, Families, and Children.

Informed Consent and Contextual Factors

The content of what you provide in informed consent forms or verbally depends, in part, on the context of the professional service. Some common contextual features include experimental or unconventional treatments, families in high-conflict situations, third-party assessments, and forensic services.

You should inform patients when you are recommending unconventional or experimental treatments, including information on treatment alternatives and the risks and benefits of the proposed treatment (Standard 10.01b, Informed Consent to Therapy).

When treating families in which there is high conflict, such as when there is a pending hearing concerning the custody of a minor child, it may be important to emphasize your policies concerning court appearances, releasing information unrelated to treatment to third parties, payment for non-therapy-related services, and more. If you are assuming a hybrid role as a treating expert, then it may be especially important to review your policy concerning payment for nontherapy services. If the court appoints you as a therapist, family educator, or mediator, then it may be important to emphasize the rules and limits concerning confidentiality. We discuss this in greater depth in Section 3, chapter 5, Court Testimony.

Third-party assessments can also influence the content of your informed consent information. These may occur in independent medical evaluations, fitness for duty evaluations (e.g., preemployment and clergy evaluations), disability evaluations, recommendations to correctional facilities or law enforcement personnel, special education placements, organizational consultations, or for research projects or screenings for medical purposes (such as bariatric surgery). When conducting these evaluations, it is wise to document at the beginning of service, the purpose of the evaluation, patient access to reports (if any), and limits of confidentiality. You should get the document signed before assessment begins. Even when informed consent is not legally required, it is advisable for you to give the patient or participant a copy of the informed consent document. We discuss third-party assessments in more detail in Section 3, chapter 6, Psychological Assessment and Testing.

Some psychologists use "consumer-focused assessments," which involve patients in important decisions about assessments (Brenner, 2003). Although this is not usually done with third-party assessments, the possibility remains that it may be relevant in some circumstances.

When evaluating seminarians for candidacy into the ranks of the clergy, a psychologist routinely asked the seminarians "What do you want to get out of the process?" Most seminarians had not thought about the issues except to view the assessment as a hurdle they must jump or a potential obstacle to their career goal. However, the psychologist conducted the assessment over several weeks, instead of all at once. That way he got more than one sample of behavior, gave homework assignments, and allowed the candidates to reflect on what they could get out of the process. Although the evaluation did not consider the sincerity of the faith of the applicant, the psychologist often included questions about religious faith, personal calling, anticipated goals in the religious vocation, and more to break the ice and lower defenses. Giving feedback directly to both the applicant and the referral source allowed both to ask questions and clarify their understanding of the findings.

This technique helped the psychologist to fulfill his obligations to the third party (the denomination) and to the applicant as well. At times the candidates had problems so significant that they could not be recommended for candidacy. However, this participatory model helped them to reflect on their capabilities, limitations, and fitness for their religious vocation. (2.5)

Informed Consent and Individual Therapist Factors

Psychologists may disagree about the extent to which they self-disclose private information to patients. Some self-disclosure, such as the nature of the training and expertise of the psychologist, would appear appropriate as part of any informed consent process.

> A psychologist was contacted by an adult who wanted help in controlling his anger. Most of the problematic behaviors occurred at work, although he did mention some problems related to losing his temper with his children. The psychologist believed he could help the man with his work-related temper problems. He did note, however, that he did not have extensive experience in working with children. At the time it did not appear that the temper problems with the children were substantial (and most likely were an overflow of problems related to work). However, the psychologist did note that if there turned out to be substantial child-rearing issues, he would refer the patient to a colleague more skilled with children. (2.6)

It would also be appropriate to disclose any potential conflicts of interest or potential multiple relationships.

> A psychologist did an intake on a patient whom she learned was active in the state's Humane League. The psychologist had contact with the Humane League through occasional participation at the local chapter's annual banquet and other events. The participation of the psychologist was sufficient that it was conceivable that they might encounter each other, albeit briefly, at a state event. The psychologist discussed the possibility of brief contacts in those venues to give the patient the opportunity to assess her willingness to pursue therapy with her. (2.7)

Informed Consent and the Detailed Case Example

What would be the optimal role of informed consent in the detailed case example introduced in Section 1? Some of the problems in the case are that the patient has missed appointments without adequate notice and then bombarded the psychologist with telephone calls and e-mails. She stopped taking medications against the advice of her physician, stopped paying bills, and refused a recommendation to participate in a special group designed for individuals with her type of problems.

An informed consent procedure will not ensure that these problems can be avoided. However, an effective informed consent policy that addresses these issues at the start of treatment and throughout therapy as necessary increases the likelihood that the problematic behaviors can be reduced and gives you greater leverage in enforcing rules of treatment. Furthermore, the informed consent process can be reviewed throughout treatment as these resistances or patient obstacles to treatment emerge.

In an effort to get patients to "buy into" therapy, some psychologists will be overly nice and lenient about enforcing basic rules regarding payment, between-session phone calls, or cooperation with medication recommendations. Later, when the patient begins to deteriorate or begins to demonstrate problematic behaviors, it becomes harder to enforce the rules. The best policy is for you to enforce the rules conscientiously. One psychologist, for example, adopts a "one bite" rule, which means he confronts the patient immediately about any rule that the patient breaks but allows the patient one mistake before raising the issue of termination (see Section 3 chap. 8, Consultant or Supervisor, Diversity Issues, Conflicts in Institutional Settings, and Termination or Abandonment, for more information on unwanted terminations). In the event that you need to terminate the patient against his or her wishes, you will be able to reduce the negative consequences of that termination because you have made the conditions of participation in treatment clear from the beginning.

If it comes to a termination, the discussion should go beyond "you agreed to do this and now you have to follow through" and should focus on the clinical justification for the parameters set on treatment. Of course, the nature of some situations is sometimes best handled by avoiding a "tug of war" and deferring to the patient on whether to take medication or comply on some other issue. Nonetheless, a psychologist should never hesitate to give serious consideration to terminating a nonemergency patient who fails to comply with elements of treatment that are deemed essential. It is better to terminate a patient who is not in crisis early than to let the patient dictate clinically contraindicated restrictions on therapy that risk placing the psychologist in a role in which he or she is providing degraded treatment.

DOCUMENTATION

At the lower levels of Bloom's taxonomy, psychologists know they are required to keep records, although they may not be particularly clear about why, except for the risk management benefits of doing so. At the higher levels of Bloom's taxonomy, experienced psychologists link record keeping to patient welfare, their overall management of patient care, and overarching ethical principles. *Bloom's taxonomy applied to documentation is shown in Table 2.C.*

TABLE 2.C
Bloom's Taxonomy of Documentation

Knowledge: You know that you have to document your services.

Comprehension: You can describe to others the ethical and legally mandated minimum documentation requirements.

Application: You can document the most routine psychotherapy sessions.

Analysis: You can identify the elements of good documentation (essential components of a treatment record), your thinking processes (the "ninth-grade algebra teacher" rule described on page 46), and the purposes that the elements of good documentation fulfill.

Synthesis: You document carefully because, among other things, it reflects the careful thought processes required for quality care, communication with other treatment providers, evaluation of the progress of therapy, or other professional purposes.

Evaluation: In any given case you can provide clinical, ethical, and legal reasons why you documented the case in a particular manner.

Good records can provide the foundation for proper diagnosis and treatment. Good record keeping assists you in treatment by refreshing your memory, justifying payment to third-party payers, creating a record that you can send to future or current health providers, protecting you in the event that there are allegations of misconduct, and meeting requirements for agency reviews or accreditation. In addition, some practitioners use records to gather data for archival research.

Documentation is directly linked to patient welfare insofar as you demonstrate your analysis and thinking process and you consider the advantages and disadvantages of different options, consult with your peers, or choose and implement a professional strategy. Documentation is indirectly linked to patient care as you show compliance with institutional or legal requirements designed to ensure that your practice, as a whole, meets minimum standards of patient care. Documentation is also indirectly linked to patient care when archival research is used as a feedback mechanism or a source of data by which the overall quality of patient care in general is improved.

Documentation reflects your competence and demonstrates that you are delivering service in accordance with a reasonable standard of care. Although many definitions of competence are available, one useful one is "the habitual and judicious use of communication, knowledge, technical skills, clinical reasoning, emotions, values, and reflection in daily practice for the benefit of the individual and community being served" (Epstein & Hundert, 2002, p. 226). Although this definition was developed for use with physicians, it has application to the delivery of psychological services as well. That is, the documentation should reflect that you have knowledge relevant to the patient's presenting problem (i.e., cognitive knowledge and technical skills), that you have an adequate treatment relationship, and that you used clinical judgment in integrating that knowledge, skill, and relationship in the delivery of your services.

Documentation has unique risk management usefulness as well. From a legal perspective, the general rule is "if it isn't written down, it didn't happen." Records are given deference in disciplinary actions. Courts will generally assume that events occurred the way the records described them. If the record states that a patient was asked about suicidal ideation and denied it, then it is assumed that this is what happened. If there were a disciplinary complaint, the complainant would have a very high (and almost impossible) burden to overturn what was written in the psychotherapy record. In some cases, psychologists who have delivered an adequate level of care have been found negligent or forced to settle out of court because documentation did not sufficiently reflect that adequate standard of care. Poor or incomplete documentation can get you into trouble even if you did a good job. On the other hand, many potential malpractice cases or disciplinary cases are never pursued because the quality of documentation reflected an adequate level of care. Often the problem is not that psychologists had not done a good job, but that they were unable to demonstrate that they had done a good job.

The minimal standards for documentation can be found in the APA Ethics Code in Standards 6.01 (Documentation of Professional and Scientific Work and Maintenance of Records) and 6.02 (Maintenance, Dissemination, and Disposal of Confidential Records of Professional and Scientific Work).

More substantive details can be found in the Record Keeping Guidelines of the American Psychological Association (1993) and in state laws and state board of psychology regulations. Other sources, such as Medicare or other insurers, also provide standards for documentation. There have been detailed discussions concerning the impact of the HIPAA Privacy Rule on documentation and the relative merits of keeping psychotherapy notes separate from the rest of the patient's record. Here our concern is with the content of the patient records rather than if they are kept in a special psychotherapy notes section separate from the rest of the patient record. We discuss those issues in more detail in Section 3, chapter 4, Privacy, Confidentiality, and Privileged Communications.

What should be included in records depends on the relevant agency, state, or federal requirements. Certainly at the minimum they should include an evaluation summary, treatment goals, and session notes that demonstrate the thinking process of the professional in making treatment decisions. A relevant metaphor is that of the ninth-grade algebra teacher who gives credit for following the proper steps in solving the problem as well as the eventual answer. You get credit for correct procedures for working with the problem, even if you do not get the answer completely correct. Likewise, records of consultations with other professionals and other documents (such as patient productions or notes from other treatment providers) that influence treatment decisions will support the practitioner's actions in dealing with a complaint.

There are many different formats for keeping records. Most psychologists probably developed their record-keeping habits from their first practicum or internship placements. Nonetheless, here are some recommendations about records.

- Good records are comprehensive. That is, they include identifying information, a diagnosis (or presenting problem), a treatment plan, and sufficient information to establish the diagnosis (or understand the presenting problem) and to justify the treatment plan. The documentation should demonstrate to a knowledgeable observer that appropriate and competent treatment occurred.
- Always document consent. This is required by the APA Ethics Code (Standard 3.10d, Informed Consent). Often this can be done by securing your patient's signature, indicating that he or she received a copy of the informed consent or therapeutic agreement. In the event that you are not using such forms, you need to document in your records that there was a verbal discussion that fulfilled the informed consent requirements.
- Whenever possible, write records objectively. Problem behaviors should be described in detail (such as the circumstances under which they occur, frequency, point of onset and degree of disruption). The impact of the problem should be described (such as the impact on home, work, physical health, and relationships with others). As much as possible, the goals and objectives should be measurable and achievable (such as to reduce the frequency of panic attacks or increase the ability to leave home without having a panic attack). You should avoid more abstract goals such as to increase awareness of the inner self; healing the inner child; or where there is id, there ego shall be.

- Create records with the expectation that the patient will someday read them (this may help you to be prudent in your phrasing and descriptions). Although you may own the paper on which the records are created, you do not have complete control over their disposition. The patient, or another third party, may someday read them and control who else may see them.
- Indicate the sources and reliability of information. For example, writing "husband alcoholic" is less desirable than writing "the patient reports that her husband is an alcoholic." Writing "patient is a time bomb" is less desirable than writing "patient reports he feels like a time bomb."
- Records should be substantive, and the content should be related to the overall treatment goals. The quality of the documentation should increase as the degree of risk to the patient or to you increases. As much as possible, your records should show the connection between the presenting problems and the treatment strategies. That does not mean that you cannot change your mind about a patient, alter your diagnosis, or change your treatment plan. However, you should document why you altered your diagnosis or changed your treatment plan.
- Finally, records should be retrievable, which means that if they are handwritten, they should be legible. You should also store them securely. The exact nature of your security precautions may vary according to the location of your office (high-crime or low-crime area), the overall security of your building, and other factors.

Challenges to Documentation Recommendations

Some psychologists may argue that our conception of documentation is flawed, that such extensive documentation takes too much time and produces little benefit to themselves or their patients. They would rather spend this time on other professional tasks. Furthermore, they may argue, our conception of documentation as improving patient welfare is exaggerated and that little thought or reflection needs to go into creating the patient's record.

Other psychologists may go further and say that, aside from the time factor, keeping records in the manner we suggest actually degrades the quality of treatment. They may, for example, reference a recent statement from the American Psychoanalytic Association that states, in part, "Psychoanalysts refrain from documenting psychoanalytic treatment session by session. We believe that documenting the content of psychoanalysis seriously alters that treatment process and conflicts with fundamental clinical psychoanalytic skills" (American Psychoanalytic Association, 1995, p. 1).

Before we respond to these challenges, let us ensure that we are not attacking a straw man. We believe that we are being realistic about the need for comprehensive records. Not every psychotherapy note has to be exhaustive, although any individual psychotherapy note should be comprehensible in the context of other adjacent notes. Concise notes are fine, as long as they are comprehensive. Many psychologists use abbreviations, shorthand notations, or symbols that create no problems as long as the psychologist can translate them easily. Not all words have to be placed in sentence form. Sentence fragments are acceptable as long as others can discern the general meaning.

Also, we concede that we know many psychologists who have kept poor (or sometimes no) records for years without obvious negative consequences. That being said, we reiterate our belief in the importance of good records. While we respect the conscientious intent of our psychoanalytic colleagues, we urge psychologists to recognize that the failure to comply with the minimal standards of psychology could result in a disciplinary action if the work of these psychologists were ever to come under scrutiny. We urge psychologists to make any decision to violate a standard or law carefully and to try to find a middle ground whereby they can fulfill their therapeutic ideals while at the same time adhere to the standards of the profession.

Furthermore, we have seen the negative consequences when no notes were kept or when they were poorly kept. We are aware of psychologists who have lost substantial insurance payments when a subsequent audit revealed no notes or inadequate notes. We know psychologists who have been disciplined because the quality of their records did not substantiate the quality of care delivered. We are aware of psychologists who confused cases because they could not recall specifics of the case and their own documentation was not adequate to give them useful information. In one case the practitioner was unable to read her own notes.

Bad things can happen to good psychologists. Our considered judgment is that you and your patients are better off when you keep good records.

Documentation and the Risk Management Formula

Experienced psychologists can appreciate the link between documentation and the factors in the RM formula.

Documentation and Patient Factors

Documentation should include information about the patient and should increase as the presence of high-risk patient characteristics increases. For example, a psychologist conducted the first interview with a highly emotional patient who told dramatic stories of past abuse, failed treatments, and suicidal ideation and gestures. Such information may suggest that this is a patient who may present the therapist with significant risk management problems. There is a greater likelihood that treatment will be ineffective (or iatrogenic), a complaint will be lodged, and the behavior of the psychologist will come under scrutiny, first by the patient and later by outside groups. Consequently, greater vigilance should be taken in showing the relevant facts about the patient and how they were integrated into the treatment plan.

Documentation and Contextual Factors

Documentation should include information on the context of treatment, such as whether the patient was being seen under duress, the expectations of the patient for treatment, and other factors. Some aspects of the context are assumed (practitioners in solo practice need not document that they are in solo practice). However, other contextual factors should not be assumed, such as the presence of a cotreating psychopharmacologist or the involvement of other family members as collaterals in treatment.

A psychologist referred a patient to the hospital in an emergency. He communicated his concerns over the phone to the

> physician in the emergency room, summarized salient concerns in a letter that was faxed to the attending physician, and followed up the fax by mailing the letter to the hospital the same day. (2.8)

Documentation and Individual Therapist Factors

Documentation has its clearest impact on the individual therapist factor. That is, it demonstrates clear thinking on the part of the treating psychologist. Many psychologists find that their conceptualization of cases changes as they begin to create thoughtful notes or as they review notes from previous sessions. Also, documentation can be considered part of the context of treatment when treating a patient in an institutional setting where cooperation among treating professionals is important.

> A psychologist was treating a man with mental retardation who was displaying highly disruptive behavior in his employment in the sheltered workshop. The psychologist used a multiple baseline design to document the problem behaviors and the effect of the interventions. These data were useful in helping the facility determine that sufficient progress was being made so that they would continue the man's employment. (2.9)

At times, psychologists have found it helpful to involve a patient in the documentation process in an effort to help the patient understand the patterns that were occurring. The most obvious examples of this occur when psychologists ask patients to record behaviors or complete homework assignments. However, other psychologists have involved patients in their note-taking as a way to give feedback to patients on the psychologist's perceptions of the problems being faced or the defenses or strategies being used.

Documentation and the Detailed Case Example

As noted above, documentation serves many purposes, including promoting the quality of patient care and providing protection to the psychologist in the event of an allegation of improper conduct.

Documentation becomes especially important with high-risk patients such as this one. There is a possibility that the treatment relationship will be disrupted and the patient will be terminated (or terminate on her own) with ill feelings. There is also a possibility that the patient will make, or may actually succeed in, a suicide attempt. As noted above, all records should describe the treatment goals and processes. In this case, the quality of the documentation should be increased to describe, among other things, an analysis of the risk of suicide and efforts to reduce that risk. In these situations psychologists must often balance the short-term risks of a suicide attempt with the long-term potential for therapeutic gain. Although a short-term hospitalization may reduce the risk of suicide, it would most likely be clinically contraindicated. The note-taking should take the form of the ninth-grade algebra teacher who was as interested in the process of thinking through the problem as in obtaining the correct answer. The advantages and disadvantages of treatment options should be candidly discussed along with the reasons why a particular action was chosen.

One of the shortcomings found in many records is that they do not always include the actions that the psychologist did not take. For example, while it is appropriate to describe why the intensity of outpatient treatment was increased, it may also be appropriate to describe why the patient was not hospitalized, relatives were not notified, or a referral for medication management was not made. It is as important to describe what you did not do and why you did not do it, as to describe what you did do, especially if at a later date, there is a likelihood that what you did not do may be the basis of a complaint or lawsuit.

CONSULTATION

At the lower levels of Bloom's taxonomy, you may view consultation as necessary when you feel a general "SOS" motivated by a fear of being overwhelmed by incompetence and danger to the patient. At the higher levels of Bloom's taxonomy, you will be better able to specify the need for consultation more clearly and precisely. The type of consultation you seek will vary according to the patient characteristics, context of treatment, and your individual therapist factors. *Bloom's taxonomy of consultation is shown in Table 2.D.*

TABLE 2.D
Bloom's Taxonomy of Consultation

Knowledge: You understand the need to get consultation for high-risk patients or when involved in high-risk situations.

Comprehension: You can describe to others what a consultation is and how to go about getting it.

Application: You know when a case-specific consultation would be recommended, from whom to get it, and how to present the case.

Analysis: You can identify the different types of consultations and whether they focus on the clinical features of the patient, the context of treatment, the items in your skill inventory, the disciplinary consequences, or more than one factor in the risk management formula.

Synthesis: You view consultation as one part of the "system of protections" by which you better understand the patient; the context of treatment; the legal consequences of your behavior; or personal cognitive, emotional, or behavioral reactions that impact patient care.

Evaluation: In any particular case you can defend how consultation helped you promote patient welfare and avoid harm to both the patient and yourself.

As noted in Section 1, experienced psychologists risk developing a wide gap between their actual and perceived individual factors. (Remember: Perceived therapist factors > actual therapist factors.) You are only human, and like others, you risk overestimating your competence. However, these overestimates can be reduced if you receive high-quality feedback. Consequently, we recommend that you always seek consultation when dealing with patients with high-risk characteristics.

Consultation differs from supervision. In consultation the psychologist retains the independent ability to make decisions about a patient. In supervision the supervisor actually directs the treatment of an individual (e.g., an unlicensed trainee) who lacks the legal authority to act independently. Sometimes psychologists use these terms incorrectly and may refer to peer consultation groups as peer supervision groups. These are important distinctions, however, because they are differentiated in law.

Consultation, like documentation, helps to ensure that you are delivering services in accordance with a reasonable standard of care. To reach and maintain that goal of delivering services with a reasonable standard of care, you need to embed yourself in a protective network that gives you high-quality feedback concerning your performance. The most obvious way to ensure that quality of feedback is to develop a working relationship with your patients who feel free to tell you how they are progressing toward their goals. Other sources of quality feedback include those with whom you share your office or those whom you seek out for consultation.

Some consultations are done within an ongoing group; others are case specific. Ongoing consultation may occur in a peer consultation group or in a support group, such as Balint groups (Salinsky, 1997). We discuss peer consultation, support, and Balint groups in more detail in Section 3, chapter 1, Competence.

Often psychologists learn through incidental encounters with other psychologists. This may occur through attending continuing education programs, participating in journal clubs, supervising practicum students or interns, making professional presentations, being an adjunct or visiting faculty member, serving on the committee of the local or state psychological association, or volunteering on the board of a local mental health organization.

In addition to participating in these lifelong systems of protections, it may be necessary to get case-specific assistance on a particular patient through consultation. In case-specific consultation you seek consultation according to the type of patient problem presented, whether it involves consequential (legal), clinical, or personal factors. As noted above, always seek consultation with high-risk patients even if it appears that you have the situation under control. Other situations in which consultation should be sought include when there is a therapeutic impasse, when you have reason to perceive an increase in legal risks, when there is danger to self or others, or when you have strong reactions (either positive or negative) toward a patient. In those situations it is important that you shore up your personal data base and get feedback on the relevance or effectiveness of your personal skill inventory.

In addition to the obvious patient benefit aspects, consultation can also be viewed as an important element of personal self-care. Feelings of stress can be diminished when psychologists have the opportunity to discuss their deepest professional fears and uncertainties with competent and trusted professionals.

> A psychologist became director of a large mental health center, and he noticed that the staff often sought impromptu discussions with each other in the hallways and in a manner that threatened to violate patient privacy. Of course, he cautioned against that practice, but he also realized that the staff did not have regularly scheduled opportunities to discuss cases. The impromptu hallway consultations were the only opportunity the staff had to get feedback on cases. Consequently, the psychologist initiated supervision and peer consultation groups. (2.10)

The type and source of consultation may vary according to patient needs and the psychologist's dilemma. Consultation may be obtained from a practitioner who is also treating the patient, such as a psychiatrist who is prescribing medication for the patient. At other times, it may be desirable to have the consultant evaluate the patient directly, for example, to screen for neuropsychological disorders, to refer to a physician who will screen for the potential of a coexisting physical problem that may contribute to the patient's problems, or to refer to another mental health practitioner for a second opinion on the patient and services delivered.

Novice practitioners sometimes toss out a general cry for help. However, more experienced practitioners will clarify the "ask" or the nature of their request when they get a consultation. That does not mean that they will only accept responses related to their questions, but they help the consultant by describing the case and framing the issues as clearly and precisely as possible.

Not all consultations are created equal. Effective consultants are critical, honest, and skilled. You should not seek self-validation ("the choir") from close friends or those who have reasons not to be critical (e.g., a spouse, supervisee, or person with less training and experience than you). Also, consultations are effective if you are completely honest about the situation, including information about transference or countertransference problems or therapeutic errors. Selective presentation of facts will lead to less than optimal advice, reminiscent of the computer adage "garbage in, garbage out."

Often it is helpful to receive consultation from a clinician with a different theoretical orientation to reduce the likelihood that ideological factors are blocking awareness of other sources of explanation. For example, it may be beneficial for a cognitive-behaviorally trained psychologist to seek consultation from a psychologist with a psychodynamic orientation. Often it is desirable to seek consultation from a psychiatrist or prescribing psychologist to determine if psychopharmacological options need to be considered.

At times it may be desirable to have the consultation in writing, especially if it involved a face-to-face interview with the patient. Many more specific consultations can be done verbally, although even in those circumstances it may be desirable to repeat back to the consultant the general nature of the recommendations and to record them accordingly.

General requests for information on electronic mailing lists need to be done judiciously. It may be quite appropriate to learn the names of specific journal articles or books on a topic or the names of particular psychologists who have expertise in an area. However, detailed requests for comment on a particular case may be problematic. It is hard to give enough detail to make the consultation meaningful, and the consultant on the electronic mailing list would not have access to therapy notes and other documentation. Furthermore, giving that amount of detailed information risks infringing on patient privacy.

Challenges to Consultation Recommendations

Some might argue that we are too quick to recommend consultation and that we fail to appreciate its costs to the practitioner. Sometimes the cost may be in terms of the time spent seeking consultation with a colleague (and time spent giving consultation to a colleague in the event there is a reciprocal agreement). At other times, there are direct financial costs in paying for a consultation.

This point highlights the fact that risk management is not only a clinical decision but a business decision as well. That is, it may take time and cost money to get consultations. The same point could be made for the time put into informed consent and documentation. Of course, each psychologist will have to decide how much time to invest in each of these risk management strategies. However, those psychologists who keep the number of high-risk patients in their practice low; have good risk management habits, know the APA Ethics Code, relevant state and federal laws, and the latest update on their applications; and are well trained will have less need to invest extra time on the risk management strategies we present.

> A psychologist had a private practice in which he restricted himself to career counseling and treating patients with relatively minor disorders. He was highly proficient in those areas in which he practiced and found little need to seek consultation, although he was quick to do so when indicated. (2.11)

Consultation and the Risk Management Formula

Consultations can be specific for the dimension of the RM formula and can include requests for information on the patient's characteristics (e.g., "Is this patient's behavior influenced by his or her physical condition?"), context of treatment (e.g., "Are there special circumstances dealing with high-conflict families that I am missing here?"), or the individual therapist factors (e.g., "Am I overestimating my competence to deal with these types of patients?").

Consultation and Patient Factors

> A psychologist was treating a patient who, during the course of treatment, was diagnosed with fibromyalga. He requested information from the listserv of his state psychological association concerning books or articles about this disorder. (2.12)

> A psychologist was asked to treat a Korean woman. Although he had little experience or knowledge of Korean culture, none of the other psychologists in his city did either. Consequently, he accepted the patient but consulted with a

Korean American psychologist concerning unique cultural factors that might influence conceptualization of patient needs and implementation of the treatment goals. (2.13)

A psychologist was treating a patient who expressed a strong impulse to kill another person. The psychologist gathered extensive information on this patient, including his responses to a violence rating scale (although the scale had not been standardized on psychiatric outpatients, and he noted this fact in his interpretation). Since he lived in a state that had a duty to warn, he carefully recorded his sources of data, patient characteristics, and factors relevant to determine whether, in fact, the patient presented an imminent risk to harm others.

In addition, the psychologist recorded what he did NOT do as well as what he did do. His records reflected his consideration of various options and why he decided that another option was more clinically and legally appropriate. (2.14)

Consultation and Contextual Factors

A psychologist accepted a child in therapy. During the course of therapy, the parents decided to divorce and became involved in a bitter child custody dispute in which, among other things, allegations of parent alienation syndrome were made. The psychologist sought consultation from an expert concerning the unique factors to consider when treating families with allegations of parent alienation syndrome. (2.15)

A psychologist was asked to participate in a research project that, among other things, required him to tape-record the therapy sessions and to give pre- and posttests. Before agreeing to participate, he spoke with an experienced researcher who explained how to enlist the cooperation of patients in the study in a manner that minimized the disruption of services and complied with relevant rules and regulations. (2.16)

As a favor to a referral source, a psychologist agreed to accept a patient in the criminal justice system who was on probation. Before he took the case, however, he spoke at length to his cousin who was a probation officer in a neighboring town. That way he was better informed on the nature and type of information that probation officers typically want when they are supervising cases. (2.17)

A psychologist treated a patient with a severe and persistent mental illness who had been unemployed for many years. He sought a consultation from an attorney specializing in disability law concerning the likelihood that his patient might qualify for social security disability benefits. (2.18)

Consultation and Individual Therapist Factors

> A psychologist/teacher received a request for a consultation from a former student/family therapist who recently went through a difficult divorce. While treating a couple for marital therapy, this former student developed a very strong negative reaction to the husband. The former student wondered if her reaction was influenced by her own recent divorce. She spoke to the psychologist/teacher about the intensity of her feelings that alarmed her. After speaking with her former teacher she transferred the couple and sought therapy for herself. (2.19)

Fortunately, this therapist had sufficient insight to seek input from a trusted professional. At other times psychologists have allowed their personal skill inventory to become obsolete over time or to be filled with their personal but often faulty perspectives on life, which may have been influenced by their own continuing personal difficulties. For example, some psychologists are not aware of the latest research in therapeutic or assessment techniques. This obsolescence is more likely to occur among psychologists who are "outliers" or who do not participate in continuing education activities (except to the minimum required by a licensing board), who do not participate in professional association activities, or who otherwise isolate themselves. This perspective was supported by a recent review that found that psychologists who did not belong to a state psychological association had three times the frequency of being disciplined by licensing boards than did those who belonged to state associations (Knapp, 2005). It is hard to evaluate these data because perhaps the more conscientious psychologists selected themselves into the state association. Nonetheless, the data are consistent with the idea that isolated outliers are more likely to experience disciplinary actions (and presumably deliver a lower level of care).

Multilevel Consultations

A psychologist was treating a patient with severe depression who was not responding to a combination of psychotherapy and medication prescribed by a highly skilled psychiatrist. A medical consultation had ruled out any physical condition that could be contributing to the depression. The treating psychologist and psychiatrist recommended a direct evaluation of the patient by a third professional to cover all aspects of the patient care, including patient characteristics, context of treatment, and individual therapist factors. The consultant provided a detailed report that followed the MOST CARE model suggested by Clayton and Bongar (1994; Medical/medication needs; Overall management of the case; Specific concerns; Therapeutic alliance; Crisis intervention plans in case of an emergency; Alternative, adjunctive, or additional treatments; Risk/benefit analysis; Ethical or legal considerations).

Formats such as MOST CARE are useful in that they ensure that the major issues of concern have been addressed. Other competent psychologists use other formats such as the BASIC ID (Lazarus, 1989) or the PAINT system (Ginsburg, Albano, Findling, Kratochvil, & Walkup, 2005) that is used for adolescents. (The PAINT acronym refers to Presenting problem,

Antecedents and consequence, Identification of goals, strengths and weaknesses, Noting the context, and Treatment data.)

Consultation and the Detailed Case Example

In the high-risk case presented in Section 1, consultation becomes very important. Ongoing consultation and social support are necessary to handle the frustration that this patient generates. On a personal level the psychologist may be overwhelmed with anger and then guilt because of the anger. An ongoing support system can help to reduce those feelings or normalize them and allow the psychologist to use those feelings to better understand the clinical dynamics of the patient.

In addition, the techniques for handling the case suggest the need for a consultant with detailed information and knowledge about dialectical behavior therapy or treatments of borderline personality disorders in general. Consultation is especially important whenever there are life-endangering qualities. The general rule is never treat life-endangering patients alone. Always consult with others.

SYNERGY OF THE RISK MANAGEMENT STRATEGIES

The three risk management strategies that we have described have a synergistic effect; they are not isolated or disembodied techniques. They are designed to promote patient welfare, avoid harm, and help psychologists better fulfill their obligations to patients. For example, documentation should indicate that informed consent was obtained, or that consultation was sought, or that consultation may be obtained on how to maximize patient investment in the treatment process.

We have already described how informed consent can promote patient autonomy. Typically, psychologists do not think of documentation or consultation as ways to promote patient autonomy. Nonetheless, in some circumstances they can be. For example, patients may be involved in the content of the documentation as an exercise in helping both parties articulate the problems or progress in treatment. This is not typically done, but psychologists may be more creative in these kinds of strategies if they remember that documentations (or consultations) can be substantive acts that further patient welfare.

How much can informed consent, documentation, and consultation contribute to the welfare of this patient, reduce the risk of harm, and protect the psychologist from allegations of misconduct? Of course, the conscientious application of these principles cannot always foster positive outcomes or reduce all risk; the question is whether it can increase the likelihood of positive outcomes and reduce risks.

Consider, for example, how the three risk management principles might have influenced the relative weight of the factors in the RM formula. Think of the formula,

$$\text{Clinical risk} = \frac{(P \times C \times D)}{TF}$$

In this formula, P = patient risk characteristics; C = context; D = disciplinary consequences; and TF = therapist factors.

Would a more detailed and ongoing informed consent procedure have helped set a more therapeutic context for treatment, such as clarifying ahead of time that the failure to adhere to medication and other treatment requirements would be grounds for termination? Could this have altered the context of treatment and made the patient more open to complying with adjunctive treatments?

Would more detailed assessment and treatment notes have helped you to conceptualize the dynamics of the case and the patient's response to treatment? Would it have given you reassurance that you were providing a high level of care? Could this have altered the therapist variables (ability to conceptualize the case) and reduced the fear of consequential factors? Would ongoing or case-specific consultation have helped you to improve the quality of treatment to the patient and helped reduce some of the negative countertransference that you feel? Would this have altered therapist variables to the extent that it improved emotional competence?

RISK MANAGEMENT STRATEGIES AND DEFENSIVE MEDICINE

Defensive medicine refers to "a deviation from sound medical practice that is induced primarily by a threat of liability" (Studdert et al., 2005, p. 2609). It can include *assurance behaviors,* such as supplying additional services of marginal or no value. As applied to psychology, it can apply to getting consultations for a case in which you only want to say you got a consultation; you really do not expect the patient to benefit from the consultation. It can also consist of *avoidance behaviors,* such as refusing to treat certain patients only because they have a higher risk of filing an allegation of misconduct against you.

ASSURANCE BEHAVIORS

Some readers may claim that the risk management strategies that we are suggesting are an assurance behavior form of defensive medicine that drives up health care costs and provides little or no benefit to patients. They may claim that the documentation and consultation recommendations contribute little or nothing to patient welfare. Some may even argue that they degrade services because they divert your attention and resources away from patient care and may disrupt your relationship with patients.

Depending on the circumstances, the risk management poultices we review may or may not improve the quality of treatment. If these poultices are used only to increase your sense of personal safety, then they are unlikely to increase the quality of health care and may increase costs. We defer to your clinical judgment as to when or how to apply the risk management recommendations. You are in the best position to determine how much time you need to spend on documentation or consultation for any particular patient. You will be more likely to make a good decision if you are informed by an accurate self-perception and your services are delivered in the context of a system of safety with redundant checks on your behavior.

Furthermore, if these risk management strategies are applied pro forma only for defensive purposes and divorced from any overarching philosophy of patient care, then we agree they would risk becoming clinically meaningless or unhelpful defensive medicine exercises. However, we urge you to consider the risk management strategies from the standpoint of Bloom's taxonomy. Informed consent, documentation, and consultation, if done at the higher levels of Bloom's taxonomy, are integrated into and improve overall patient care. At the lower levels, these risk management strategies may save you from complaints and lawsuits but may add little to your management of the case. Remember that caring for patients not only means your affective feeling of concern but also your diligence ("conscientiousness, self-scrutiny, and a concern for excellence"; Peteet, 2004, p. 53) in meeting patient needs.

AVOIDANCE BEHAVIORS

Critics may also claim that our recommendation to show discretion in treating high-risk patients represents avoidance behavior that results in denial of care to vulnerable patients. Often these patients are from historically disadvantaged groups that have had a high rate of victimization. Instead of reaching out to help these individuals, it could be argued that our risk management recommendations tend to discourage psychologists from treating them by encouraging psychologists to refer them to community agencies that are traditionally underfunded and often staffed with uncredentialed mental health providers.

We are not saying that you should avoid all high-risk patients. Indeed, the moral principle of distributive justice (the fair distribution of health care resources; Beauchamp & Childress, 2001) would suggest that you should make a special effort to treat those needing treatment, those who other health care providers might avoid. However, the moral principle of distributive justice needs to be balanced with the moral principles of beneficence (promoting welfare of others) and nonmaleficence (avoiding harming others).

Consequently, we are saying that you should make an informed decision to treat such patients and to recognize that sometimes, despite your best intentions, your treatment may not be beneficial and may, in fact, harm them. Good intentions are not enough; they need to be informed good intentions. Even informed good intentions can lead to angry patients who look for ways to retaliate.

In addition to your personal response to individual patients, we ask you to consider the public policy issues that are involved. We agree that public mental health services are underfunded. We have all been involved with our state psychological associations, the APA Practice Organization, the Association for the Advancement of Psychology, and other groups to promote adequate funding for public agencies. We urge you to do the same.

Eight Essential Points to Remember

1. The purposes of informed consent are to (a) maximize patient participation in the treatment process, (b) avoid creating a sense of betrayal, (c) explain office policies, and (d) explain billing and payment policies ahead of time.

2. Informed consent is a process, not a one-time event.

3. Informed consent is especially important when conducting evaluations with consequences.

4. It is difficult to overestimate the importance of good documentation.

5. Good records should explain what was done and the reasoning behind why those decisions were made. In high-risk situations, good records should also explain what was not done and why not.

6. When in doubt, get high-quality consultation that focuses on the areas of clinical knowledge, disciplinary consequences, or your personal skill inventory.

7. Consultations are most effective when you select someone who is objective, not beholden to you, and willing to be critical of what you have done and who views things from a different perspective and values patient welfare above sparing your feelings.

8. You will be better able to apply the risk management recommendations of informed consent, documentation, and consultation if you have a higher understanding of what they mean.

Chapter 1: COMPETENCE

Competence means the ability to perform according to the standards of the profession. Pope and Brown (1996) described competence as involving three factors: knowledge, technical skills, and emotional competence.

Generally, psychologists' graduate programs and supervised experiences will have helped them acquire the necessary knowledge and technical skills, and their mastery of the content for the psychology licensing examination will have furthered their goal of becoming knowledgeable. Typically, psychologists' areas of competent practice are derived from the content of their graduate programs, practica, internships, and other supervised experiences, subject to some kind of external control. After becoming licensed and with some experience, most psychologists feel comfortable stating that they are competent in certain areas of practice, such as in the treatment and assessment of adults, health psychology, neuropsychology, or another domain of practice. It may be helpful to consider competence from the standpoint of Bloom's taxonomy (see Table 3.1.A).

Furthermore, some psychologists are specialists in that they have received more training, experience, and expertise in a certain domain of practice through additional supervision, course work, or postdoctoral training. Psychologists may, for example, have received a diplomate from the American Board of Professional Psychology or a certificate from the College of Professional Psychology. Specialists typically spend a large portion of their time working in their area of specialty. Most psychologists are unlikely to earn specialty standing in more than two areas of practice, since the very nature of being a specialist involves having a large portion of one's practice dedicated to work in that specialty.

Psychologists are best able to contribute to the public welfare when they view competence as a dynamic and interactive factor. Remember the risk management formula:

$$\text{Clinical risk} = \frac{(P \times C \times D)}{TF}$$

In this formula, P = patient risk characteristics; C = context; D = disciplinary consequences; and TF = therapist factors.

At first appearance it looks like competence is identical to the individual therapy factors or personal skill inventory described in Section 1. However, competence is not a fixed entity but varies according to the unique needs of your patients, context of treatment, and your life circumstances. For example, psychologists with a very strong personal skill inventory will be able to work well with a wide range of patients. However, even those psychologists may apply it with patients or in situations beyond their range of effectiveness and increase their risk of practicing incompetently. On the other hand, psychologists with more limited personal skill inventories may be aware of their limitations and consequently select patients or situations carefully and ensure that their skills will be applied where the likelihood of success is high. Again, look at competence from the standpoint of Bloom's taxonomy (see Table 3.1.A).

TABLE 3.1.A
Bloom's Taxonomy of Competence

Knowledge: You can identify the mutually agreed upon goals (based on the patient's diagnosis or presenting problems) and the professional services (such as interventions) that should be used.

Understanding: You can describe or define the goals of treatment and describe the interventions used.

Application: You can implement an intervention appropriate to the treatment goals with a patient in the context of a professional relationship.

Analysis: You can identify the components and sequence of the interventions that you implemented, the elements of your professional relationships, and their relationship to specific agreed upon treatment goals given your individual therapist factors, including emotional resources, time resources, and skill inventory appropriate for this patient in this context.

Synthesis: You can integrate the components of your intervention within the context of an overall professional relationship given your individual therapist factors, including emotional resources, time resources, and skill inventory appropriate for this patient in this context.

Evaluation: You can justify the assessment and intervention strategies you used, how they were related to the patient's problems and goals, and how they were appropriate considering the totality of your individual therapist factors and their appropriateness for this patient in this context.

Dr. Smith was a highly respected psychologist. When her spouse became disabled, the entire burden of family income fell on her, including the burden of paying for her children's college expenses. She began to work longer hours and accept patients whom she ordinarily would have referred elsewhere. She accepted a high-conflict family, and because she lacked the time to respond quickly to the many phone calls, she became alienated from one of the parents. A complaint before the licensing board followed.

Although the complaint was not founded and she was exonerated by the licensing board, it nonetheless represented

> a treatment failure and a burden for Dr. Smith to defend herself before a licensing board investigator. Although Dr. Smith might have been competent to deal with this family when her life was less hectic, she was not competent to deal with them when her professional resources were more taxed. (3.1.1)

Awareness of the extent of one's competence is one of the factors in a psychologist's individual skill inventory. The care with which psychologists make decisions about the application of their skills depends on how accurately they judge their abilities and resources. Those psychologists who consistently overestimate their abilities or resources will find themselves in situations in which they are less likely to perform in a competent manner.

Fortunately, most patients have fairly routine problems. Nonetheless, psychologists need to be cautious when dealing with high-risk patients, such as those who are involved in litigation, present a threat of harming others, or have a serious personality disorder. If you have been treating a patient who begins to present a condition that you do not feel competent to treat, discuss the matter with an experienced colleague. If appropriate, refer that patient to another psychotherapist for evaluation or treatment.

You should know when to pass up the opportunity to treat certain patients. Some patients have complex needs and are best treated in an institution or where a team approach is available that includes coordinating services during therapist absences and emergencies, 24-hour coverage, availability of psychiatric and medical care, and access to hospital or day treatment programs if needed. Individual psychologists who see such patients will need more skills or more resources to help them. That is not to say that all of you should refer all of your patients with serious personality disorders or other serious disorders. Nonetheless, if you do accept them as patients, you need to appreciate the emotional and time demands that they will place on you. Many psychologists restrict themselves to only one or two such patients at any given time.

> Dr. Jones agreed to accept a patient with a serious personality disorder and chronic suicidal ideation for therapy. Dr. Jones was proficient in the treatment of such disorders, had received advanced training, and had a strong network of supportive professionals. The next day she received a referral from another patient with a similar symptom presentation. She declined this referral, recognizing that her ability to respond to the needs of this patient (and indeed her entire caseload) might be compromised by the presence of one more highly disturbed patient in her caseload.
>
> Dr. Jones recognized the limits of her individual therapist factors. She had the self-awareness to understand that she could not help everyone. She avoided "runaway compassion," or the belief that she has to help everyone. She also understood that the legal right to treat does not mean a legal mandate to treat. (3.1.2)

A common situation occurs when one parent in a high-conflict family wants you to treat the child, but the other parent objects. Even if you are legally allowed to treat that child, at times the family conflicts over therapy make the very act of therapy iatrogenic. Sometimes it is best not to treat. You need to weigh these situations carefully and consider whether your ability to help the child will outweigh the harm caused by the added tension of providing treatment with a family that is partially opposed to your efforts.

Again, forethought, thought, and afterthought are important. Think about your strengths and where you want to concentrate your efforts ahead of time. Get quality feedback on your strengths and weaknesses as they relate to your desired areas of practice. Think back on your experiences and determine where you need more work.

EMOTIONAL COMPETENCE

The American Psychological Association's "Ethical Principles of Psychologists and Code of Conduct" (APA Ethics Code) requires psychologists to be alert to early signs of personal problems that may prevent them from fulfilling their professional obligations. Sometimes unresolved personal problems can cause psychologists to act impulsively or to be insensitive to the needs of their patients. If psychologists neglect their self-care, they may be more prone to disrespecting their patients, denigrating the importance of their work, feeling an array of dysphoric emotions, or making more clinical mistakes (Pope & Vasquez, 2005).

Compassion fatigue is especially likely to occur when psychologists treat patients who have had severe traumas or who otherwise have great personal needs. Psychologists may need to distance themselves from their patients' problems to be effective. They may need to limit the number of needy, seriously disturbed, or taxing patients with whom they work. Psychologists' individual therapist factors may be adequate to take one patient with a serious personality disorder, but by doing so, they limit their flexibility in taking on a second such patient. The emotional and time strain produced by one such patient limits their flexibility in handling subsequent patients.

When you become aware of personal problems (e.g., fatigue, burnout, depression, or substance abuse) that could significantly impair the quality of your work, the APA Ethics Code requires that you address them, and in the meantime, limit, suspend, or terminate work-related duties. You are especially likely to make errors when you are undergoing personal crises or stresses. One of the paradoxes is that you are more likely to engage in denial when you are emotionally compromised, thus making it more difficult to identify your vulnerable state.

> A psychologist had a friend from graduate school who had just gone through a divorce. He contacted his psychologist friend, and they had lunch together. It was a way for the psychologist to express his concern for his friend and to offer assistance or nurturance if it was needed. (3.1.3)

Of course, your goal should not be just to avoid impairment but to maximize your physical and emotional health. You need to be aware of your physical and mental needs. You benefit when you take routine care of your basic physical needs such as diet, rest, exercise, and medical care and make certain that you feel adequately refreshed in the morning. You should show equal concern for your mental health by taking time to nurture your support system and enjoy your friends and family members.

In their landmark survey of psychotherapists from many countries, Ronnestad and Orlinsky (2005) found that a dimension of practice, which they called "stressful involvement," was reflected in defensive, therapeutically destructive coping strategies and demoralization. These defenses were more likely to occur among psychologists who worked in institutional settings with little social support. On the other hand, many other psychologists experienced what Ronnestad and Orlinsky called "healing involvement," characterized by constructive involvement, affirmative involvement in work, and flow during therapy sessions. They emphasized the importance of continuous personal growth experiences for psychologists throughout their careers.

Ideally, you will be continually moving toward greater self-awareness through the use of self-reflection. Of course, this can sometimes come through supervision or personal therapy. However, it may also come through keeping a diary of important clinical experiences, group consultation, or Balint groups (Salinsky, 1997)

Unfortunately, some psychologists will be unable to meet the minimum standards of their profession as a result of physical or mental disabilities. Fortunately, many licensing boards or state psychological associations have developed colleague assistance programs. The nature and procedures for these programs varies from state to state, but typically they provide a means for impaired psychologists to receive treatment and offer the option that they can continue in, or return to, professional service (Barnett & Hillard, 2001).

COMPETENCE WITH DIVERSE POPULATIONS

As the American population becomes more diverse, all psychologists will be more likely to encounter patients from diverse cultural, ethnic, racial or religious backgrounds. Ideally, everyone who requests mental health services should be able to receive them from someone who understands his or her culture.

You will be more effective when you recognize that patients from diverse backgrounds can express their distress and react to psychological treatment in unique ways. You should be aware of the unique needs or perspectives of patients who are from diverse religious backgrounds, are members of sexual minorities, or have physical and mental disabilities, and you should strive to learn from such patients about their special cultural expressions that may interact with your mental health services. Invite diverse patients to share their perspectives and collaborate with you in understanding their needs. Follow the APA "Guidelines on Multicultural Education, Training, Research, Practice, and Organizational Change for Psychologists" (APA, 2003) and "Guidelines for Psychotherapy with Lesbian, Gay, and Bisexual Clients" (APA, 2000).

Fortunately, information on how to respond more effectively to individuals from cultural or linguistic minorities is emerging (see, e.g., APA, 1993, 2003; Hansen, Pepitone-Arreola-Rockwell, & Greene, 2000; Stuart, 2004).

Also, a body of literature is emerging on the unique clinical concerns of patients with same-sex attraction. You will be more effective if you have familiarity with this literature (see, e.g., Lasser & Gottlieb, 2004; Pachankis & Goldfried, 2004; Schneider, Brown, & Glassgold, 2002).

The Ethics Code allows limited exceptions to competence that can be made in emergencies or when working with closely related problems in underserved geographic areas (Standard 2.02, Providing Services in Emergencies).

In emergencies, when psychologists provide services to individuals for whom other mental health services are not available and for which psychologists have not obtained the necessary training, psychologists may provide such services in order to ensure that services are not denied. The services are discontinued as soon as the emergency has ended or appropriate services are available.

Nonetheless, if you continue to deliver services under these circumstances, you should acquire competence through study, supervision or consultation.

MAINTAINING COMPETENCE

How do you ensure that you are maintaining your competence (keeping up with the knowledge base of the field, ensuring adequate technical skills, and maintaining emotional competence)? Knapp and Keller (2004b) found that psychologists rated interaction with colleagues as the source that did the most to develop their professional skills. Other sources were continuing education (CE) workshops, newsletters, professional and scientific conventions, and journal articles. Of course, these global ratings failed to give specifics concerning the type of colleague interactions, CE programs, or other sources and how they related to the development or maintenance of any particular skill. Nonetheless, the ratings suggest that professional development is likely to be enhanced by participation in activities that increase one's connections with peers, such as through peer consultation groups, listservs, or attendance at professional meetings. Finally, continuing education programs themselves may facilitate interactions among colleagues. For example, in their review of the literature on continuing medical education (CME), Davis et al. (1999) found that interactive CME programs (those that included case discussions, role plays, discussion groups, etc.) tended to produce better patient outcomes compared to didactic presentations.

The failure to maintain one's competence has been called "practitioner decay," although that might not be the best term to describe this phenomenon. It is true that some psychologists may have been competent, but their basic interpersonal skills declined over time. However, it is also possible that some were not entirely competent from the beginning. Nonetheless, there is some evidence consistent with the theory that the skills of some practitioners fall behind acceptable standards over time. Choudhry, Fletcher, and Soumerai (2005) found that the quality of performance of physicians was inversely related to their years of practicing. Also, Handelsman (1997) found that Colorado psychologists who had been licensed more than 15 years were more likely to have an ethics charge levied against them.

The reasons for this vulnerability to lapse into substandard quality of service delivery are not known. Perhaps over time psychologists overestimate their competence. They can compensate for this tendency by receiving high-quality feedback. It is important for psychologists to embed themselves in a "system of protection."

SYSTEMS OF PROTECTION (REDUNDANT SYSTEMS)[1]

The literature on medical errors may be relevant here. According to the Institute of Medicine (2000), between 44,000 and 98,000 hospital patients die each year because of preventable medical errors. These errors included such mistakes as administering an incorrect medication (either the wrong medication was given to the patient; the patient was given a medication that was known to cause an allergic reaction in that individual; the incorrect dose of a medication was given; or the patient was given medications in combination when it should have been known that the interaction of these medications would have an adverse effect). Other errors included laboratories that mixed up the results from different patients, surgeons who operated on the wrong patient, and more.

These medical errors were frequently caused by the breakdown of communication among staff members. For example, a physician might not read the nurse's notation in the patient's chart; a pharmacist might not read the physician's prescription accurately (perhaps the pharmacist was in a hurry or perhaps he or she misread the physician's scrawl); or a physician who had a history of scolding nurses who questioned his or her orders or who asked questions about patient care might intimidate other health care personnel from presenting him or her with useful information relevant to patient outcomes.

In the ideal system, the likelihood of an error is reduced when health care personnel check on each other. For example, if a physician orders an unusual prescription of medication, the pharmacist or nurse should feel free to double check with the physician.

These systemwide problems occur primarily in institutional settings. The interventions include medical procedures in which patients are essentially passive participants and which, of necessity, involve many health care professionals. These situations have direct application to psychologists working in hospitals or large agencies.

On the surface these findings do not appear applicable to outpatient practices. However, further thought suggests otherwise. Even those psychologists who work in a solo practice should not consider themselves as working alone with patients. First, the patient should be part of the treatment team and should feel free or encouraged to help direct his or her treatment by identifying goals, giving feedback on what works and what doesn't work, and more. Second, psychologists should, when appropriate, involve family members or significant others in the treatment process,

[1] From "Could the Titanic Disaster Have Been Avoided? Or Promoting Patient Welfare Through a Systems Approach, by S. Knapp, 2003, August, *The Pennsylvania Psychologist, 63*, 4, 18, 36. Copyright 2003 by the Pennsylvania Psychological Association. Adapted with permission of the Pennsylvania Psychological Association.

perhaps as collateral contacts. Third, psychologists should be part of an ongoing consultation group that will give feedback on their general skill level, needs of particular cases, and ongoing professional development in assessment and treatment.

Finally, you should provide yourself with a redundant system of protection when possible. For example, one psychologist made a point of randomly double checking his scoring whenever he administered a standardized psychometric test. Another psychologist routinely gave patients with a risk of suicide a brief screening instrument of suicidal ideation to supplement the interviews he had with them. Sometimes the screening instrument picked up suicidal ideation that was not detected in the interview.

It is also possible to view the three essential components of risk management as a method of increasing redundant systems of protection. For example, obtaining *informed consent* should involve patients in the decision-making process and ensure that they feel comfortable raising issues relevant to the progress and success of therapy. Also, *documentation* should, ideally, be a time when you can reflect on your intervention and determine the extent to which you are proceeding toward your goals. Finally, *consultation*, which is especially important when working with high-risk patients or when working in high-risk contexts, could be considered another form of redundant protection insofar as the consultant gives feedback on the quality of treatment provided.

CONSCIENTIOUS FURTHER EDUCATION

All psychologists want to continue to grow and improve as they progress through their careers. They can do that through "reflective practice, ongoing learning, critical thinking, and self-care" (Elman, Illfelder-Kaye, & Robiner, 2005, p. 373). However, even among the best practitioners, a gap will usually exist between the best known intervention and how they commonly practice. The top practitioners and researchers may have cutting-edge knowledge of what works best with a particular disorder, but there is a gap of at least a year before that knowledge gets published, a longer gap before the most well-read practitioners read and incorporate the findings into their practices, and a still longer gap before the practices become generally incorporated by the average practitioner. To the extent that a new procedure requires specialized training and supervision, the time period will be further extended.

Psychologists sometimes say that there is so much to learn and they have limited time to invest in continuing education. We recommend that you focus on those situations, patients, or problems that you are most likely to encounter in your practice. Psychologists also ask how they should invest their time. Rather than focus on low-risk or low-probability events, it is better to invest your time on the high-risk or high-probability situations.

For example, every psychologist treating mental illnesses can expect to encounter patients with a high risk for suicide or who are perpetrators or victims of domestic violence, and competence in the evaluation and treatment of such patients is essential. However, the likelihood of encountering a duty-to-protect situation in which a patient threatens an identifiable third party (other than in domestic abuse situations) is far lower. Consequently, it would be more prudent for the average psychologist to take a continuing education course in suicidology or domestic violence than in a less common area of practice. Needless to say, psychologists should not overlook the dangers involved with low-risk or low-probability situations. Such situations do occur and involve the potential for serious harm to the patient, the psychologist, or the public in general.

MOVING INTO NEW AREAS OF PRACTICE

Periodically psychologists may wish to branch out and practice in areas of psychology in which they did not receive education, training, or supervision in their graduate programs. Although your preparation as a psychologist may have provided you with general skills that apply to that new area of practice, you may need additional study, training, consultation, or supervised experience to become competent. The general rule is that you should seek consultation or guidance before stepping outside your areas of competence. The reason for this is that psychologists must acknowledge their own vulnerability to error and misinterpretation. When they overestimate their skill level and areas of competence they become especially vulnerable to allegations of incompetence should something go wrong. Consultation with other professionals is a useful way to gain feedback on your skills.

You can acquire a specialty or proficiency credential from a well-respected organization such as the American College of Professional Psychology, the American Board of Professional Psychology, or a similar organization. Such credentials are typically based on a work product or examination demonstrating professional achievement. As a word of caution, however, it may not be worthwhile to acquire credentials from "vanity boards" that "grandparent" a large number of practitioners in exchange for a fee.

> A psychologist who has not been in clinical practice for almost 20 years, routinely receives invitations to be grandfathered into a number of specialty boards (all of which have the same address). His philosophy is that any board that offers to grandfather him is not worthy to join. (3.1.4)

Of course, a special credential might not exist for all areas of specialty or subspecialty. Consequently, psychologists sometimes will need to create their own system of feedback. Belar et al. (2001) described a self-assessment program to help psychologists determine the competencies they need before expanding into clinical health psychology. The methodology they used is applicable for psychologists who are considering moving into other new areas of practice, too. Some of the questions Belar et al. encouraged psychologists to ask are whether they have the necessary basic scientific knowledge (biological, cognitive-behavioral, social, and developmental bases of behavior and their interactions), basic knowledge of interventions, technical skills in implementing the interventions, and knowledge of the unique features of the professional context (policy, ethical, legal, and other professional issues concerning the service).

Our description of competence according to Bloom's taxonomy may be relevant here as well. Ideally, when you expand into a new area of treatment you will be performing at the higher levels within the taxonomic system before you practice independently. That is, you will be able to analyze, synthesize, and evaluate the patient, context, and skill factors needed for effective professional service.

EMERGING AREAS OF PRACTICE

Levant et al. (2001) described emerging areas of practice for psychologists in the 21st century. Those areas include health psychology, personal coaching, organizational interventions, Internet therapy, and prescriptive authority. The APA Ethics Code provides very general guidelines for moving into new areas of practice, stating that psychologists should

> undertake relevant education, training, supervised experience, consultation or study. (Standard 2.01c, Boundaries of Competence)

Today, psychologists have expanded opportunities to move into new areas of practice, such as electronic media (Ragusea & VandeCreek, 2003), which could include telephone therapy or e-mail therapy. Others are moving into personal coaching for which well-developed standards of practice have not yet been established. It is not feasible to go back to school to get a doctorate in coaching, in part because no such specialized academic programs exist. Nonetheless, you may need some in-depth training and supervision in the new area of practice. You need to get an experienced person in the area you are moving into to be your consultant for a year or two so that you can be assured that the experience gap in your technical competencies does not cause harm to your clients.

PSYCHOPHARMACOLOGY

Every psychologist involved in health care needs to understand basic psychopharmacology (Barnett & Neel, 2000). You need to know enough about the proper use of psychotropic medications so that you can discuss those treatment options with patients. Many disorders, such as depression or anxiety disorders, can be treated with either medication or psychotherapy, although the research indicates that a combination of both may work best. Also, about 50% of patients in psychotherapy are on psychotropic medications at some point in their treatment (Borkovec, Echemendia, Ragusea, & Ruiz, 2001). You will be in a position to monitor your patients' responses to medication, and if necessary, communicate your observations to the treating psychopharmacologist. Some of the questions to ask include "Are you feeling better since you started taking the medication?" "Are you taking the medication as prescribed?" "Are you experiencing any side effects?" It may be helpful to inform the patient what side effects are common with the prescribed medication. When ascertaining whether patients are taking their medication, it is important to ask patients how often they are taking a drug and what the dosage is. For patients who are unable to recall such facts, it may be indicated to query further to ensure that they are taking medications as prescribed.

Many medication errors occur because of the lack of communication between health care personnel. If you are coordinating treatment with prescribing professionals, you should be careful to inform them of any significant changes in patient behavior or other relevant information, such as lack of adherence to medications or use of self-prescribed herbal remedies.

Since most psychologists are not, at this time, authorized to prescribe medications, they should be careful about making medication suggestions to physicians or other prescribing professionals. Nonetheless, many physicians will ask psychologists for their opinions concerning the appropriate medications to prescribe. Decisions about what psychologists can or cannot say depends to a large extent on the interpretations of the scope of practice by the licensing boards, but most would agree that properly trained psychologists can make general recommendations about medications to physicians or other prescribing professionals while acknowledging that the final choice is up to the prescriber.

Prescribing psychologists will face unique liability issues. Of course, the prescribing psychologists will have to face such issues as warning patients about side effects of medications, prescribing off-label, and monitoring the interactions of medications with other medications and herbal and other alternative remedies. In addition, there may be pressures on prescribing psychologists to treat patients with more serious mental illnesses who have overall treatment needs that differ substantially from the depressed or anxious patients who make up the bulk of the caseload of most psychologists. When treating patients with serious mental illnesses, prescribing psychologists need to be especially sensitive to such issues as competency to consent to treatment, confidentiality with family members (who may be in a caregiver role), and the clinical literature on psychosocial rehabilitation treatment. In addition, psychologists must be aware of differences in attitudes, beliefs, and responses to medication in diverse racial and cultural minority groups.

At this time it is not known how often prescribing psychologists will be involved in "split treatment" in which one professional prescribes and manages medication while a second professional provides psychotherapy. Those arrangements can work well if the prescriber and the psychotherapist communicate freely and frequently. They can work poorly if good communication does not occur.

INNOVATIVE TREATMENTS

Innovative treatments range from those that have real promise of cure to those that may have some legitimacy but get misapplied or misused to those that are pure quackery. For example, during the 1940s, many psychiatrists began to practice psychosurgery for a wide range of serious mental disorders. Despite claims of widespread success, the methods used to evaluate the results were crude; patient protection measures were poor or nonexistent; and it is now believed that many patients were irreversibly harmed by these procedures (Valenstein, 1986). Nonetheless, recently there has been a resurgence in interest in the potential effectiveness of psychosurgery with a narrow range of mental conditions.

Many desperate parents saw facilitative communications as a method of overcoming autism and other serious and pervasive disorders, even though the research on this intervention was not supportive (Jacobson, Mulick, & Schwartz, 1995). Other treatments such as the Orgone Box, the "love treatment" (involving sexual relationships with patients), "Z" therapy (tying up patients and poking and taunting them), and rebirthing therapy lack any professional or scientific support.

On the other hand, there may be positive developments in the ability to help individuals with innovative techniques. Many conscientious and well-informed psychologists are considering the therapeutic benefits of transcranial magnetic stimulation for depression, light therapy for seasonal affective disorders, or other treatments. More research is needed in these new interventions.

You must ask when a new treatment is a fad and when it is an innovation. These decisions require you to evaluate the relevant scientific data and professional evidence. You should be able to review the evidence (whether it is experimental studies, single-case studies, quasi-experimental designs, case histories, or other sources of data). You should be able to articulate a rationale for why certain techniques were used with a particular patient. It is not sufficient to justify the use of a new technique by saying that the technique helped or was successful in some research study. It is necessary to justify why this technique was used with this particular patient.

You need to use care when engaging in alternative or complimentary treatments, such as treatments involving herbal remedies or touch. Herbal remedies are especially problematic because the dose or strength of the pills or tablets sold in stores is not standardized, and the herbs may interact with existing prescription or nonprescription medications the patient is taking. Therapies involving touch raise concerns because the meaning of the touch is always in the eye of the beholder, and the therapist's intentions may be misinterpreted by patients with special needs for affection. If the interpretations are not quickly corrected, touch can lead to charges of inappropriate touching, boundary violations, negligence, or sexual misconduct.

These comments are not intended to imply that the use of all herbal or touch treatments is inherently unethical. But they may increase the legal risks to the practitioner. You can decrease those risks by informing patients of the innovative and experimental nature of any new treatments, documenting the treatment and the patient's response in detail, and seeking consultation when indicated. If the proposed treatment involves herbal remedies or vitamin supplements, it may be wise to consult with the patient's physician or other prescribing professional before recommending these treatments. You should document why you thought that the particular treatment was appropriate for this particular patient. The blanket recommendation of touch therapy for all patients, for example, raises questions as to whether the unique benefits of this therapy for this patient were being considered. Certainly, high caution should be used when recommending these treatments with high-risk patients.

Competence Applied to Detailed Case Example

It may be useful to review the issue of competence from the standpoint of the case example presented in Section 1 (see page 26). Here are some questions that you should ask yourself before undertaking to treat this patient.

Do you know enough about serious personality disorders and their treatments, such as dialectical behavior therapy or other professionally derived theories for the treatment of serious personality disorders? Do you have the technical skills for handling relationship and parasuicidal issues that may arise? Do you have the emotional strength to handle the anger that may be directed at you? Are you free of rescue fantasies or do you have your rescue fantasies under control? Are you able to say no to clinically contraindicated requests by the patient? Do you have the outside resources that may be needed in this case, such as access to a psychopharmacologist, partial hospitalization program, or inpatient unit if necessary?

At this time in your career do you have the emotional and time resources to initiate treatment with a high-risk patient? Do you already have too many high-risk patients on your caseload? Do you have a heavy caseload or heavy personal demands at this time that will tax your energy in the event that this patient gets into a crisis? Do you consider the risks in treating such patients by looking at patient characteristics, context of treatment, and your individual therapist factors?

Seven Essential Points to Remember

1. Being competent involves knowledge, technical skills, and emotional competence.

2. Being competent is not identical to the set of your individual therapist factors. Instead, competence can also vary depending on the patient characteristics, context of treatment, and the extent of your previous commitments.

$$\text{Clinical risk} = \frac{P \times C \times D}{TF}$$

where P = patient risk characteristics; C = context;
D = disciplinary consequences; and TF = therapist factors.

3. It is wise for psychologists to focus on promoting their emotional health (by ensuring that their physical and emotional needs are being met) as part of their strategy to avoid impairment.

4. Psychologists should strive to be competent with individuals from diverse cultural or linguistic backgrounds.

5. Psychologists can do more to maintain the quality of their care if they incorporate a system of protection (redundant systems) into their daily practices.

6. Psychologists who move into new areas of practice need to ensure that they have received appropriate training before doing so and ongoing outside consultation and feedback once engaged in the new practice area.

7. All psychologists who treat patients with mental illnesses should have basic knowledge of psychopharmacology.

Chapter 2: MULTIPLE RELATIONSHIPS AND BOUNDARIES

Boundary violations are one of the most common sources of disciplinary actions that psychologists face. Charges of boundary violations may be filed with the American Psychological Association (APA) Ethics Committee; state psychological association ethics committees; the state licensing board, in the form of a malpractice suit; or all three at the same time. In some states, sexual contact with a patient may also be grounds for criminal charges. Sexual contacts with patients are especially likely to result in disciplinary actions, although nonsexual multiple relationships can also result in disciplinary actions.

Standard 3.05a, Multiple Relationships, of the APA "Ethical Principles of Psychologists and Code of Conduct" (Ethics Code) states,

> A multiple relationship occurs when a psychologist is in a professional role with a person and (1) at the same time is in another role with the same person, (2) at the same time is in a relationship with a person closely associated with or related to the person with whom the psychologist has a professional relationship, or (3) promises to enter into another relationship in the future with the person or a person closely associated with or related to the person.

Thus, a psychologist who is in a concurrent business relationship with a patient would be in a multiple relationship. A psychologist who had a business relationship with a close friend or relative of a patient would also be in a multiple relationship.

Concurrent relationships also need to be considered when a psychologist is providing individual and group therapy to the same person at the same time. Concurrent relationships may also occur when a psychologist is involved in more than one professional role with a patient, such as being a treating expert and evaluator for a personal injury case (see Section 3, chap. 5, Court Testimony, for more information on treating experts). More information on concurrent multiple relationships is provided in Section 3, chapter 3, Working with Couples, Families, and Children.

At other times, multiple relationships may be consecutive. A psychologist who is treating a patient with whom he has had (or will have) a business or social relationship is engaging in a consecutive multiple relationship. A promise of a future relationship is also a multiple relationship. For example, a consecutive multiple relationship could occur if a psychologist offers to enter into a business arrangement with a patient as soon as therapy ends.

Standard 3.05a, Multiple Relationships, of the APA Ethics Code explains that psychologists should refrain from entering into a multiple relationship if it

> could reasonably be expected to impair the psychologist's objectivity, competence, or effectiveness in performing his or her functions as a psychologist, or otherwise risks exploitation or harm to the person with whom the professional relationship exists.

It is important to note that multiple relationships are not inherently unethical and sometimes they are unavoidable. However, psychologists must ensure that any multiple relationship could not be expected to exploit or harm the patient.

UNAVOIDABLE MULTIPLE RELATIONSHIPS

Standard 3.05b of the APA Ethics Code states,

> If a psychologist finds that, due to unforeseen factors, a potentially harmful multiple relationship has arisen, the psychologist takes reasonable steps to resolve it with due regard for the interests of the affected person and maximal compliance with the Ethics Code.

Some unavoidable encounters may be intense, while others are more incidental. Consider, for example,

> A psychologist attended a football game and found that a family he was seeing for family therapy (parents and their two young children) had seats adjacent to his. The patients politely said hello and were willing to leave it at that, but their children recognized the psychologist and wanted to engage in more detailed conversations. (3.2.1)

Although these encounters are more likely to occur in small towns and rural areas, they can also occur in urban communities. For example, a psychologist belonged to the local Buddhist Temple and received referrals from other Buddhists in the area. Although he did not treat those who regularly attended his own Temple, he did treat other Buddhists even though there was a possibility that they might encounter each other coincidentally through their common religious affiliation.

Many psychologists in this situation adopt the "you first" rule, meaning that they instruct the patients that they have to acknowledge the psychologist first in a public setting; the psychologist will not take the initiative to acknowledge the patient.

TREATMENT BOUNDARIES

The crucial feature is whether the multiple relationship would impair the objectivity of the treatment relationship. Relationship factors are extremely important in ensuring the success of psychotherapy. Some may argue that they are even more important than specific therapeutic techniques in producing positive outcomes. The relationship factors related to good patient outcomes could include the ability to form a therapeutic alliance; collaborate in establishing treatment goals; show empathy, positive regard, and congruence; manage countertransference; and repair disrupted alliances (APA Division 29 Steering Committee, 2001).

The term boundaries refers to the context in which this productive relationship occurs. Perhaps the salient feature of the boundary is that the focus of the relationship is on the welfare of the patient, not the psychologist. It is helpful to distinguish between the terms boundary crossings and boundary violations. (Guthiel & Gabbard, 1998). Boundary crossings refer to any activity that moves therapists away from a strictly neutral position with their patients. Boundary crossings may be helpful or harmful. A boundary violation is a harmful boundary crossing.

Common examples of boundary crossings include limited patient-oriented self-disclosures, exchange of token gifts, and nonsexual and socially acceptable touching. The risks of these boundary crossings are generally low. Properly trained psychologists can determine when the disclosure of personal information to patients can have therapeutic benefits, when the exchange of token gifts is a mere social formality or a nonpathological expression of appreciation, or when a gentle touch or a hug could have a therapeutic benefit.

A boundary violation could occur if the psychologist or patient interprets the boundary crossing as harmful. For example, a patient might construe a gift, therapist self-disclosure, or a hug as a step in moving from a professional to a social or potentially a sexual relationship or an attempt to initiate a concurrent or consecutive inappropriate multiple relationship. Because boundary crossings are subject to being interpreted by some patients as boundary violations, it is important to have a therapeutic rationale for boundary crossings.

> A psychologist who works in a rural and religiously conservative state often has patients or prospective patients ask her if she is a Christian. She anticipates this question from patients or prospective patients and has a response consistent with her comfort zone for self-disclosure. Although she is a Christian, she declines to disclose her religious affiliation. Instead, she has learned that most patients or prospective patients are trying to discern if she will allow them to discuss their religious beliefs in a nonjudgmental atmosphere. (3.2.2)

At this time it may be appropriate to recall the risk management formula introduced in the Preface.

$$\text{Clinical risk} = \frac{(P \times C \times D)}{TF}$$

In this formula, P = patient risk characteristics; C = context;
D = disciplinary consequences; and TF = therapist factors.

BOUNDARIES AND PATIENT FACTORS

Otherwise benign boundary crossings are more likely to be problematic when they are done with patients with high-risk factors. Psychologists encounter some of the most disturbed persons of society. They may challenge boundaries, solicit sexual favors directly or indirectly, or react with extraordinary rage to relatively minor events.

In one case a patient complained of harassment because the psychologist contacted him (with his documented consent for clinical reasons as explained ahead of time) by phone between sessions. In another case a patient complained because, after the session, the psychologist went out to his car and drove away (the psychologist had parked his car in close proximity to the patient's car). Another patient became furious when her psychologist took a month off from treatment to give birth. The patient alleged that the pregnancy was a planned event designed to allow her therapist to "abandon" her. Of course, these complaints appear frivolous to us (but not to the patients involved). We mention them only to describe how the perceptions of patients can lead to serious results. It is easy to see how these patients could further distort any deviation from strict professional roles. Any touch, no matter how benign, could be eroticized; and any self-disclosure, no matter how discreetly and therapeutically indicated, could be construed as an effort to turn the professional relationship into a social one.

We are not raising these red flags to dissuade you from touching or self-disclosing to all patients. Remember, we considered such advice to be one of the false risk management principles discussed in Section 2. However, you need to be aware that some patients may grossly misconstrue relatively innocuous boundary crossings. Consequently, you need to have a clinical justification for your actions. Some psychologists may, as a result of their therapeutic orientation, eschew all touching (other than handshakes) and reject all gifts, no matter how innocuous or small. Other psychologists engage in limited self-disclosure and accept token gifts. Both, however, should be able to justify their decisions based on clinical grounds that focus on promoting patient welfare. The risk management recommendations we suggest later in this chapter will greatly reduce the potential for negative consequences to any boundary crossing.

BOUNDARIES AND CONTEXT

Any concurrent or consecutive multiple relationship may become problematic if it is accompanied by another high-risk factor. For example, it would be unwise to be in a multiple relationship with a patient who has been diagnosed with a serious personality disorder. Also, if a family is seeking help because of a high-conflict divorce or is seeking assistance in ongoing litigation, then any multiple relationship has a greater likelihood of creating problems or being misconstrued. In other words, any time patient or context characteristics suggest high risks, psychologists should be especially prudent about engaging in a multiple relationship or crossing boundaries.

> A psychologist began evaluating a claimant for a court case in which she alleged serious emotional distress as a result of an accident. Shortly after the evaluation began, the claimant announced to the psychologist, "I saw you in therapy 10 years ago." The psychologist checked his records, and indeed he had seen the woman 10 years earlier. She had a different surname at the time. He discontinued the evaluation and notified relevant parties of the unexpected multiple relationship. (3.2.3)

This psychologist wisely understood that a multiple relationship in a high-risk context might disqualify him from his current role. Consider a slightly different scenario.

> A psychologist started an evaluation with a couple seeking marital therapy. Shortly after the evaluation began the wife announced to the psychologist, "I saw you in therapy 10 years ago." Indeed he had seen the woman 10 years earlier. She had a different surname at the time. He paused the evaluation to determine if this prior relationship would compromise his effectiveness as a marital therapist. (3.2.4)

In this case, the husband stated that because the psychologist was so conscientious about discerning his feelings he had more confidence that the psychologist would be a fair and helpful marital therapist. With some marital therapy cases such a previous multiple relationship might make treatment clinically contraindicated, although the risks are far lower than those found in a forensic case.

Many psychologists provide home-based treatments, such as with older adults who have mobility problems or when conducting behavioral interventions in the home (Knapp & Slattery, 2004). No doubt, much clinically indicated work occurs in such settings. Nonetheless, psychologists who work in patients' homes need to be especially scrupulous about boundaries. When services are delivered in patients' homes, there is a greater likelihood that they may adopt a "guest" schema as opposed to a professional schema. They may be more likely to engage in polite social conversation, serve refreshments, or otherwise drift away from the therapeutic purpose of the visit. While some latitude may be clinically indicated, it is wise to redirect the interaction to more professional topics. Psychologists need to use discretion when deciding whether to conduct home visits, especially with high-risk patients.

Often boundaries get challenged through apparently innocuous comments by neighbors or social acquaintances. For example, a neighbor called a psychologist at home about an apparently minor problem dealing with her child's nighttime routine. While not wishing to be rude, the psychologist was aware that the brief phone conversation with the neighbor was no substitute for a detailed history and that there might be more complications than could be discerned over the phone. Her comments were circumspect, and she noted that some of the mother's questions could only be answered through a more thorough examination.

Similarly, psychologists need to ensure that they do not make casual comments at parties or other social gatherings that could be construed as giving professional advice. Friends of friends or social acquaintances may pressure psychologists for brief and simple solutions to complex interpersonal or psychological problems.

> A psychologist was asked to participate as an instructor in her church's Women's Spiritual Retreat Weekend that was advertised as a weekend of "prayer, reflection, Bible study, and spiritual renewal." However, on Friday night one of the participants threatened suicide and made superficial cuts on her wrist. It later came out that she had displayed these behaviors before and that the assistant pastor had specifically asked the psychologist to come to the retreat to assist with this problem parishioner. Of course, the psychologist had no idea of the hidden agenda behind the invitation to be an instructor for the weekend. (3.2.5)

The well-meaning assistant pastor did not know that psychological services could only be administered in the context of a professional relationship. The psychologist declined to interview the parishioner but had a long discussion with the pastor concerning professional boundaries and better ways to ensure that a disturbed parishioner does not upset the weekend for the other parishioners.

BOUNDARIES AND INDIVIDUAL THERAPIST FACTORS

Certain therapist factors increase one's ability to make wise decisions concerning the maintenance of proper boundaries. Perhaps the first is the *general knowledge of how to develop and maintain effective psychotherapy relationships*. Effective psychologists have an awareness of general psychopathology and especially those disorders in which difficulty in maintaining boundaries is likely to occur.

Psychologists need to have *ethical decision-making skills* to judge when a patient, licensing board, ethics committee, or jury is likely to construe a multiple relationship as exploitative or harmful. One of the factors to consider when dealing with the potential of a multiple relationship is the availability of alternatives. In some small communities you may have fewer options for dealing with multiple relationships than in larger urban areas. If you are working in a small town where there are only two or three psychologists and 5,000 people, you will undoubtedly be faced with some multiple relationships. At times, a community or town is so isolated that you will find no alternatives that are equal or better than the services you can offer. In that situation you have fewer options than if you live in a larger urban area; nonetheless, being in a small town or rural area in and of itself provides an inadequate defense against charges of boundary violations.

Technical competence comes into play because effective psychologists have learned through supervised training and experience how to establish and maintain helpful psychotherapeutic relationships. Emotional competence is important as well. Effective psychologists have the *self-awareness* necessary to determine when personal feelings may interfere with their therapeutic relationships. Finally, they are more likely to be embedded in a redundant system of protection whereby others can provide a check on their judgment. Consulting with colleagues on a regular basis provides such a redundant system of protection.

Sometimes the threat to boundaries can be subtle, such as the potential for psychologists to impose their religious beliefs on patients. Obviously, psychologists should not use their therapeutic influence to proselytize for their own religion. However, sometimes the issue becomes nuanced, for example, when patients present religious beliefs in a manner that seems harmful to their mental or physical well-being. Consider the following example:

> Dr. Green accepted a patient who requested therapy to help her with her depression. In the first session the patient revealed that she was having substantial marital problems that she attributed to her "proud spirit" and her failure to submit to her husband as commanded by her religion. Twice in the session she cited the Biblical passage from Titus 2:4-5 ("young women [should be]...submissive to their husbands") to justify her need to be submissive. (3.2.6)

Dr. Green, who is both a feminist and a Christian, believes that the patient has selected a passage out of context, and she could have quickly cited numerous other passages and themes to contradict the interpretation that Christianity requires women to blindly submit to their husbands. The first interview leaves Dr. Green with the impression that the husband's misogynistic beliefs are fueling the patient's depression.

However, Dr. Green knows that she needs to probe how the patient is defining submission; she has not tapped the depths, complexities, nuances, or contradictions of the patient's belief system; she should not necessarily assume that the wife's report is normative for her denomination; and an interview involving the husband might give important information to clarify the marital situation. Finally, although religious beliefs appear to be impacting her psychological functioning, Dr. Green is aware that the reverse could be true.

In proceeding with the case, Dr. Green will respect the religious traditions of her patient and will refrain from imposing her beliefs on her patient. In fact, if the patient's religious beliefs do significantly contribute to her depression, then Dr. Green will strive to promote a healthier manifestation of faith, rather than try to undermine that faith (Rucker, Hite, & Hathaway, 2005).

RISK MANAGEMENT APPLICATIONS

The risk management strategies of informed consent, documentation, and consultation can help reduce risks associated with multiple relationships. The informed consent process is relevant in that it is important to discuss the potential ill effects of a multiple relationship with patients ahead of time. For example,

> A psychologist had agreed to represent his local club in a community council that was established to help victims of a local flood. When he attended the first meeting he saw that one of his current patients was there representing another club. During the next treatment session the psychologist spoke to the patient concerning any discomfort or potential negative effects that this would create. (3.2.7)

This psychologist understood that informed consent was not a one-time event but an ongoing process that had to be revisited from time to time as events in therapy unfolded. He understood that according to the higher levels of Bloom's taxonomy, the informed consent process was geared toward improving patient welfare and increasing patient autonomy. Fortunately, this psychologist understood how to use the informed consent process to further the patient's treatment goals.

Of course, the manner in which the autonomy-enhancing discussion occurs is as important as whether it occurs. A genuine concern for the welfare of the patient is conveyed by body posture, nonverbal cues, and the specific choice of words when discussing delicate and potentially difficult topics.

It is advisable to document all multiple relationships and why you believe that each was, was not, could become, or would likely become clinically contraindicated or exploitative. The facts or circumstances of the case should be laid out, and the reasons for the conclusion given. Always document unavoidable multiple relationships and how efforts were made to act in accordance with the APA Ethics Code. It may be desirable to document all incidental social contacts and how they were handled when the patient or context suggests a high-risk situation. Of course, you should always seek consultation when problematic multiple relationships occur.

Consultations will help psychologists to consider the benefits and drawbacks of a proposed boundary crossing or how an unavoidable boundary crossing was handled. Ideally the consultant will consider the characteristics of the patient, the context of the services provided, the goal of the boundary crossing, and the nature of the psychologist-patient relationship. Often the very process of discussing the patient with a consultant will help psychologists to clarify their goals, and the advantages, and disadvantages of the boundary crossing.

SEXUAL VIOLATIONS

At first glance, it would appear difficult to say anything novel or useful about sexual exploitation. Every psychologist knows that sexual violations are unethical, in many jurisdictions illegal, and a major source of disciplinary actions against psychologists.

Offenders are more likely to be middle-aged or older male psychologists who have sexual relationships with younger female patients. Nonetheless, some same-sex relationships are reported, and sometimes female psychologists engage in sexual exploitation, although the frequency of these encounters is far less than the frequency among male psychologists. Sexual exploitation can also occur when psychologists have sexual contact with former patients or with relatives of patients (such as the parent of a child patient).

Some have argued that whenever boundaries are crossed, the psychologist and patient find themselves on a slippery slope and are likely to move from a social to a sexual relationship over time. Of course, not all boundary crossings are inevitable invitations to sexual exploitation, and we would not want the fear of sexual exploitation to discourage you from engaging in therapeutically indicated boundary crossings. Although every case of sexual misconduct started with a boundary crossing, not all boundary crossings lead to misconduct. Correlation does not imply causation.

The frequency of sexual misconduct by psychologists appears to be decreasing, although the reasons for this are not clear. Perhaps it is because licensing boards are becoming more aggressive in prosecuting cases of misconduct that come to their attention. Several states have criminalized sexual contact with patients. Other states have mandated reporting requirements in place that require psychologists to inform the licensing board whenever they treat a patient who had sexual contact with a former psychotherapist. Patients also are becoming better educated and sophisticated about the inappropriateness of such behavior. Perhaps the decrease is purely an artifact of the shifting demographics of professional psychology wherein more women (who tend to have substantially lower rates of sexual misconduct) are entering the profession. Perhaps all of these factors have played a role in reducing rates of sexual contact. On the other hand, the apparent decrease may be due to the proactive way that graduate schools, continuing education programs, and consultation services (such as those provided by the Trust or state, provincial, and territorial psychological associations) are addressing patient relationships, psychologists' self-care, and the interrelationship between the needs of the psychologist and the likelihood of the exploitation of a patient.

In any event, the goal is to reduce the frequency of sexual offenses even more. One step might be to look at sexual offenders and determine what common factors appear to be associated with sexual offenses and what can be done to reduce their frequency. Not all psychologists are at equal risk of offending sexually. Certainly a few psychologists have serious personality disorders (such as narcissism or sociopathy) or have paraphilia. Some may argue that these individuals are the cause of the problems and should never have become psychologists in the first place. Probably no amount of education is going to dissuade them from these violations. When detected, they should be removed from the profession as quickly as possible. Unfortunately, the repeat offenders and the true predators account for a very small number of psychologists who have been sanctioned for sexual misconduct.

Other psychologists who have offended have encountered patients in a context that makes them vulnerable to becoming "love sick," a state wherein they convince themselves that they have acted with the purest of romantic motives. They may find themselves unusually attracted to a patient. They may find "rescue fantasies" activated by a particularly vulnerable or grateful patient. Or, they may find themselves treating a patient who uses the idealization or seduction of others as interpersonal strategies.

These psychologists may be especially at risk if they have had inadequate training in handling countertransferential feelings or have had a recent stressor in their private lives (e.g., spouse has had an affair, spouse or child dies, business failure or severe financial problems, or too much stress in the practice). Serious personal stressors can blind even the best practitioner. Psychologists may be arriving at a dangerous point if their sexual fantasies are aroused or if they have convinced themselves that they can handle a little more closeness with a particular patient. It is with these individuals that proactive educational techniques focusing on handling treatment relationships and self-care can probably do the most to reduce the likelihood of reoffending.

Another strategy might be to focus less on the characteristics of the few who are at risk of becoming offenders and more on the general issues of improving treatment relationships and self-care for all psychologists. The large majority of psychologists who have sexual feelings toward patients do not offend. Nonetheless, the overall quality of treatment may be degraded because of these feelings. The inability to acknowledge counter-transference feelings and deal with them so they do not have a negative impact on therapy may result in those feelings going "underground" and being unprocessed. When the feelings are acknowledged in a safe setting, psychologists may be better able to handle those feelings productively.

INDIVIDUALLY FOCUSED RISK MANAGEMENT SUGGESTIONS

On an individual level, the risk management strategies designed to protect one from becoming vulnerable to sexual temptations are similar to strategies designed to protect one from other unhealthy boundary violations. Psychologists should be technically competent in relationship skills, act to ensure their emotional competence, embed themselves in a protective social framework, and have considerable self-awareness.

Ask newly licensed psychologists if they ever expect to have sex with a patient during their career and 99+% emphatically would say no. Yet current data suggest that a few, 2% to 3% of psychologists, will have a sexual relationship with at least one patient sometime during their careers. On the other hand, the vast majority of psychologists will have strong romantic feelings toward certain patients that, while not leading to sexual behaviors, may nonetheless impact the quality of treatment.

Properly trained psychologists recognize that they will have strong feelings toward patients. They will also have enough self-awareness that they know how to handle these feelings productively and have the technical skills to continue to help patients when strong feelings arise. If the feelings continue to interfere with effective treatment, and the issues are not overcome through consultation, personal therapy, or supervision, it is highly recommended that the psychologist transfer the patient to another professional.

PROFESSIONWIDE RISK MANAGEMENT STRATEGIES

Another way to approach this issue might be to move away from the individual dyad level of analysis and look at societywide or professionwide interventions. Some might argue that sexual misconduct is a private act with private consequences for both the patient and the psychologist who is at risk of being disciplined. To carry the argument further, one might say that these things happen, so get over it. The only damage is to the psychologists and their patients. To a very limited extent this is true. However, every psychologist suffers when one psychologist has sex with a patient, and every current or potential patient can suffer as well to the extent that public confidence in the profession of psychology is decreased. Current or potential patients who learn of this misconduct will be that much less likely to trust their psychologists or even to seek psychotherapy in the future. In addition, sexual misconduct often makes the press and can become a front page issue. This could have deleterious effects on all therapy during the time of the exposé in that patients and therapists may need to take valuable treatment time to deal with the media coverage.

One might believe that the remedy for sexual misconduct has to come at an individual level. To a large extent this is true. However, every psychologist can contribute to a professionwide atmosphere that makes sexual misconduct less likely to occur.

It is also possible to view sexual contact as an outgrowth of degraded professional relationships that have lost their focus on treatment and have become a sexualized social experience. If so, then the level of intervention shifts from being just how psychologists can stop this individual from engaging in sex with this patient to include the question of how psychologists can help all psychologists improve the quality of their professional relationships with all of their patients. In other words, how can all psychologists better handle the feelings generated in psychotherapy? There may be a need to shift the culture of psychology so that there is an increased emphasis on self-awareness and relationship maintenance. How can psychologists shift the culture of psychology?

Here is what some psychologists have done to improve the profession's ability to deal with relationship issues.

- One psychologist was assertive in keeping in touch with colleagues and reaching out to those who might not be doing well emotionally. She checked on her friends, asked how they were doing, and went out to lunch with them when they appeared to be struggling.

- A psychologist participated in the colleague assistance program of her state psychological association. She counseled other health care professionals who were doing poorly and participated in self-care education.

- A psychologist served on the continuing education committee of her local hospital's behavioral health unit that presented workshops on relationship management.

- A psychologist participated in a study on treatment factors in psychotherapy and in a study on how psychologists responded to sexually inappropriate behaviors.

- Another psychologist read books and took continuing education courses on supervision and incorporated self-awareness as an important component of the supervisory experience. This included an effort to engage in self-care and normalize sexual feelings when they arose in treatment.

> • And finally, another psychologist, realizing that counter-transference feelings she was having with a particular patient were threatening to get out of control, sought consultation to assist with the treatment and personal therapy to resolve the feeling without additional interference with the therapy. She shared her experience and her problem-solving thinking when she presented continuing education workshops. (3.2.8)

Do you have further ideas about how the profession might be better able to address these issues? If so, please communicate them to us.

Seven Essential Points to Remember

1. Multiple relationships are not necessarily unethical or harmful. Multiple relationships that are exploitative or clinically contraindicated should be avoided.

2. Boundary crossings are deviations from a strictly neutral therapeutic position; boundary violations are harmful boundary crossings.

3. Psychologists should be extremely cautious about boundary crossing or engaging in multiple relationships with patients with high-risk features or when treating patients in high-risk contexts.

4. Psychologists should be especially prudent about informed consent, documentation, and consultation when crossing boundaries or engaging in multiple relationships with high-risk patients or in high-risk contexts.

5. Although the frequency of sexual exploitation is decreasing, it remains a major source of complaints against psychologists.

6. Sexual exploitation can be reduced if individual psychologists focus on technical skills in maintaining boundaries, ensuring their emotional competence, and embedding themselves in a system of protection.

7. Sexual exploitation can be reduced if all psychologists recognize that strong feelings, including sexual feelings, will arise during the course of therapy with certain patients. Continuing education programs, graduate training, supervision, consultation, and other venues can be used to help psychologists learn how to control, modify, or channel those emotions to productive ends.

Chapter 3: WORKING WITH COUPLES, FAMILIES, AND CHILDREN

Another source of a significant number of complaints against psychologists is working with couples, families, and children. This is especially likely to occur in high-conflict families or when there is a contested custody case.

In chapter 3, we review problems in working with couples, families, and children. More specifically, we review issues of informed consent when working with couples, consent and confidentiality when treating children, and special challenges when working with high-conflict families and doing child custody work.

INFORMED CONSENT ISSUES WITH COUPLES AND FAMILIES

The American Psychological Association's "Ethical Principles of Psychologists and Code of Conduct" (APA Ethics Code) provides guidance when psychologists treat several persons in a relationship. Standard 10.02a, Therapy Involving Couples or Families, of the APA Ethics Code states,

> *When psychologists agree to provide services to several persons who have a relationship (such as spouses, significant others, or parents and children), they take reasonable steps to clarify at the outset (1) which of the individuals are clients/patients and (2) the relation the psychologist will have with each person. This clarification includes the psychologist's role and the probable uses of the service provided or the information obtained.*

The general rule is that psychologists should avoid situations in which they have conflicting loyalties. Consider this example:

A psychologist is treating a wife individually. During the course of treatment, the wife brings in her husband for conjoint sessions. However, the relationship between the couples deteriorates and both wish to have individual sessions with the psychologist. (3.3.1)

Here it is important for the psychologist to have followed Standard 10.02a, Therapy Involving Couples or Families, and clarified to all parties the nature of the relationship with each of them. Ideally, when the husband first came in for sessions with his wife, the psychologist would have explained that the wife was his patient and that the husband was there as a collateral contact only to further the treatment of the wife. If this step had been taken, the husband would have been more willing to accept the fact that the psychologist had the primary treatment obligation to his wife and could only refer him to a therapist of his own.

However, a number of other situations may occur when treating families. Consider, for example,

> A psychologist is treating a couple for marital problems. However, the relationship between the couple deteriorates. The husband discontinues therapy, and the wife requests individual sessions with the psychologist. (3.3.2)

Again it is important for the psychologist to have followed Standard 10.02a, Therapy Involving Couples or Families, and clarified to all parties the nature of the relationship with each of them. Ideally, when the couple first came in for sessions, the psychologist would have identified who was the client. Perhaps in this situation the psychologist considered both parties to be his clients, and the marriage was the focus of the treatment. If the husband dropped out of treatment, then the psychologist would need to determine if the husband no longer wished to continue in treatment, and if not, to formally terminate the relationship with the husband and then consider the clinical advantages and disadvantages of continuing therapy with the wife as the primary client. Although legally the psychologist may continue treatment with the wife, there may be clinical considerations not to do so. For example, the psychologist needs to ask whether there is a likelihood that couples therapy will resume, and if so, whether seeing the wife individually would create a perception that the psychologist is now biased.

> A psychologist was treating a couple for marital problems, but decided the optimal way to proceed was to provide individual therapy sessions to each of them. At one point the wife decided that she wanted a divorce, while the husband was using the individual therapy sessions to help preserve the marriage. (3.3.3)

Again, Standard 10.02a, Therapy Involving Couples or Families, should guide the behavior of the psychologist. Ideally the psychologist clarified with both parties that he was seeing them individually for their agreed upon purpose of saving the marriage. Perhaps he cautioned them that he would only provide such treatment if they agreed that he could exchange information obtained in sessions with one to assist in the sessions with the other (although certainly he would use such information with discretion). Consequently, the wife knew at the point she told the psychologist of her intent to get a divorce that this information would be conveyed to her husband. She should also have understood that the purpose of her individual sessions was to preserve the marriage, and if she no longer shared this goal, the individual sessions with this psychologist might end.

Each of these situations points to the importance of the risk management (RM) formula we have been using and especially of the informed consent process. Unless the informed consent process was implemented scrupulously, there would have been a potential for misunderstandings, ill feelings, or a sense of betrayal. In each of the three scenarios above, it may have been necessary for the psychologist to review the conditions of treatment before every session to ensure that the patients (or the collateral contacts) did not misconstrue the psychologist's role. Documentation of these informed consent procedures is indicated as well.

CHILD AND ADOLESCENT TREATMENT

Informed consent and confidentiality issues will also occur when working with children. Who can consent for treatment may vary according to state law. In some states, adolescents, depending on their age, may consent for mental health treatment on their own. In other states, they cannot. In some states, either parent may give consent for a child to receive treatment. In other states, the right of a child to receive treatment may require the consent of both parents if there is court-ordered joint legal custody.

The APA Ethics Code Standard 3.10b, Informed Consent, states,

> For persons who are legally incapable of giving informed consent, psychologists nevertheless (1) provide an appropriate explanation, (2) seek the individual's assent, (3) consider such persons' preferences and best interests,...

Consequently, if the child is not legally able to give consent, you should nonetheless, share the proposed information in a manner appropriate for the child' mental and social development. What you would say to the average 5-year-old will differ from what you would say to the average 11-year-old. Also, you should seek to secure the assent (or agreement) of the individual for treatment and consider his or her preferences and best interests.

The informed consent process is especially important in negotiating the boundaries of privacy between an adolescent, the adolescent's parents, and you.[1] Parents who bring their rebellious adolescents into treatment may feel helpless in the face of apparently intractable problems. They may expect you to protect their child from his or her dangerous experimentations with alcohol or other drugs, sex, or criminal behavior. Their anxiety may prompt them to see you as an extension of their parental control, and they may attempt to intrude in therapy in ways that are understandable but counterproductive.

On the other hand, adolescents may start distrusting you if they see you as an authority surrogate for their parents. This tension can be confronted constructively through the therapeutic process by negotiating the parents'

---

[1] From "Resolving Some Areas of Continuing Confusion," by E. Harris, 2003, Winter, *MassPsych: The Journal of the Massachusetts Psychological Association, 47,* 18–22, 29. Copyright 2003 by the Massachusetts Psychological Association. Adapted with permission of the author.

access to information about treatment. Parents can be encouraged to give up their legal right of access to information so that you can provide the adolescent with a protective space where he or she can build a therapeutic alliance and make therapeutic progress.

In doing so, however, you need to clarify to all parties what kind of information will be shared and under what circumstances. Sometimes the sharing of information is dictated by institutional policy or state or federal law, such as when a state law permits adolescents to seek treatment on their own in a drug and alcohol facility.

Unfortunately, at times an adolescent may not trust the therapist and may "game" the therapy regardless of the limits placed on confidentiality. This is a difficult clinical situation, especially if the adolescent continues to engage in dangerous behavior, including using drugs or committing other criminal acts. Where parents have a legal right to information, many psychologists only accept adolescent patients with the understanding that they will be able to give general information to parents concerning the overall progress of treatment (and productive use of time) and that they have the discretion to share information with parents when the life or safety of the adolescent or a third party is endangered. Exactly where that line is drawn will depend on the intensity, frequency, and seriousness of the behavior and your decisions as to when parental involvement would or would not be helpful. Such decisions are context dependent and include questions such as the likely response of the parents, the damage to the therapeutic process, and the willingness of the adolescent patient to eventually disclose and work on the problematic behaviors personally.

Even in those settings in which adolescents may control the release of information independently, some of you may insist that adolescent patients agree to release information to parents so that they can bill insurance companies, be alerted as to whether you are using the time productively (e.g., is the adolescent showing up for sessions?), or be informed of the need to make a referral, if necessary.

Sometimes these issues become difficult to manage. When, if ever, should you inform parents that their child is cutting himself or herself if the cutting is not likely to be lethal? What about failure to eat? How much risk should there be in sexual behavior before a parent is notified? What about same-sex activity? The parents may agree to treatment with the expectation that you will encourage heterosexual interests, but the patient may not share that goal.

The Health Insurance Portability and Accountability Act (HIPAA) Privacy Rule also allows parents to enter into "agreements of confidentiality," or binding agreements to waive their entitlement to access a child's records to allow more privacy and facilitate effective therapy. If the parents have joint legal custody, the permission of both parents is required. In states that allow minors to independently consent to treatment and/or control the dissemination of treatment information, such a contract can be an effective way to provide parents with access to the information about the treatment that you consider important to ensure effective parental participation (and payment for) the treatment. Of course, the ordinary exceptions to confidentiality apply to adolescents as they do to other patients. We provide more information on the Privacy Rule in Section 3, chapter 4, Privacy, Confidentiality, and Privileged Communications.

A psychologist was treating an adolescent who lived in a state where parents had to consent for treatment and controlled confidentiality. As was her usual informed consent procedure, the psychologist made an agreement regarding confidentiality with both the parents and the adolescent present, noting that she would protect the privacy of the adolescent's communications in therapy but would inform parents if the adolescent acted in a manner that threatened her life or safety. The psychologist also noted that these decisions concerning what constitutes a threat to safety can sometimes be ambiguous and that the parents would need to trust the psychologist about when that line was crossed and the parents needed to be notified. "For example," the psychologist stated, "I may learn that your daughter is using drugs or having sex. I may or may not disclose that to you depending on my perception of the risk involved and whether it is a one-time slip or a pattern."

Over the course of treatment the girl disclosed an increasingly disturbed pattern of "hooking up" with men she met over the Internet. The psychologist urged her to refrain from this behavior, which she promised to do. But, over the months, she had difficulty adhering to her promise during periods of stress. The psychologist then reminded the girl of their original agreement that she had the option of informing her parents of behavior that threatened her life or safety. After considerable discussion, the psychologist told the girl that she had to develop a safety plan that included using her parents as a resource to curtail this behavior.

The psychologist listened to the girl's objections and insisted that she understand the concerns for her safety, and they negotiated the process by which the parents were to be informed. (3.3.4)

This psychologist accurately saw informed consent at the higher levels of Bloom's taxonomy whereby it was incorporated into her overall treatment process and relationship. In this case, the informed consent process involved the parents as well as the identified patient. The parents gave their consent for treatment based on the premise that the psychologist would take appropriate action in the event the life or safety of their daughter was at stake. For her part, the risks to the daughter were high enough that she needed external controls to protect her from impulsive actions.

The difficulty for the psychologist in this example would become apparent if the psychologist had decided not to inform the parents of this potentially dangerous behavior by the patient and the patient hooked up with an individual who seriously physically harmed the patient. This was an extremely difficult decision to make, and all relevant factors of the RM formula had to be taken into consideration in order to provide for the welfare of the patient.

No one format for these agreements of confidentiality is appropriate for every psychologist. Psychologists vary in the extent to which they can tolerate dangerous high-risk behavior among adolescents. Some psychologists may prefer to have agreements that adopt a lower threshold for notifying parents (such as anytime the welfare or safety of the adolescent is at risk), while others will adopt a higher threshold (such as immediate danger to oneself or others). It is crucial, however, that the patient and parents understand the standards used by the psychologist ahead of time.

TREATMENT OF HIGH-CONFLICT FAMILIES[2]

Naive psychologists who fail to attend to the nuances of treatment issues with high-conflict families may inadvertently deliver substandard therapy (Greenberg, Gould, Gould-Saltman, & Stahl, 2003). Even assuming that appropriate parental consent has been obtained, psychologists who are legally allowed to treat a child should consider a number of clinical factors before going ahead with treatment. At times it may be clinically indicated to refuse such cases, especially if the marital turmoil created by the very act of getting therapy outweighs any benefit that the child may experience from therapy. While therapy is generally beneficial, there are some highly charged situations that doom to failure any therapeutic attempts. It is always recommended that prior to initiating treatment of a minor, the therapist obtain the consent of both parents if legal consent is required. If one parent refuses, the stress related to the conflict between the parents may prohibit any success in the therapy for the child. Also, seeing a child without the knowledge of both parents may inadvertently reinforce the idea that the nonconsenting parent is bad or cannot be trusted, and it may place a barrier between the child and that parent to the detriment of the child.

Of course, in unusual situations it may be legal and clinically indicated to involve only one parent. In those situations, however, prudent psychologists seek consultations. Nonetheless, experienced psychologists often find that parents will frequently respond favorably to a fair and open invitation to participate in treatment or at least to give consent to treatment. Sometimes the opposition to treatment is not so much opposition to treatment per se but anger at the fact that the parent was not even consulted about his or her opinions concerning the need for or the direction or nature of therapy.

The policy of refusing to treat some families under some circumstances is a good risk management strategy, but more importantly, it is a risk management strategy that is linked to the overarching moral principles of beneficence (promoting the welfare of others) and nonmaleficence (doing no harm). That is, you need to make an informed decision as to whether your potential to help the family exceeds your potential to harm them. When you look at competence from the standpoint of Bloom's taxonomy, you remember that, at the higher levels, the evaluation of competence considers the context in which treatment occurs. Consequently, it is not our intent to cast doubt on your skill or expertise. It is to recognize that sometimes your best use of your skills and expertise is to determine up

---

[2] From "Treating Children in High-Conflict Families," by S. Knapp and J. Lemoncelli, 2005, October, *The Pennsylvania Psychologist, 65,* 4. Copyright 2005 by the Pennsylvania Psychological Association. Adapted with permission of the authors.

front if your services can in fact benefit the child and parents or if the situational factors are such that no intervention should be made at the time absent resolution of the more fundamental underlying problem between the parents. None of us has the wisdom of Solomon (The Bible, I Kings 3:16-28), and sometimes the correct course of action is not clear. No doubt many of you can do much good for these high-conflict families, and we are not trying to discourage you from treating them. We are encouraging you to make an informed decision as to whether to treat them, how to treat them, and what might be considered to pave the way for unencumbered therapy in the future.

If you decide to go ahead and treat the child, you should remember that treatment with divorcing families often differs substantially from treatment with typical families. Ordinarily psychologists assume that the parent is coming to treatment voluntarily. However, some parents in high-conflict cases have been ordered into therapy by a court or have been strongly encouraged to enter therapy by their attorneys.

Ordinarily, you assume that parents present information accurately. However, in high-conflict families the presenting parents may give slanted reports and attempt to use the therapy to promote their own agenda. The emotions generated by the divorce may override sound parental judgment.

Ordinarily, you assume that parents are acting in the best interest of the child. However, in high-conflict families parents may request treatment for benign-sounding reasons, but their real agenda may be to improve their relationship with the child in preparation for a pending custody evaluation or to use the child to get information against the other parent in the upcoming custody evaluation. In addition, one parent may be on his or her best behavior in hopes that the psychologist will "side" with him or her during the custody hearing.

This is not to say that divorcing parents are always coerced into treatment, lie, or put their personal needs above those of the child. Very often divorcing parents are magnanimous in how they relate to each other and the child. They put their ill feelings aside and focus on doing what is best for the child. However, the risks for these problem behaviors increase when families are divorcing, usually as a direct function of the level of acrimony between the parents.

Regardless of whether both parents agree to treatment, it may be desirable to establish parameters of treatment ahead of time. These include an understanding that the purpose of therapy is for treatment only and not for making custody recommendations. You may inform parents that you will not be discussing the case with any attorneys or any court (some psychologists say they will only discuss the case with a court-appointed custody evaluator upon receipt of a court order or the appropriate releases from all the necessary parties). In addition, some psychologists require parents to pay for all services, even for time spent talking to a custody evaluator and time spent talking to an attorney explaining that they will not make a custody recommendation.

In Section 3, chapter 9, The Reluctant Business Person, we discuss payment issues, and we argue that psychologists should ordinarily refrain from "nickel-and-diming" patients with charges even if they are covered in the psychologist/patient therapeutic agreement. Nonetheless, we believe that it is often clinically indicated to be firm about insisting on payment for forensic or forensic-like services when treating high-conflict families. Requiring payment for such services substantially cuts down on clinically contraindicated or frivolous requests for information.

Finally, when the custody conflict is especially vicious, it may be prudent to get a court order for treatment. This ensures that neither parent can waffle on consent or use the threat of withholding consent to advance a clinically contraindicated agenda. Nonetheless, when you agree to see families on the basis of a court order, you need to clarify who will be paying for services; what, if any, unusual confidentiality limits apply; and to whom (if anyone) to send reports.

The treatment of high-conflict families takes on special considerations, for example,

> A child's therapist was asked to do a custody evaluation by one or both of the attorneys involved because he already knew the family situation and was liked by both parents. (3.3.5)

Of course, in these situations you would reject the offer, noting that the Guidelines for Child Custody Evaluation in Divorce Proceedings of the APA (1994; APA Child Custody Guidelines) generally prohibit such a change in roles (there are narrow exceptions, such as in isolated or frontier areas where the availability of mental health professionals is limited). Ideally, the requesting parent would understand the therapeutic reasons behind the rule (e.g., the quality of therapy is compromised when forensic and treatment roles are mixed; there is a high risk of alienating one or more of the parents by participating in such roles; and such opinions by treating psychologists are based on less information than opinions expressed by custody evaluators). Nonetheless, at times some parents seem unable to appreciate these reasons, and it may be prudent to bolster the arguments with the statement, "in any event, the APA Child Custody Guidelines prohibit me from providing such an evaluation and expressing an opinion."

> A psychologist was treating a child in a high-conflict family. During the course of treatment, the psychologist received a phone call from the mother asking him to send a summary of the treatment to her attorney.
>
> Since the psychologist was a covered entity under HIPAA, the mother had a right to receive a summary of treatment. However, the psychologist was concerned that there might be actions that would compromise the neutrality of his therapy. Consequently, as part of his informed consent procedure he informed both parents that he would not be releasing information to third parties unconnected with treatment (except for a court-appointed evaluator with the consent of the parties controlling confidentiality). He also informed parents that they would be billed for all time spent related to the custody case, even if it included speaking to parents or attorneys about why he would not be involved in the custody dispute.

> The psychologist believed that the child would benefit most from a therapeutic setting in which the child felt safe and removed from the turmoil of the custody decision. Although he was normally generous in providing incidental services to patients without charge, the psychologist billed the mother $30 for the 15-minute phone call in which he explained again the reason he would not be involved. He strongly believed that such bills would discourage parents from nontherapeutic demands on his time. (3.3.6)

Remember the RM formula,

$$\text{Clinical risk} = \frac{(P \times C \times D)}{TF}$$

In this formula, P = patient risk characteristics; C = context; D = disciplinary consequences; and TF = therapist factors.

You will often find high-risk patients in this high-risk context.

High-conflict families include patients in litigation and often patients with serious personality disorders. Some argue that the patients in high-conflict families are only manifesting behaviors representative of personality disorders in the context of the stressful custody fight. Others might say that the conflicts are expected manifestations of the underlying personality disorders of each parent. Whether or not these are true personality disorders is irrelevant in this context. What is relevant is that the family members are expressing projection, rigidity, splitting, and other behaviors that seriously interfere with healthy functioning. Consequently, it is very important to use the risk management strategies (informed consent, documentation, and consultation) in these situations.

CHILD CUSTODY

Child custody evaluations are the number one context in which parents complain to licensing boards (although a very high percentage of these complaints are dismissed and relatively few result in disciplinary actions). Most of the complaints are lodged against psychologists who voluntarily assume the role of custody evaluator. Other complaints are lodged against psychologists who perform court-ordered therapy, parent education, or other services. In addition, psychologists who are treating patients who are involved in custody disputes in some way may sometimes get involved, albeit unwillingly or unknowingly, in an allegation of misconduct.

Psychologists often evaluate children in anticipation of custody litigation.[3] Who gets custody of children when a marriage dissolves is a difficult legal and moral question. Primary custody, joint custody, and visitation rights are

[3] From "Some (Relatively) Simple Risk Management Strategies" by E. Harris, 2004, Spring/Summer, MassPsych: The Journal of the Massachusetts Psychological Association, 48, 27–28. Copyright 2004 by the Massachusetts Psychological Association. Adapted with permission of the author. Also from "Child Custody and Custody-Related Evaluations and Interventions: What Every Psychologist Should Know," by S. Knapp and R. Baturin, 2003, March, The Pennsylvania Psychologist, 63, 3–4. Copyright 2003 by the Pennsylvania Psychological Association. Adapted with permission of the authors.

all fraught with difficulty. For better or worse, our system of government del-egates the decision making on child custody to local courts. If the parents are having difficulty reaching a custody arrangement, the courts may order them to mediation or another alternative dispute resolution. If none are available, or if those means fail, the courts may order psychological evaluations to assist in making those determinations.

Typically, the court or a private party arranges for the evaluation that is designed to help the court decide the custody arrangement that is in the best interest of the child. The process used to conduct these evaluations should correspond to the APA Child Custody Guidelines. Among other things, these evaluations should address the needs of the children, not the parents. The needs of the parents are well articulated; they each believe that they are the best parent and they each want custody of the children. Custody evaluations typically involve psychological testing and interviews with all relevant parties (parents, stepparents, relatives, significant others, the children, and sometimes the teachers and neighbors, as appropriate). Related to custody evaluations are "focused evaluations," which may be an update of a previous evaluation or a record review in which a psychologist reviews the work of a previously conducted custody evaluation.

Psychologists who conduct custody evaluations work in the area of prac-tice that has the highest risk of engendering a licensing board complaint. Many contested cases bring about the worst in the individuals involved, and the dynamics may appear similar to those of a borderline personality disor-der. In such situations, interpretations of the behavior of another person may be governed by the principle that "the friend of my friend is my friend, and the friend of my enemy is my enemy." If one parent perceives that the psychologist is more favorable to the other parent, then the parent may vil-ify the psychologist and have no hesitation about reporting him or her to a licensing board.

Although there is little objective evidence, it is clear to many psycholo-gists that attorneys involved in custody disputes may leverage their cases by getting the client to file a licensing board complaint against the psychologist evaluator if it appears that the recommendation will not be favorable to the party the attorney represents. While such a complaint may have little effect on the current case when the judge makes the final decision as to the ade-quacy of the evaluation and testimony, having a history of licensing board complaints can do significant damage to one's reputation and practice.

Psychologists do make errors that are likely to engender disciplinary actions, such as mixing therapy and evaluation; sending out information without having a release of information form or court order; failing to get consent of parents or a court order when conducting an evaluation; mak-ing substantial scoring errors on tests; not performing the work in a time-ly manner; or showing clear, unsubstantiated, and unsupported bias in the report and recommendations.

As noted above, the APA Child Custody Guidelines state that psychol-ogists ordinarily refrain from mixing therapy and custody evaluations. However, even treating psychologists who do not intend to provide a cus-tody recommendation may inadvertently do so, thinking that they are per-forming a good service. For example, sometimes attorneys will phrase requests in a deceptively innocuous manner, such as asking the treating psychologists to comment on visitation arrangements. Naive treating psychologists may do so without realizing that any comment about the custody arrangements is crossing the line into a custody evaluation.

Complaints also have been made against psychologists conducting child custody evaluations for failing to report child abuse, for reporting child abuse, for making factual errors in the background statements about the child or family members, for interpretation errors, for showing bias, for selecting tests allegedly irrelevant to the conclusions, or for misinterpreting the tests. The use of projective tests (e.g., Draw-A-Person, Thematic Apperception Test, Children's Apperception Test, Bender Gestalt, and Rorschach) can leave the psychologist subject to severe cross-examination. If you use these devices, be sure you have an in-depth familiarity with the instrument and can justify their use in this clinical situation.

Allegations of misconduct may result in disciplinary action, although it is difficult for a licensing board, in the absence of clear negligence, to find cause. Custody evaluators, of course, like other psychologists, have to report suspected child abuse. We urge psychologists to interpret their state laws literally. Do not believe that because another health care professional is involved in the case that you do not need to report suspected or known abuse. Such laws typically require reporting when the psychologist suspects or believes that abuse has occurred. Thus the threshold for reporting is low. It does not necessitate certainty nor does it require the psychologist to verify the accuracy of the report. Even if, on a statistical basis, the probability of founded reports is substantially lower when they are made in the context of a custody dispute, child abuse does occur and must be reported when the necessary threshold is reached. Unfortunately, in highly charged custody cases it is not unusual for one parent to accuse the other of child abuse. The situation becomes more difficult when such reports are received and the psychologist needs to consider the allegation and report as required.

Some parent support groups are very aggressive about reporting psychologists who do custody evaluations to the point that such allegations are often a tactical weapon designed to intimidate evaluators or create an apparent conflict of interest that will result in removing the psychologist from the case. Some parents have been coached to plant inaccurate information in the child's history so that they can have grounds for alleging negligence on the part of the psychologist if they do not like the conclusions in the report. They may, for example, report that the child started a private school in February 2005, when in fact the child started the private school in March 2005. Although this fact may be irrelevant to the issues facing the court, it nonetheless creates an impression of sloppiness on the part of the psychologist. More importantly, Web sites now provide information for husbands and for wives with considerable advice on how to respond to the psychologist's questions and tests that are part of the custody evaluation. Divorce proceedings may represent life and death struggles with no-holds-barred; for each parent the stakes are extremely high.

Other allegations such as bias, faulty selection of tests, or faulty interpretations are difficult to prove. Nonetheless, care must be taken to ensure an appearance of fairness. In one instance, a complaint was based on the fact that the psychologist spent more time interviewing one parent than the other. The time differential was entirely justified by the circumstances. Nonetheless, the mere appearance of unfairness was sufficient to prompt a complaint.

Attorneys vary considerably in the manner in which they handle custody disputes. It has been said that clients pick the attorneys most likely to reflect their personal styles. However, the obligation of attorneys is to their clients, not to you. Some attorneys attempt a more restrained and moderate approach, recognizing that the long-term welfare of the family will be best ensured by fair play during the divorce and custody proceedings. Others, sometimes with an exaggerated sense of self-righteousness, demonstrate unrestrained aggression toward the other parent or the custody evaluators if it suits their purposes, even if it means harming the child in the process.

It takes *special skills to be a child custody evaluator.* Simple *competence as a child clinical psychologist* is necessary but not sufficient. Some skills of child clinical psychologists are relevant, such as knowledge of child development (including normal developmental stages), family systems, parenting skills (including the match between parents and children), psychological testing (including the degree of confidence to place in the sources of data and information on the psychometric properties of the tests), child and adult psychopathology, report writing, and basic professional ethics. In addition, *competent custody evaluators know the basic workings of the legal system, professional ethics as applied to forensic practices, the unique clinical features that are likely to occur in high-conflict families* (such as serious allegations of misconduct by one parent against the other, exaggeration of small concerns into major issues, and similar features that occur when parents are locked in battle), *how to testify in court,* and *how to write forensic reports.* Finally, it is necessary to *have the personality to tolerate the stresses of child custody work* including resilience, comfort and confidence in one's work, problem-solving abilities, conflict tolerance, and a sense of humor. The average competent clinician should not enter the custody arena without substantial additional education, supervision, or consultation.

The rules and procedures of a child custody court vary from state to state, and even within the same state, may vary from county to county. In one rural county the family court judge took a special interest in the quality of child custody evaluations. He held informal educational meetings with the child custody evaluators and local family law attorneys, attended judicial education programs on family law, and kept up on the professional literature on custody cases. He set a prochild atmosphere that permeated his court and demanded high-quality service from all professionals.

However, in an urban county, the family court was seen as a transitory and unpleasant assignment until more prestigious judicial appointments could be obtained. Although the basic standards of judicial conduct were maintained, few judges felt a long-term investment in the quality of the work they provided.

We have noted that it is unethical for a treating psychologist to provide a custody recommendation because an appropriate evaluation has not been performed, and there is a fiduciary obligation to the client that has an inherent bias. In addition, those involved in treatment should avoid giving testimony on individuals who have not been their clients, even if they have been involved as a collateral contact.

The role of a treating psychologist should be, at the most, to provide information to court-appointed custody evaluators. However, even that role has risks; the information may not be conveyed accurately or it can be taken out of context. You may find that the cautious language you used over the phone is greatly distorted in the final report. Consequently, many psychologists follow up such phone consultations with custody evaluators with a written summary of their perception of the conversation.

ALTERNATIVE DISPUTE RESOLUTION AND OTHER ROLES

Many people have become dissatisfied with using litigation to resolve disputes because of the time and cost involved. In addition, litigation tends to force parents into adversarial roles. Consequently, several methods of alternative dispute resolution (ADR), such as arbitration or mediation, have been applied to family disputes. These ADRs differ in terms of their degree of confidentiality, the extent to which they are legally binding, and the qualifications of the persons who perform them. The particular ADR used depends on the state laws and local rules. Mediators have their own training programs and standards of conduct. Often mediators are attorneys, but they may also be psychologists and other mental health professionals.

Psychologists are often requested to intervene without having the parents go to court. Such situations may arise when there is a concern about the alienation of a child from his or her parents, the desire of a child to modify the visitation schedule to accommodate changing interests, or a concern about the child management procedures of one or more of the parents. The term "reunification therapy" is generally used when the goal is to reconcile a child with a parent (or a parent with a child). Parenting classes are generally conducted in an educational format and are designed to address common problems encountered by families. Some parenting classes may be tailored to families that are undergoing a divorce. In coparent counseling, psychologists meet with the parents to help them consider the best manner in which to work together to promote the welfare of (or minimize the harm to) their children. Of course, psychologists may provide therapy to the child, either of the parents, or to the family. When judges refer a family for therapy, it is desirable to identify the specific issue that prompts the judge to make the referral. Whenever possible, a psychologist who is providing therapy to a child in a custody dispute should attempt to get an agreement from all parties to protect their neutrality in providing treatment for the child.

Whenever a judge or attorney refers a parent for psychological services, be it therapy or parenting classes, it is desirable for the psychologist to have the goals and nature of services clarified ahead of time. The specific term used for the intervention is less important than the question of whether the psychologist has the skills necessary to deliver the service requested. The psychologist and the parents should understand ahead of time the limits of confidentiality and whether a report will be written. If a report is to be written, the psychologist and the parents should know the general content of the report, such as any recommendation on the custody arrangement.

Whether a psychologist should apply for third-party reimbursement for these services depends on the nature of the service. A parenting class will probably not qualify for reimbursement, whereas therapy may. It is very unwise to "relabel" something in order to gain access to insurance coverage. Whether coparent counseling or reunification counseling qualifies for insurance reimbursement depends on if the intervention is designed to alleviate a mental disorder in the identified patient and if the services are covered under the parent's health insurance policy by the managed care company.

On a final note, many prudent psychologists involved in custody work stress the importance of having a clear court order before proceeding with any evaluations or intervention in such cases.

Seven Essential Points to Remember

1. It is important to clarify obligations when treating more than one person in a relationship (see APA Ethics Code Standard 10.02, Therapy Involving Couples or Families).

2. The treatment of children and adolescents involves special issues regarding informed consent and confidentiality. The rules may vary from state to state or even within the same state depending on the treatment setting.

3. The treatment of high-conflict families requires a special awareness of the unique clinical features that such families are likely to manifest.

4. The risk management "poultices" of informed consent, documentation, and consultation are very important when treating high-risk families.

5. Psychologists who perform child custody evaluations should follow the APA Child Custody Guidelines and relevant state laws.

6. Participation as a custody evaluator requires special skills in addition to those held by otherwise competent child clinical psychologists.

7. Psychologists may perform valuable roles in alternative dispute resolution or other roles helping divorcing families. However, these roles involve disciplinary risks as well. Clear court orders are important.

Chapter 4: PRIVACY, CONFIDENTIALITY, AND PRIVILEGED COMMUNICATIONS

Privacy is the constitutional right of individuals to choose for themselves whether or when to reveal private information. Privacy overlaps but is distinguished from confidentiality and privileged communications. Confidentiality is the duty imposed on professionals to keep information disclosed in professional relationships in confidence. It is embedded in ethics codes and state laws but also in the federal Health Insurance Portability and Accountability Act (HIPAA) Privacy Rule (hereinafter referred to as the Privacy Rule). Privileged communications is a legal term that refers to the legal right of individuals to withhold information in judicial proceedings under limited circumstances.

Throughout most of this chapter we emphasize the application of the risk management (RM) formula introduced in the Preface and the application of risk management strategies using therapeutic discretion and prudence. However, in this chapter we give relatively more emphasis to understanding basic information about the legal system and its impact on the practice of psychology. For example, we note that you still must use your professional judgment on important issues such as how much effort to place into preventing accidental breaches of confidentiality and how to handle patient requests for records. Nonetheless, much of the content, by necessity, involves a somewhat didactic presentation.

BASIC FACTS ABOUT CONFIDENTIALITY

Privacy and confidentiality are cornerstones of effective psychotherapy. As stated by the United States Supreme Court in *Jaffee v. Redmond* (1996),

> Effective psychotherapy...depends upon an atmosphere of confidence and trust in which the patient is willing to make a frank and complete disclosure of facts, emotions, memories and fears. Because of the sensitive nature of the problems for which individuals consult psychotherapists, disclosure of confidential communications made during counseling sessions may cause embarrassment or disgrace. For this reason, the mere possibility of disclosure may impede development of the

confidential relationship necessary for successful treatment. (p. 340)

Psychologists are required to protect patient privacy by virtue of the American Psychological Association's "Ethical Principles of Psychologists and Code of Conduct" (APA Ethics Code), provisions of their state's licensing law (which typically adopts the APA Ethics Code or a version of it or the Association of State and Provincial Psychology Boards [ASPPB] Code of Conduct), and other statutes and case law. The general rule is that psychologists must keep patient information confidential. They do not gossip about patients or permit the unauthorized release of patient information except in specific situations as required or permitted by law. This means, among other things, that psychologists take special care in how they create, store, and dispose of records. There are also rules regarding patient access to records.

The special rules governing the release of patient information in court proceedings are referred to as privileged communication laws. These laws deal with the circumstances in which courts will accept confidential information into the legal proceedings. Other rules regarding patient releases, subpoenas, or court orders deal with the circumstances under which psychologists are required to release information into court.

Most rules governing confidentiality are found in state laws. However, the Privacy Rule, which went into effect in April 2003, establishes minimal nationwide standards for confidentiality of patient information. Moreover, the Privacy Rule has a preemption clause; it holds that any state law that is more protective of patient privacy will trump the minimum standards in the Privacy Rule. Because mental health laws tend to be more protective of patient privacy than other laws dealing with health care records, the Privacy Rule has had little impact on the day-to-day manner in which psychologists handle confidential information. We describe these minimal changes below.

The Privacy Rule requires each covered entity to appoint a Privacy Officer who is responsible to develop and implement privacy protections. Among other things, Privacy Officers ensure that each patient receives a Privacy Notice, all staff members are trained in confidentiality issues, and the other confidentiality requirements are met. Because certain aspects of HIPAA are scalable (meaning that the measures to implement it vary according to the size and needs of the organization), most solo practitioners serve as their own Privacy Officer, and in small practices, one owner or employee can be appointed the Privacy Officer.

EXCEPTIONS TO CONFIDENTIALITY

The exceptions to confidentiality are determined by the standards in the APA Ethics Code and the relationship of these standards to the peculiarities of state and federal law. The exceptions to confidentiality may occur either through the actions of the patient (such as by signing an authorization to release information) or through an exception created for public policy reasons. The public policy exceptions include consultations with other professionals, the mandated reporting of suspected child abuse, a patient's mental or emotional status when the patient has raised this issue as part of a legal proceeding, or a malpractice suit against the psychologist filed by the patient. Other mandatory reporting laws found in some but not all states include reporting of elder abuse, medical errors, impaired professionals, professionals who have sexually abused patients, professionals who have committed serious ethical violations, and impaired drivers. More detail on these mandated reporting requirements is found in Section 3, chapter 7, Assessing and Treating Patients Who Are Potentially Suicidal or Dangerous to Others. The point is that there is no substitute for knowing the laws in your state.

The APA Ethics Code permits psychologists to consult with other professionals concerning a patient so long as you

> do not disclose information that reasonably could lead to the identification of a client/patient.

and you limit the disclosure

> to the extent necessary to achieve the purposes of the consultation. (Standard 4.06, Consultations).

Most psychologists prefer a broader right of consultation that allows them to identify the patient if it is appropriate to the consultation, such as with the referral sources, the patient's primary care physician, or the patient's psychiatrist. The laws and regulations in some states permit such consultations, as does the Privacy Rule. However, the laws and regulations in other states are silent with regard to such consultations. The APA Insurance Trust (the Trust) recommends that even when permitted by state law, you include your consultation policy as part of the informed consent agreement that your patients sign.

There is an exception that permits psychologists to release information to Worker Compensation referees in some states. Discretionary disclosures when clinically indicated may include a breach of confidentiality when needed to protect a patient with a high risk of suicide or in most states to protect an identifiable third party from violence (we discuss this topic in greater detail in Section 3, chap. 7, Assessing and Treating Patients Who Are Potentially Suicidal or Dangerous to Others). Other narrow exceptions include collections for payment of bills and giving confidential information to the executors or personal representatives of the estates of deceased patients (in most states).

Confidentiality with minors varies from state to state. You need to consider who controls the confidentiality of minors. If parents control the information, then you need to consider how much to involve the parents in the information exchange and whether to use an agreement of confidentiality (see Section 3, chap. 3, Working with Couples, Families, and Children).

BREACHES OF CONFIDENTIALITY

Most psychologists are scrupulous about the protection of patient privacy. Seldom do they gossip or talk about their patients in public places or display identifiable confidential patient information openly. However, some psychologists are indiscreet about patient information and may tell stories about patients at parties or to their close friends. Even though they may believe that the patient is not identifiable, such an assumption might not always be warranted. Furthermore, such "entertaining" stories may give an impression that these professional psychologists are not taking the problems or privacy of their patients seriously.

Also, an accidental breach of confidentiality can occur in any professional setting. When psychologists have their offices in their homes, professional mail may get mixed up with personal mail or messages from the answering machine may be played too loudly and be overheard by members of the family. The conversations of psychologists meeting for a lunch consultation may be overhead by others sitting nearby. In large institutions, extra protections for patient records stored on computers may be needed. In any setting, voices may sometimes bleed through the office walls and ceilings, patient charts may be left unattended, and staff members may forget that they need permission before leaving messages on the answering machines of patients.

According to the Privacy Rule, the Privacy Officer is responsible for training support staff members (and documenting that training). Within your office, patient privacy should be everyone's business. In the ideal environment all of the staff members (clerical, billing, and professional) will be looking out for the welfare of the patient and each other. When threats to patient privacy arise, each staff member should feel comfortable addressing the issues with each other. All psychologists are human and may be unaware of how their behavior presents a threat to confidentiality.

Psychologists should also have "business associate" agreements. Business associates are non-health-care professionals with whom you contract but whom you do not employ and who have a legitimate reason to get protected health care information. Business associates would include billing services, bookkeepers, and attorneys. A business associate agreement ensures that these associates will respect the confidentiality of the information that you provide them.

PRIVILEGED COMMUNICATIONS

The term privileged communications refers to a limited right to withhold information from a court. Within the United States the first privileged communication laws were developed to ensure that clients would be able to share all relevant information with their attorneys without fear that the attorneys could later be required to testify against them in court. However, in creating privileged communication laws, the legislatures balanced the interest of fairness in justice against other social policies to determine the exception to the general rule of admitting all evidence into court. That is, the likelihood that a court could reach an erroneous conclusion increases every time evidence is withheld from the court because of a privileged communication law. Because fairness in dispute resolution is a high social value, legislators have been reluctant to create privileged relationships, and courts have tended to interpret them narrowly.

Although some may argue that privileged communication laws are based on a constitutional right to privacy, courts have been reluctant to accept such arguments (Knapp & VandeCreek, 1987). Instead, most legislatures have enacted psychologist-patient privilege laws primarily out of utilitarian concerns. That is, the overall public good is promoted when patients can receive therapy without unnecessary worry that their communications will be made public. Some degree of privacy is necessary for effective psychotherapy.

Privilege laws exist in every state for the attorney-client, husband-wife, and priest-penitent (or clergy-communicant) relationships. Many states also have privileged communication laws for the social worker-client, sexual assault crisis counselor-client, domestic abuse counselor-client, and journalist-source relationships.

All states have a privileged communication law for psychologist-patient relationships, although the scope of these laws varies enormously from state to state. In some states the protections are quite extensive; in other states they are very limited. In any event, in every state these laws all have some exceptions, and unless their application is clear, will be narrowly construed by the courts. Privilege laws are enacted state by state and usually profession by profession so that patients of different mental health professionals in the same state may have quite different protections. A psychotherapist-patient privilege exists in all federal courts. Here are some exceptions that apply in some states, depending on the privilege statute or the common law interpretation that the courts have given to the statute. There is no substitute for learning the relevant rules that apply in your state.

Most state privilege laws include an exception when patients place their mental status into litigation as part of their claim or defense. In addition, once they have made their mental health a part of the litigation, patients may not selectively edit what gets admitted without special permission from the court. In some states, courts hold that any time parents seek custody of a child, they are entering their mental health into litigation and the privilege would not apply. The privilege typically does not apply during a hearing for a civil commitment to a hospital or if individuals enter their mental health into litigation, such as when they present a plea of insanity or diminished mental capacity or if they initiate a suit alleging emotional harm (such as a malpractice suit). The privilege does not apply to court-ordered examinations. The courts in many states have carved out additional exceptions for when a patient self-releases information about the treatment or when the patient's behavior is inconsistent with an expectation of privacy. Most state laws allow you to pursue patients who do not pay their bills but limit the information that you may release to collection agencies to that which is necessary to collect the debt. If a patient threatens your life, you may seek a restraining order.

In some jurisdictions the privilege may only apply to those professional relationships that involve the diagnosis and treatment of a mental or nervous disorder; other professional communications may not be covered. In some jurisdictions the privilege may apply only to the information shared by the patient, while in others it will include collateral contacts with family members or others who are present to further treatment. In some jurisdictions it covers supervisees; in other jurisdictions, it does not. In many jurisdictions judges have discretion to waive the privilege if it is necessary for the administration of justice.

This list of potential exceptions is not given to imply that the privilege is completely toothless. Indeed, it provides meaningful protection for many patients. Not all of the exceptions apply in all states. However, this list of exceptions across all states was given to illustrate the idiosyncratic manner in which privilege laws are written or the idiosyncratic manner in which courts interpret the privilege laws under similar circumstances. While you should be familiar with the privilege statute and its exceptions in your state, you should always refer patients to a mental health attorney when they have questions about unique circumstances such as whether their communications will be protected if they are involved in an unrelated lawsuit.

The privilege exists for the benefit of the patient and belongs to the patient.

> A psychologist received a court order to testify but refused to do so, noting that she was invoking the "psychologist privilege" even though the patient wanted her to testify. She did not realize that she had no standing to invoke the privilege (except in some states in which psychologists have a narrow obligation to invoke the privilege on behalf of the patient if the patient cannot be located). (3.4.1)

The privilege only deals with the circumstances under which patients may block psychologists from sharing information with the court. It is not up to the psychologist to determine that a patient has waived the privilege. It is up to the judge, after hearing arguments from attorneys, to make a final determination. Psychologists, for their part, can only release records with a signed patient release of information form (authorization) or court order.

> A psychologist received a phone call from an attorney who told him that he was sending a subpoena to turn over patient records, that the patient had waived her privilege by introducing her mental health into litigation, that the subpoena was binding on the psychologist, and that the failure of the psychologist to honor the subpoena would be construed as contempt of court, and he could be subject to imprisonment or fines if he refused to comply. The psychologist, who had neither a release from his patient nor a court order, sent in the records. He was later disciplined by his state licensing board. (3.4.2)

This psychologist failed to appreciate that privileged communication laws deal only with the criteria that the courts use for admitting evidence into court. These laws do not permit psychologists to make the decision about whether to release such records. Of course, the psychologist also failed to realize that the attorney was not acting on the psychologist's behalf and had no legal obligation to ensure that he understood the relevant state laws governing his profession. Unfortunately, such misrepresentations by attorneys are common.

Patients should be given some information about privileged communications at the start of treatment, presumably in a Privacy Notice or another informed consent document. The amount of information given needs to be tailored to the needs of individual patients. More extensive information should be given to patients who are involved in litigation or where it is anticipated.

SUBPOENAS AND COURT ORDERS

In general, a psychologist may only disclose information with the consent of the patient or in response to a court order.[1] The receipt of a subpoena alone without the consent of the patient does not override this requirement. A court order, however, overrides the need to obtain patient consent.

A subpoena is a document issued by an attorney instructing the recipient to provide documents or to be present to give oral testimony. The exact form of a subpoena may vary from jurisdiction to jurisdiction, but it typically includes a signature or stamp of the clerk of court, prothonotary, or an attorney.

A court order is a document issued by a presiding judge that instructs the recipient to provide documents or oral testimony. The exact form of the court order may vary from jurisdiction to jurisdiction, but it typically includes identification of the case and the signature of the judge.

Psychologists are required to respond to a subpoena, but they are prohibited from releasing records merely upon the receipt of a subpoena. In most instances the psychologist should inform the releasing party, in writing, that the receipt of a release of information form (authorization) signed by the patient is required prior to releasing information in response to a subpoena. If no such release is forthcoming, the psychologist should advise the requesting party that he or she is waiting for further instruction from the presiding judge. California, a state that is often imitated legislatively, allows notification of the patient to accompany a subpoena and requires submission of the information if the patient does not file a formal objection.

Unfortunately, many attorneys do not understand that psychologists have limited discretion for releasing records. Attorneys representing patients (or sometimes attorneys representing parties adverse to the patient's interests) may misinform psychologists of their legal obligations and instruct them to release records in response to a subpoena alone. Do not be bullied by these tactics. It is best to seek legal consultation in situations in which the requirements are unclear.

A court order issued by the presiding judge does compel the release of records or testimony as specified in that order. Although you may feel very strongly about the obligation to protect patient privacy, you need to remember that there are other competing social values in play, and judges, with their wealth of experience in the law and the social obligation to ensure the administration of justice, are entrusted to balance competing demands and make such choices. Our experience is that judges, as a whole, are conscientious (often impressive) public servants who will consider the welfare of your patient and the overall public good. As a rule, they have no desire to cause needless harm to anyone. If you have a good reason to challenge a court order, most judges will want to learn of your concerns.

When dealing with the courts, the first risk management rule is "Treat all judges with respect." In the rare situations in which you wish to challenge a court order, we recommend that you obtain legal counsel to avoid any behavior that gives direct or indirect appearance of contemptuous

[1] From "Practical Considerations When Responding to Subpoenas and Court Orders," by S. Knapp, A. Tepper, and R. Baturin, 2003, August, *The Pennsylvania Psychologist, 63*, 5, 16. Copyright 2003 by the Pennsylvania Psychological Association. Adapted with permission of the authors.

behavior on your behalf. Some battles are best left to others.

> A psychologist received a subpoena from an attorney asking for the release of patient records. The attorney followed up the subpoena with a phone call in which he claimed that the psychologist would be in contempt of court if he failed to send the requested information. The experienced psychologist was not intimidated by such tactics. She called her patient, and the patient, upon consultation with his attorney, decided that he did not want the information released. The psychologist then sent a brief letter to the attorney who sent the subpoena that stated she would only release patient information with a release signed by the patient or a court order. (3.4.3)

If the patient, upon consultation with his attorney, had wanted the information to be released, the psychologist would have acquired the appropriate release from the patient and sent the records. This experienced psychologist was wise enough to ensure that the patient had consulted with his attorney before any decision was made. If the patient had been a child, she would have ascertained if the patient had been appointed a guardian ad litem.

HIPAA PRIVACY RULE[2]

We now turn our attention to a brief review of the Privacy Rule and some of the more salient issues that may apply to your practice. At times, our discussion may appear detailed and arcane, but we believe it is important for you to understand the reasoning behind the public policy involved and our recommendations. Furthermore, as we note below, some issues in the Privacy Rule have not yet been resolved. We urge you to keep abreast of current developments.

The Privacy Rule applies to any licensed health care provider who electronically transmits or hires someone to electronically transmit protected health care information in one or more covered transactions. All covered transactions involve communications with insurance, managed care, or third-party payor entities. Once an electronic transmission occurs, the Privacy Rule thereafter applies to all of the psychologist's activities involving protected health care information. For now, psychologists who have not transmitted information electronically in one or more covered transactions are not covered by HIPAA. However, psychologists who receive reimbursement from third-party payors electronically are likely to be covered in the future if and when electronic billing or electronic utilization reviews are required.

For those who are not covered entities but who bill clients directly with the expectation that they will pay out of pocket or seek reimbursement from third parties on their own, the future is uncertain. For those with an entirely self-pay practice or who exclusively engage in non-health-care activities, such as forensic services, the Privacy Rule will most likely not apply. However, as

[2] From "Resolving Some Areas of Continuing Confusion," by E. Harris, 2003, Winter, *MassPsych: The Journal of the Massachusetts Psychological Association, 47,* 18–22, 29. Copyright 2003 by the Massachusetts Psychological Association. Adapted with permission of the author.

soon as a psychologist transmits a bill or other covered information electronically, the entire Privacy Rule will apply to the entire practice. In addition, as the rules of HIPAA become more prevalent in health care, it is possible that some future court will rule that some of the standards of HIPAA, such as a Privacy Notice at the start of therapy, will become mandatory for all health care providers. As the electronic creation and storage of records becomes more prevalent, it is possible that some current proposals (which have widespread support across the political spectrum) to mandate electronic records will become law. Since it is difficult to implement the Privacy Rule suddenly, we recommend that all psychologists understand the Privacy Rule and assume that it will apply to them in whole or in part at some point in the future.

The Privacy Rule has been in effect since April 15, 2003. The current APA Ethics Code has been effective since June 1, 2003. Many psychologists have tried to understand and integrate these complex regulatory changes into their practices. However, the implementation process has exposed confusion and uncertainty concerning (a) informed consent, (b) psychotherapy notes, (c) forensic services, and (d) psychological testing. We review each of these four areas below.

INFORMED CONSENT

We already reviewed informed consent as a risk management strategy in Section 2, and we discuss the application of informed consent as a risk management strategy throughout Section 3. However, here we are just referring to the informed consent requirements found in the Privacy Rule.

The Privacy Rule mandates that covered entities must give patients a Privacy Notice (Notice Form) that details their rights involving the release of information. It is important to note that while some aspects of the Privacy Rule are scalable, the requirement to give patients a Privacy Notice and all that the notice must contain is not scalable. Obtaining the patient's signature by the end of the first professional contact showing that the Notice Form was received generally satisfies this requirement. If patients refuse to sign the acknowledgment that they received the Privacy Notice, then you can note that the patients were offered and refused to sign the acknowledgment. The Notice Form must comply with both the Privacy Rule and state law according to the preemption analysis prescribed within the Privacy Rule. Therefore, the actual content of the Notice Form will differ from state to state. In addition to the notice requirement under the Privacy Rule, the Ethics Code requires that you obtain the informed consent of patients before initiating professional services or as soon as feasible (Standard 3.10, Informed Consent).

Some of you may view these requirements as "new" burdens that interfere with good treatment. However, as we discussed in Section 2, these informed consent requirements are not very different from what always has been considered to be essential for effective psychotherapy. Psychologists, perhaps more than other health care professionals, are well aware that confidentiality serves as the foundation of therapeutic services. The problem with the Privacy Rule is that it substantially adds to the amount of information that should be presented to patients, and since this information is also required to be distributed by all other health entities, the Privacy Rule is very likely to diminish the significance of the content. Since as psychologists you were already required to maintain confidentiality and to provide a substantial amount of informed consent content, this additional content required by the Privacy Rule could diminish, rather than enhance, the basic autonomy principles underlying the informed consent responsibility.

The Trust and the APA Practice Organization (APAPO) developed the home study product, *HIPAA for Psychologists,* as a resource tool to assist you in meeting these requirements.[3] *HIPAA for Psychologists* includes three important downloadable documents: (a) the required Notice Forms researched to comply with the specific requirements of statutory law and regulations in each state; (b) the Explanation Form, a document that explains to the psychologist the requirements in each jurisdiction; and (c) the Psychologist-Patient Agreement, a document addressing the major informed consent issues that should be provided at the end of the first session so patients can read, discuss, and sign it at the next session. The use of these documents will vary depending on the modality of services and types of patients seen. The rationale for developing two separate informed consent documents rather than one more elaborate document was that the Psychologist-Patient Agreement (which is a redesigned form of a sample generic informed consent document that has been distributed by both organizations for some time) is more user friendly and is much more relevant to what actually takes place in most psychotherapy than the Notice Form, much of which concerns issues that rarely arise in most practices.

HIPAA requires that you give the Privacy Notice to patients and receive acknowledgment by the end of the first professional contact in which the psychologist receives protected health care information. We recommend that the Psychologist-Patient Agreement, which is a more user friendly informed consent document, be given to the patient at the same time as the Privacy Notice, but that a signature not be sought until the beginning of the second session after the psychologist has given the patient an opportunity to discuss its terms and conditions. In practice, few patients read the document carefully, and few ask questions. This approach requires a brief verbal statement about the limits of confidentiality at the beginning of the first contact to prevent uninformed and potentially damaging statements.

If the patient is a child, the documents should be given to and discussed with the parent or legal guardian who brings the child for services. If the state allows minors to consent to treatment independently, they should receive the Notice Form instead of the parent or legal guardian. More information on privacy and confidentiality with adolescents can be found in Section 3, chapter 3, Working with Couples, Families, and Children.

The Explanation Form provided with *HIPAA for Psychologists* provides the basic information that you need to know about the interaction of the laws in your jurisdiction and how these laws interface with the provisions of the Privacy Rule. Unfortunately, this is a complicated area of psychology/law interface, and the relevant documents require careful reading. Nonetheless, as we discussed in Section 2, when done properly, a careful discussion of the salient issues in these documents can augment treatment and strengthen the therapeutic relationship.

---

[3] Psychologists can access this information at www.apait.org or www.apapractice.org.

PSYCHOTHERAPY NOTES

A second area of confusion caused by the Privacy Rule involves psychotherapy notes. We reviewed the risk management features of documentation in Section 2, and we discuss the use of documentation as a risk management strategy in specific chapters (see chaps. 1, 2, 7, and 8 in Section 3). Here we only address the special topic of psychotherapy notes as defined by the Privacy Rule.

The Privacy Rule provides special protection of confidential mental health information by permitting the practitioner to keep some types of confidential information in psychotherapy notes. Under the Privacy Rule, insurance companies may not require the patient to release information contained in psychotherapy notes as a condition of coverage. In addition, the psychologist may not be required to release information contained in psychotherapy notes to the patient unless mandated by state law. Unfortunately, there is much confusion in the field regarding the advantages and disadvantages of psychotherapy notes.

Initially there was confusion as to whether keeping psychotherapy notes was required or optional. On the one hand, it could be argued that such notes would be required to fulfill the obligation to maximize patient confidentiality. On the other hand, it could be argued that such an obligation would not make sense in states whose laws give patients complete access to their records, including psychotherapy notes. Keeping psychotherapy notes would seem unnecessary for psychologists who provide primarily behavioral therapy and do not depend on analysis of transference or for psychologists who are performing evaluations. Further, if psychotherapy notes were obligatory, it could stimulate disputes between patients and psychologists about the location of specific patient information. These disputes could develop into licensing board complaints with patients alleging that the psychologist should have put more or less information in clinical records as opposed to psychotherapy notes. Fortunately, conversations between the Trust, APAPO, and the U.S. Department of Health and Human Services (HHS) confirmed that HHS intended that the separate designation of records entitled psychotherapy notes is at the discretion of the practitioner.

The confusion regarding the appropriate use of psychotherapy notes is partially a result of poor regulatory draftsmanship as well as a lack of guidance for when to use and when not to use psychotherapy notes. The Privacy Rule itself is somewhat vague about psychotherapy notes, stating only that they include

> notes recorded (in any medium)...documenting or analyzing the contents of conversation during a private counseling session or a group, joint, or family counseling session and that are separated from the rest of the individual's medical record. (45 C. F. R. 164.501)

Psychotherapy notes do not include documentation related to the

> modalities and frequencies of treatment furnished, results of clinical tests, and any summary of the...diagnosis, functional status, the treatment plan, symptoms, prognosis, and progress to date. (45 C. F. R. 164.501)

If read expansively, psychotherapy notes would seem to include all information that describes what took place in any psychotherapy session. However, it is clear that psychotherapy notes must be kept separate from the general medical record so, for example, the notes that you write in the log on the ward of a medical hospital as part of a consultation would not be considered psychotherapy notes because they are not separated from the rest of the medical record.

> A psychologist working in a nursing home two days a week knew that the information he wrote in the patient's chart in the nursing home would be read by the entire staff. Although Medicare laws required him to document his meetings in the nursing home chart, he was circumspect about what he placed in those records. On the other hand, he kept more detailed patient records in the patient charts that he kept in his private office. (3.4.4)

Some practitioners have suggested that the option of keeping separate records permits them to keep very sparse clinical records, putting the meaty information about treatment in the more confidential psychotherapy notes. This seems a very attractive option given practitioners well-founded concerns about privacy and the intrusiveness of managed care companies into the psychologist-patient relationship. The clinical records could be limited to an initial treatment plan, dates of treatment, changes in the treatment plan, and session notes (e.g., "June 10, psychotherapy, 50 minutes, discussed problems with parents"). This may be poor advice for a number of reasons. First HHS, in its commentary accompanying the Privacy Rule, provided guidance that would be inconsistent with this strategy.

The rationale for providing special protection for psychotherapy notes is not only that they contain particularly sensitive information but also that they are the personal notes of the therapist, intended to help him or her recall the therapy discussion and are of little use or no use to others not involved in the therapy. Information in these notes is not intended to communicate to, or even to be seen by, persons other than the therapist. Although all psychotherapy information may be considered sensitive, we have limited the definition of psychotherapy notes to only that information that is kept separate by the provider for his or her own purposes. It does not refer to the medical record and other sources of information that would normally be disclosed for treatment, payment or health care operations.

It is reasonable to conclude that the clinical record, excluding psychotherapy notes, must at least be adequate to meet professional documentation guidelines. The records must be comprehensive enough to adequately document and share what transpired in the treatment with a future treating professional and with other health care providers who might be treating the patient for some other condition. If one is seeking insurance reimbursement, the records (or the treatment report forms of the patient's managed care organization [MCO]) must include sufficient information to justify medical necessity and to survive a retroactive utilization review.

Another way to determine what information should be kept in the clinical record and what should be kept in psychotherapy notes is to consider the rules that determine access to both sets of records and determine how much patient privacy psychotherapy notes actually provide. Based on the 10-year experience of the Trust Risk Management Program, access to provider records is most commonly sought (a) by the patients and/or their guardians or legal representatives to examine and/or receive a copy of the records, (b) for release as potential evidence in litigation in which the patient is a participant, and (c) by health insurers or MCOs for eligibility and accountability purposes. The more access a state law provides to psychotherapy notes in these three situations, the less sense it makes to keep them.

PATIENT REQUESTS FOR INFORMATION

While there are a few exceptions, in most states the Privacy Rule provides either the same or greater access by patients to protected health information (i.e., the clinical record) than does existing state law. According to the preemption doctrine, the statute or rule that provides the patient with the greatest level of access preempts (or overrides) the more restrictive statute or rule. Under the Privacy Rule, the primary ground for refusing patients' request for copies of their clinical records is that in your professional judgment it is

> reasonably likely to endanger the life or physical safety of the individual or another person. (45 C. F. R. 164.524 (a) (3) (i))

If records are withheld under this provision, you must provide a justification for the judgment in your record and provide an appeals process that may be difficult and expensive to implement.

Since the Privacy Rule does not require psychologists to provide patients access to their psychotherapy notes, current state laws governing patient access to medical and mental health records would take precedence and regulate access to psychotherapy notes. A few states have no laws governing record access. Most commentators believe that in these jurisdictions the actual records (i.e., the content of the records and the paper on which it is written) belong to you, the provider, who could restrict or deny patients access to them. However, patients could almost always obtain a copy of their complete record through the legal process.

Many states have laws that provide patient access to mental health records unless in the professional's judgment the release would damage the patient. Often, these states require that the threatened damage be "substantial" or "serious" and that providers document their reasons for refusal in their records. Many also give patients the right to forward the records to another provider of their choice. Some states require that a summary of the record be provided to the patient as an alternative to the actual record. However, others have laws that give patients complete access to their records including both clinical records and psychotherapy notes.

The more access to records a state law provides to a patient, the less privacy protection psychotherapy notes enjoy. In states where access is greater than that provided by the Privacy Rule, the rationale for keeping psychotherapy notes is diminished. We encourage psychologists to know the law in their states about patient access. This information is available to you from your state association, mental health attorneys in your state, and *HIPAA for Psychologists* for your state.

CLINICAL FEATURES OF PATIENT ACCESS TO RECORDS

Up to this point we have discussed only the legal requirements concerning patient access to the records. However, these requests have clinical implications as well, which require some judgment on how to respond. When patients request access to their records, it is often helpful to think clinically first. Ask "why does this patient want the record?" Often the request for records is an indirect way of asking other questions such as "What does my psychologist really think of me?" or "Am I really going crazy?"

When possible, it is best to address the underlying clinical issue first and ask about the patient's goal. Often you can address the clinical issue without giving the patient access to the records or by showing him or her a limited portion of the records.

The harm from the occasional request by patients for their records can be avoided either by keeping a second set of psychotherapy notes for certain patients who appear especially vulnerable or by being very tactful in the manner in which you write all your clinical notes. However, in some situations patients will insist on seeing their notes and have the legal right to them, although seeing the notes may be harmful to them. For example, some patients may request to see their records, which will include, among other things, the patient's presenting problem and diagnosis. Because patients have a right to know their diagnosis as part of their protected health information, you need to consider the consequences of providing the patient with the diagnosis. The conditions under which you can withhold the protected health information from patients are exceedingly narrowly defined as explained above and are unlikely to be met in the large majority of clinical situations. Given that reality, should you, for example, give a patient the diagnosis of borderline personality disorder (BPD) or a similar diagnosis indicating a serious mental disorder, especially if you work in a state that grants patients full access to all their records? On the one hand, it could be argued that giving such a diagnosis to a patient might harm the patient. For example, it may limit the patient's ability to get life insurance or get accepted into the military or a high-security occupation, may prejudice future health care providers, or be upsetting to the patient. On the other hand, it can also be argued that such a diagnosis should be given if it is accurate, regardless of whether it is upsetting to the patient, just as a medical diagnosis should be given even if it is upsetting to the patient.

To ease the potential burden on the patient and assist the psychologist in making decisions about assigning such diagnoses, it may be useful to consider the RM formula here. Your decision making should include awareness that inaccurate or inadequate diagnosis is a common disciplinary complaint (it is often included as negligent practice in the list of common disciplinary complaints reported to ASPPB). If the diagnosed condition, such as BPD, is the focus of treatment, it may be desirable to find a way to fulfill the potentially incompatible obligations to present information accurately, respond to the request by the patient, and minimize harm. For example, it may be possible to involve the patient in the development of the treatment plan, including a behavioral description of the presenting problems in a manner that is consistent with BPD. It may be better to share the diagnosis with the patient up front and describe it and its implications in therapy, rather than to have the patient learn the meaning and implication of the diagnosis from a Web site or other informal source of knowledge.

These situations require clinical judgment. For example,

> One patient periodically asked the psychologist, "What do you think of me?" "What are you going to put in your notes about me?" The patient showed other signs of suspiciousness and self-consciousness. The psychologist suspected that her patient might eventually request the records, so the psychologist was careful in how she phrased her thoughts in her notes, clarified the diagnosis with the patient in lay terms, and offered to show her notes to the patient on occasion. (3.4.5)

REQUESTS FOR INFORMATION TO BE RELEASED AS POTENTIAL EVIDENCE IN LITIGATION

All states have psychologist-patient privilege statutes that allow patients to prevent information in their psychologist's records from being admitted as evidence in a legal proceeding. However, these privilege laws typically include exceptions, such as when patients place their mental health at issue in a case or when a court has ordered an examination (more detail on privileged communication laws can be found earlier in this chapter).

Privileged communication laws do not distinguish between clinical records and psychotherapy notes. When you receive information requests in the early stages of litigation, you may want to offer a summary of the record to protect your patient's privacy at least to some degree. In general, this is not a good strategy. Attorneys are rarely going to be satisfied with a summary that you have prepared; they usually want to examine the actual content of records to see how they can use it to their advantage and to prepare for its use by their adversaries. Furthermore, attorneys, particularly attorneys opposing a patient, are likely to believe that you may edit the material in ways that reflect your biases in favor of the patient or your work with the patient and interfere with their best legal arguments. Psychologists who are compelled to turn over records in a legal proceeding will undoubtedly end up turning over the entire record including psychotherapy notes. Offering a summary may actually hurt the patient because the opposing side is likely to request the entire record, and if you are called to testify, the opposing side may attempt to discredit your testimony by pointing out differences between the summary and the original record.

REQUESTS BY THIRD PARTIES FOR REIMBURSEMENT

Perhaps the most confusing aspect of the release of psychotherapy notes occurs when trying to ascertain what information a health insurer or MCO can require as part of its claims review or utilization management process to determine whether requested services are within the policy contract or are "medically necessary." (Note this restriction does not apply to health insurance requests to determine coverage eligibility or to requests from other insurers such as disability or life insurance companies.) Health insurers and MCOs cannot require patients to turn over their psychotherapy notes as a condition of coverage. However, they can refuse to pay claims or even demand recovery of funds already paid if your documentation in the clinical record cannot establish medical necessity on a prospective or retrospective basis.

If the clinical record is insufficient to demonstrate medical necessity, then you will have to go back to the patient and ask permission to submit the information contained in the psychotherapy notes, in whole or in part, or ask the patient to pay for the service out-of-pocket. Further, if the clinical record is insufficient to establish medical necessity on its own, the initial impression of the insurance company may be that the documentation was inadequate to justify services, thus making the review process more onerous. Psychologists are more likely to be targeted as outliers if their clinical records are inadequate to justify services in the first place.

Many psychologists have been subjected to Medicare audits. Often, the sole problem is that these audits identify inadequate documentation, but this is sufficient to allow Medicare to recover all payments for those sessions for which adequate documentation does not exist. Most MCOs regularly audit participating providers, and if the records of these providers are deemed inadequate, the company can also demand repayment. Since the audits often take place after the treatment is over, you may not be able to get the separate authorization required to release psychotherapy notes to use in those audits. Recently, an insurance company audited the records of many mental health professionals and determined that many of the records were inadequate. The company initiated claims for repayment, many of which, based on extrapolation formulas, involved many thousands of dollars. While these demands were withdrawn as part of a settlement because of the lack of established standards for record keeping, they point out the need to have adequate clinical records that can independently establish medical necessity. Providers would have a difficult time using their psychotherapy notes to establish that.

Unfortunately, other psychologists have had to repay money. The repayment and any associated legal costs are not covered by professional liability insurance (see chap. 11, Professional Liability Insurance—Don't Practice Without It).

Given the limited privacy protection accorded psychotherapy notes and the additional administrative time required to keep two sets of notes, many psychologists have decided to forgo keeping psychotherapy notes and to keep a single record. Psychotherapy notes would seem to make the most sense for psychodynamically oriented psychologists in states that do not allow patients access to these notes who wish to keep the analysis of the process of the therapy relationship and other psychodynamic formulations separate from the more behavioral descriptions of what happened in the session. These types of notes were often referred to as "process notes" before the advent of the Privacy Rule. If your records adequately document the presenting problem, treatment plan, and progress, MCOs should not need the additional information contained in psychotherapy notes. The primary interest of the MCO is in clinical necessity and not in embarrassing personal details or transference and countertransference issues.

FORENSIC PSYCHOLOGICAL SERVICES

We discuss forensic psychological services in more detail in Section 3, chapter 5, Court Testimony. However, here we discuss the application of the Privacy Rule to forensic services. The Privacy Rule has also caused confusion concerning the extent to which it applies to forensic services. One could argue that those who provide only forensic services are unlikely to be covered by the Privacy Rule because their services do not generate protected health care information. However, many of you have mixed practices and the provision of one single covered transaction triggers the application of the Privacy Rule to one's entire practice, including one's forensic work.

The Privacy Rule defines protected health information so broadly that it would be very difficult to argue that forensic psychological services do not involve protected health information. While the Privacy Rules mandates a sweeping right of patients to access protected health information (45 C. F. R. 164.24) and to request amendments (45 C. F. R. 164.526) of protected health information contained in a health care professional's records, it specifically exempts

> information compiled in reasonable anticipation of, or for use in, a civil, criminal, or administrative action or proceeding. (C. F. R. 164.524 (a) (ii))

When forensic psychologists are hired directly by attorneys, their work, in almost all cases, can be deemed to fall within this exception because any other interpretation would be in conflict with the very strong attorney-client privilege that includes materials prepared by retained experts as attorney "work products." Such information, therefore, would be governed by state laws relating to access to information, and forensic psychologists could impose the same limits to access forensic information that existed before the Privacy Rule went into effect.

Therefore, the Privacy Rule has not greatly impacted forensic practices when you are working for attorneys. Regardless, forensic psychologists need to give a Notice Form or an Informed Consent Contract to the person being assessed before services are provided. Most prudent forensic psychologists already have had such informed consent agreements. Such a form would have to meet the formulaic requirements of the Privacy Rule and would probably include more information about the exceptions to confidentiality than was previously included in such contracts. A sample forensic contract (pre-HIPAA) can be downloaded from the Trust Web site (www.apait.org). Most forensic psychologists would probably need a similar contract for the attorney requesting the services. These contracts can be quite complex, but the Privacy Rule does not require any changes in these documents.

Of course, many of you present information in court as fact witnesses, as treating experts (see chap. 5, Court Testimony), or in other roles in which you are not covered by the attorney-client privilege. You would arguably then be covered by the Privacy Rule, assuming that you are an otherwise covered entity.

Also, if you perform nonforensic third-party evaluations, such as independent medical examinations, in which there is no reasonable anticipation that the services will be involved in administrative or legal proceedings, you are subject to the Privacy Rule access to information requirements. Psychologists who perform Social Security disability determinations have been informed that the previous federal rules prohibiting patient access to psychologists' records have been preempted by the Privacy Rule.

It is important to note that our conclusions about the Privacy Rule, along with the conclusions of many others, are subject to differing perspectives. Some commentators have come to different conclusions, and for example, believe that all information collected for third-party evaluations that does not contain protected health information is not covered by the Privacy Rule.

PSYCHOLOGICAL TESTING

We provide more information on psychological testing in Section 3, chapter 6, Psychological Assessment and Testing. However, here we review the impact of the Privacy Rule on psychological testing. Among the most significant changes of the 2002 Ethics Code are the standards pertaining to patient access to test data and test materials. The 1992 Ethics Code stated that you should not give test data or materials to individuals who are not qualified to use them. This standard (2.02b, Competence and Appropriate Use of Assessments and Interventions) was designed to protect patients from receiving confusing or potentially misleading information and to protect the reliability and validity of psychological tests by limiting the publication and distribution of test questions and answers.

The 1992 provisions created several problems for psychologists. In most states, court rules considered this material, if not protected by privilege, as admissible evidence, particularly if the report was based in part on testing. Many judges were reluctant to grant a request that the material be released only to another psychologist or another mental health professional or to issue protective orders requiring that the parties not rerelease information beyond what was required for the specific case. Psychologists who refused to turn over raw data in response to a valid subpoena or court order faced credible threats of contempt motions from the requesting attorneys.

In some states, patient access laws require psychologists to release all materials to patients, including raw data, although some have argued that federal copyright laws override state record access laws. Other states prohibit release to untrained individuals and prohibit courts from issuing court orders to obtain the information. Furthermore, forensic psychologists who were retained by attorneys to do testing or to analyze testing by someone else could not very well refuse to provide the hiring attorneys with as much of the testing as was necessary to help the attorneys understand how they reached the conclusions and to defend them in court, if necessary. Finally, with the advent of the Internet, many test protocols or manuals can be obtained online. Many Web sites provide sophisticated advice on how potential test takers can "beat" the psychological tests. It is not unusual to see test manuals in used book stores or for sale on eBay.

Although agreeing to turn over test data to another psychologist was a plausible solution to ensure appropriate review, interpretation, and copyright protection, some commentators recommended that courts and attorneys should have greater access to copyrighted tests (Lees-Haley & Courtney, 2000). The question remained how one was to determine that another provider had the requisite skill and knowledge to review and interpret the test results. The idea was to keep the material out of the hands of lawyers who, it was thought, would use test materials to "coach" their patients. This also overlooked the fact that some mental health attorneys frequently knew more about psychological testing than many psychologists. Attorneys have argued that they need direct access to test information to represent their clients effectively. At times it was difficult for attorneys to find a qualified psychologist to interpret the test results, and retaining a second psychologist placed a financial burden on patients. Furthermore, the extant draft of the HIPAA Privacy Rule held that the test report and test data must be available to patients and their attorneys on appropriate request, unless release would cause serious physical harm to the requester. This was the context of developing law when the APA Ethics Code Task Force redrafted the APA Ethics Code.

The 2002 APA Ethics Code changed long-standing ethical policy on this issue. The Code first established new definitions for test data and test materials to help clarify what had formerly been an almost epistemological debate. Standard 9.04, Release of Test Data, in the 2002 Ethics Code states,

> *the term* test data *refers to raw and scaled scores, client/patient responses to test questions or stimuli, and psychologists' notes and recordings concerning client/patient statements and behavior during an examination. Those portions of test materials that include client/patient responses are included in the definition of* test data.

This last sentence means that if patient responses are written on the test protocols, such protocols are converted to test data. The term *test materials* refers to "manuals, instruments, protocols, and test questions or stimuli and does not include *test data*" (Standard 9.11, Maintaining Test Security). Unless prohibited by law, test data must be provided to the client/patient unless to do so would cause "substantial harm or misuse or misrepresentation of the data or the test" (Standard 9.04, Release of Test Data).

Psychologists were required to make reasonable efforts to maintain the integrity and security of test materials and other assessment techniques consistent with law and contractual obligations. One gray area left unresolved by the 2002 APA Ethics Code was how to address the conflict between the requirement of release of data and the contractual obligations to test publishers that prohibit release where state law does not directly resolve the question, especially when the test stimuli or questions appear on the same page as patient responses and turn the test materials into test data.

It is not surprising that test publishing companies are greatly concerned about these developments, particularly the provision that would convert test materials, which the companies consider proprietary, to test data where data and materials are merged. A series of communications between and among test publishers and HHS has failed to resolve all of the issues to everyone's satisfaction, and conscientious readers can still find uncertainty in the response given by HHS. The legal issues are complex. Nonetheless, the test manufacturers have interpreted the response of HHS as permitting psychologists to withhold test materials (protocols and other stimuli) as legally protected "trade secrets." Under this analysis, materials could not be converted to data by the inclusion of client/patient answers or other identifying data.

Harcourt Assessment, Inc., one of the largest test publishers, sought an advisory opinion as to whether either federal copyright law or legislation protecting trade secrets overrode the Privacy Rule. They were told that copyright law did not negate the access provided by the Privacy Rule. However, HHS responded,

> *Any requirement for disclosure of protected health information pursuant to the Privacy Rule is subject to Section 1172 (e) of HIPAA, "Protection of Trade Secrets." As such, we confirm that it would not be a violation of the Privacy Rule for a covered entity to refrain from providing access to an individual's protected health information to the extent that doing so would result in a disclosure of trade secrets.*
> (Campanelli, cited in Harcourt, 2005, p. 1)

Harcourt interprets this letter as requiring psychologists to comply with their contracts with test publishers that prohibit dissemination of test record forms or protocols to attorneys, patients, or others who claim that they are entitled to these documents under HIPAA. If Harcourt is correct, the part of the Ethics Code that states that including patient answers on test protocols converts the protocols to test data would violate federal law and thus be invalid. Unless a court decision overrules Harcourt's interpretation, we believe that you should comply with it.

We advise you to act in accordance with your contracts with test publishers and refrain from sending copyrighted test materials to patients. Noncopyrighted materials would not qualify as trade secrets and would be governed by the 2002 Ethics Code and would need to be sent to patients. This means that patient answers on copyrighted materials should, to the extent possible, not be included on question sheets or other test protocols, since that arguably converts the entire document to test data.

The Privacy Rule gives patients a right to receive all test data. Practically, this would require a psychologist to manually separate the answers and questions. When test data are requested by a patient, you can respond either by whiting out the questions or stimuli or putting the answers on a separate sheet of paper before sending them. If one adopts this latter approach and the material is subpoenaed, then whiting out the questions and stating why they have been redacted is the only appropriate response. Copying the answers on a separate sheet of paper and submitting that paper rather than a redacted original would be problematic under the rules of evidence in most states.

If you receive a subpoena with appropriate authorization from your client/patient, you should not send test questions and test stimuli to the requesting attorney, citing the fact that these materials are protected by the Federal Trade Secrets Act and stating that they, therefore, can only be supplied in response to a court order. You should keep a copy of your contracts with test publishers as well as the test publisher's legal interpretation. These documents should be sent to the subpoenaing attorney to substantiate your position and thereby avoid threats of contempt actions. It is very unlikely that a state court would cite you for contempt for a good faith attempt to conform to state law. Also, forensic psychologists can include in their Business Associate Agreements with the lawyers that the lawyer will not voluntarily redisclose any test materials given to them by the psychologist unless required to do so by law.

Obviously this will take time to sort out. The Trust will monitor developments closely and provide information on our Web site as soon as more definitive information is available. At this time, patient requests for test data should be honored and requests for test materials resisted.

HIPAA SECURITY RULE

For covered entities, the Privacy Rule applies to all communications of patient information, whether they are through oral, written, or electronic means. However, the HIPAA Security Rule (hereinafter referred to as the Security Rule) applies to the manner in which information is stored electronically. The APAPO developed a home study on the Security Rule as a resource tool to assist you in meeting these requirements. You may purchase this home study program from the APAPO at www.apapractice.org.

The Security Rule requires you to determine the risks to the accessibility and privacy of patient records that you store electronically and to take precautions to minimize those risks. As such, you need to analyze your existing storage systems, identify where there are gaps, and close those gaps (Holloway, 2005). Electronic information storage includes electronic organizers, cell phones, computer records, and other electronic devises.

The Security Rule consists of three types of standards, some of which contain specific implementation standards and others that do not. Administrative standards involve questions such as how you protect privacy in your office. Do you have rules and procedures, training, and consequences for persons who violate the rules and procedures? Physical standards refer to limits of access to the places where information is stored, including such things as locks on doors, passwords, virus protection, and firewalls. Technical standards refer to the actual format or structure of records, such as whether they are encrypted and which staff members have access to this information (such as through the use of passwords).

The Security Rule has two different types of specifications. "Required" specifications must be implemented as written. "Addressable" specifications allow you more discretion to tailor the particular standard to your own practice. You may implement the standard as it is, or you may implement an alternative standard, but you must explain in writing why the alternative standard accomplishes the objective better. Look at each issue;

think about what you are doing; and document how you are trying to comply with it.

Just as the Privacy Rule was more flexible for smaller practices, the Security Rule also invokes the principle of scalability that allows smaller practices to choose implementation strategies that are appropriate to the size and sophistication of the data storage system. For example, a small office with limited storage of patient data might not need to purchase an encryption program. As long you as you make a good faith effort to comply with the Security Rule and document the reasons for your decisions, you will be in compliance.

You must do a risk analysis, which means you must look at the ways that you store electronic information and how you protect it. You need formal written policies and procedures. You have to document how you looked at these risks and how you are complying with the law, although you have a lot of discretion about how to comply.

Seven Essential Points to Remember

1. Most violations of confidentiality occur when psychologists accidentally allow the confidentiality protection mechanisms to break down. Responding to a subpoena for records without proper consent represents a major area of breach of confidentiality.

2. Psychologists are responsible to train and monitor their employees on procedures to protect patient privacy.

3. State and federal laws generally permit patients access to at least some portion of their records. You should attempt to handle most requests for patient records clinically.

4. Privileged communication laws, which have numerous exceptions, deal with the right of patients to withhold information from court.

5. Except in narrow circumstances specified in law, psychologists should only release patient information upon receipt of a valid patient release or a court order.

6. The Privacy Rule has certain ambiguities regarding its application to forensic services and access to test materials.

7. The Security Rule provides standards for protecting the security of electronically stored data.

Chapter 5: COURT TESTIMONY

Many psychologists find court involvement stressful and will go to great lengths to avoid it. Nevertheless, most psychologists will, at some time in their careers, have some involvement with the judicial system. Those who have no knowledge of the judicial process run an increased risk of exposing themselves to legal liability.

Otto and Heilbrun (2002) classify psychologists into those who are forensic specialists (have a high level of intensive and in-depth training in forensic psychology), those who are proficient (have some training in forensic activity related to their areas of practice), and those who are legally informed clinicians (know basic information about the legal system and know when they are moving into a forensic role). It may be realistic to add a fourth category, the legally uninformed clinician who is rarely called on to work with attorneys or do forensic work and who knows very little about forensic issues or the experience of testifying. In this chapter we review the basics of practicing within the legal system so that you will be legally informed clinicians and know how to reduce your legal exposure.

More information on the court system can be found in Section 3, chapter 3 (Working With Couples, Families, and Children), chapter 4 (Privacy, Confidentiality, and Privileged Communications, which includes discussions of the HIPAA Privacy Rule and forensics), and chapter 6 (Psychological Assessment and Testing).

As you may recall from our risk management (RM) formula,

$$\text{Clinical risk} = \frac{(P \times C \times D)}{TF}$$

In this formula, P = patient risk characteristics; C = context; D = disciplinary consequences; and TF = therapist factors.

Patients who are involved in legal cases are a high-risk group. As we noted in Section 2, the litigation may reflect a more pervasive orientation toward handling problems; the litigation itself may produce more aggressive or narcissistic behavior on the part of the patient; or the role of being in court may place you in a position where you are or appear to be acting against the best interests of your patient or client.

THE AMERICAN LEGAL SYSTEM

The American legal system is adversarial. It seeks the truth by presenting and evaluating positions and arguments from opposing points of view. It is a dialectic dispute resolution process governed by a complex set of formal and informal procedural rules (known as the evidence code). Within this system, the judge's role is to be a referee who ensures that the appropriate rules are followed, instructs the jury about the legal rules governing the dispute, and considers and rules on the attorneys' motions and objections.

Within this system, the attorney's role is to convince the jury by providing them with the narrative of his or her client's case concerning the events that happened. To do this, attorneys may present evidence in the form of witness testimony, documents, and demonstrations that support this narrative. The attorneys may argue for an interpretation that supports their client's narration. They may refute evidence and interpretations presented by the other side. They also act to protect their clients by objecting to what they perceive to be unfair practices by the other side's attorney. Attorneys may also advocate with the judge for appropriate instructions to the jury.

Within this system, the role of the jury is to consider all of the evidence and assign appropriate weight to it. The jury decides what most likely happened and which narrative to believe. They apply the legal rules contained in the instructions from the judge to the facts, and they reach a decision as to which side prevails. The jury may also determine the consequences, such as what damages will be awarded or what penalties will be imposed.

Within this system, the psychologist's testimony, records, and opinions are considered as evidence and are governed by the rules of evidence. Any involvement with the legal system and lawyers, whether voluntary or involuntary, is considered a forensic activity. The activities of psychologists in the forensic arena are governed by several standards within the American Psychological Association's "Ethical Principles of Psychologists and Code of Conduct" (APA Ethics Code), such as Standard 2.01f, Boundaries of Competence, which states, "When assuming forensic roles, psychologists are or become reasonably familiar with the judicial or administrative rules governing their roles." Psychologists do not need to be forensic experts. However, when they act in the forensic arena, they need to make some effort to have a working knowledge of the rules governing their participation.

Psychologists who work in the forensic arena may benefit from becoming familiar with the revised draft "Specialty Guidelines for Forensic Psychologists" promulgated by APA Division 41 (Committee on Ethical Guidelines for Forensic Psychologists, 2006). Although these have never been adopted formally by APA, many psychologists have found them to be useful guidelines for forensic psychologists to follow.

In order to facilitate the fairness of judicial proceedings, the doctrine of testimonial immunity protects a witness's testimony. A witness cannot be sued for his testimony. In addition, psychologists who are appointed by the court to perform certain functions such as custody evaluations are protected from suit by the related concept of judicial immunity. This immunity is limited to litigation, however, and does not protect a psychologist from a licensing board complaint.

PSYCHOLOGISTS AS WITNESSES

While mental health professionals appear in court for many reasons, they are frequently called as expert witnesses. Many of you do not want to appear in court at all and may go to great lengths to avoid doing so. Some may even require patients to sign a contract at the start of therapy stating that the patient will not require you to appear in court. Perhaps you want to avoid being in a potential dual role with patients in which you must answer questions in court that may interfere with a productive treatment relationship. Perhaps you have had a bad experience in court in which you felt attacked and possibly humiliated. Perhaps you are afraid of losing a day's income or more by having to appear in court. Perhaps you have heard stories from colleagues and believe that providing such services will be too stressful.

We sympathize with you. Certainly there are cases in which attorneys have taken liberties and acted without proper concern for the welfare of the patient or the treating mental health professional. At times attorneys will call a psychologist as a fact witness (for which the psychologist receives a nominal fee for travel or parking) and then try to direct questioning in a manner that elicits expert testimony. At other times attorneys have been insensitive to the schedules of psychologists and have bullied them into canceling a day's worth of appointments, without informing them that the judge might, in fact, be more considerate of their time demands and willing to reschedule their testimony or allow them to testify over the phone or make other accommodations.

There have been situations in which attorneys have lied and misrepresented the legal obligations engendered by a subpoena and threatened the psychologist with legal action for failing to respond to a subpoena when, in fact, the subpoena from an attorney alone does not permit the psychologist to reveal information. Some attorneys may act out of ignorance and be unaware that state laws typically grant greater legal protection to the records and testimony of mental health professionals than they do to the records of other health professionals. Other attorneys may deliberately try to mislead you and rationalize their behavior by stating that they are only zealously advocating for their client and are not responsible for representing your interests.

Attorneys vary considerably in their knowledge of mental health law, tactfulness, and sensitivity to the legitimate needs of other professionals. The great majority of attorneys act with highly commendable virtue when dealing with their clients, other parties, and psychologists. On the other hand, a few attorneys will, either deliberately or because of ignorance, attempt to induce you to violate the law and place you in jeopardy of disciplinary actions. Typically, the attorney working on behalf of your patient will treat you with courtesy. However, that attorney is not working for you, has no fiduciary relationship with you, and has no obligation to work to reduce your discomfort or protect your interests. You need to know the basics of the legal system.

Basic Information About Psychologists as Witnesses

Every one of you will probably during the course of your careers end up in court on behalf of a patient, probably more than a few times. The "no-court" provisions in contracts are not foolproof. Although they may dissuade patients from trying to get you involved in a court case, they cannot prevent a judge from ordering you to testify, if necessary. A court may view a no-court contract as contrary to public policy and fail to recognize it (Woody, 1997). Furthermore, as a professional with obligations to your patient, there may be times when the welfare of your patient requires you to testify in court.

The reasons that you want to avoid testifying may not, in the opinion of the court, represent good policy reasons.

> A patient was seriously injured in an automobile accident during the time she was in therapy. She entered her mental health into litigation, alleging that the automobile accident caused mental as well as physical damage. She signed a release that permitted her psychologist to release her treatment records to her attorney so the attorney could determine if the records would support her claim of mental damage from the accident. The psychologist refused, noting that "sharing the notes in court would harm the patient because of public embarrassment," and that "these notes are mine." (3.5.1)

The psychologist failed to consider that the patient has the right to decide about sharing the records (principle of respect for patient autonomy). As an autonomous individual, the patient has to decide, albeit with input from the psychologist and the attorney, whether pursuing the case for mental damage is worth more than whatever embarrassment might occur from admitting the evidence into court. Furthermore, the psychologist is wrong in stating that the "notes are mine." Although the psychologist may own the paper on which the notes are written, the patient has an interest in what happens to those notes and may, with informed consent, authorize their release to a third party. Finally, the release of the records is to the patient's attorney who, like the psychologist, is in a fiduciary relationship with the patient and bound to act to promote the welfare of the patient. In order to represent the patient properly, the attorney needs to know the content of those records.

> A psychologist was treating a patient with a serious personality disorder who became involved in a traffic accident during the course of therapy. The patient sued the other driver, alleging that she was seriously harmed mentally by the accident. However, the treating psychologist believed that the patient had a long-term mental condition and was only slightly harmed by the accident. The psychologist had to tactfully but clearly convey to the patient and her attorney the general nature of his prospective testimony. His patient was furious with him. However, it was better that he told the patient up front rather than to have the patient learn about his opinions in court. (3.5.2)

Nonetheless, here are some suggestions that will greatly reduce the negative aspects of your occasional appearance in court. First, when treating high-conflict families for whom your participation in court would be clinically contraindicated (see the discussion in Section 3, chap. 3, Working with Couples, Families and Children), you can specify in the psychologist-patient agreement your unwillingness to testify in court (although do not expect this to be binding in all circumstances). Also, for all patients you can specify clearly that if you are to provide forensic services, the patient will pay you at your forensic rate for all time spent on the court case (including but not limited to phone calls, preparation for the case, record copying and mailing, time traveling to and from the court house, travel and parking expenses, time testifying, and time spent in the court room waiting to be called for testimony). This provision will do more to reduce frivolous requests to be in court than anything else. Finally, you can reduce your worry by understanding basic information about courtroom procedures (We provide more information about payment under the heading, Getting Paid for Your Time, below).

Having a court order to perform therapy with a child, couple, or an individual patient does not require you to perform that therapy. More than one psychologist has been surprised by a prospective patient who appears with a court order specifying that he is she is to do therapy with so and so. One psychologist had a patient appear with such an order and then announce, "The court may order me to appear, but I am not going to pay you a penny." Another psychologist received five minutes of verbal abuse that accompanied the explanation that "The judge has ordered me here, so you have to take this abuse from me."

Of course you do not have to treat such patients. If no specific individual is named in the court order, then it is not incumbent on you to treat that individual. If you are specifically named in the court order, then it is a courtesy to the court to explain in writing why you will not be treating the individual, if you decide to refuse the case. Any reason you give is adequate. Perhaps the needs of the patients are outside of your areas of expertise, or your schedule is already booked solid.

> One psychologist interviewed a man who announced that he could not pay for any of his court-ordered therapy. The man explained that he had to pay the attorney a retainer of $5,000 and could not afford any more expenses. The psychologist elected not to see the patient. (3.5.3)

> One psychologist took a court-ordered patient even though it meant adding to an already heavily booked schedule. However, he wanted future referrals from the court and took the case as a courtesy to a potential future referral source. (3.5.4)

Fact and Expert Witnesses

A psychologist may be called upon to serve in one of several roles as a witness. In a trial, both sides present a narrative of events that supports their desired resolution of the dispute. The decision maker (jury) evaluates the factual evidence and decides the dispute based on instructions provided to them by the judge about the relevant law in their jurisdiction. Each of the attorneys will call witnesses to present facts who they know from their personal experience and experts who have been qualified based on their ability to provide guidance in areas in which a layperson does not have sufficient knowledge or expertise to reach a conclusion. *Fact witnesses* are those who have firsthand knowledge of facts that are relevant to the case at issue before the court. They are only allowed to testify about what they know and cannot opine as to what the facts mean in the case. A pure fact witness cannot give opinions or testify about something that was said to them by another person. Such hearsay testimony is generally prohibited, since the person who communicated the knowledge is unavailable to be cross-examined.

Other witnesses are considered *expert witnesses*. State law will determine what professionals qualify as expert witnesses on specific topics. However, the general rule is that an expert witness has knowledge in an area that is directly relevant to the dispute and is beyond the knowledge base of the average layperson. In addition, expert witnesses can take the factual situation and draw conclusions related to the issue in dispute. Therefore, expert witnesses are expected to bring information on a specialized branch of knowledge to the court. What qualifications an expert should have and what subject matters are appropriate subjects of their expertise are questions that forensic specialists and courts regularly debate.

A psychologist who has been qualified as an expert by the court is allowed to give a full range of opinions, including speculative or hypothetical opinions. Expert opinions are not personal opinions; they should be opinions based on scientific evidence. If you cannot provide scientific evidence for your opinion, then it would be prudent to respectfully decline to offer an opinion.

Many of you have treated a patient and have become a witness in litigation in which your services were relevant to your patient's lawsuit. The patient may have brought suit against other parties in which the patient asserted that as a result of the other party's negligence, the patient was emotionally damaged. Another common situation is a highly contested divorce involving child custody issues with a family or child you have treated. Sometimes your patient is involved in a criminal proceeding, and you are called to challenge your patient's veracity. When you provide professional services to a patient and are later called to be a witness in a lawsuit, your role is neither purely that of a fact witness nor an expert witness. You are either a *percipient expert* or a treating expert. What distinguishes expert witnesses from fact witnesses is that expert witnesses have relevant specialized knowledge beyond that of the average person; this knowledge may qualify them to provide opinions as well as facts.

Psychologists and psychiatrists who provide patient care can usually qualify to testify as treating experts in that they have specialized knowledge not possessed by most individuals to offer a clinical diagnosis and prognosis (Greenberg & Shuman, 1997). Percipient experts are "those individuals who have specialized training and experience but who are not retained for the purpose of litigation" (Caudill & Pope, 1995, p. 104). However, when psychologists testify as a treating expert, they are only allowed to opine about issues that are directly related to the services that they provided. In addition, the hearsay rule does not apply because the communication between the therapist and patient comprise much of the data on which the treating expert bases his or her professional opinions.

To clarify the responsibilities of a treating expert, consider the following example:

> A psychologist is treating a patient for depression and for problems at home and work. The patient reports and believes that he became depressed after a recent traffic accident. During treatment he brings suit against the other driver, asserting that the other driver negligently caused the accident. Because the patient has placed his emotional state at issue in this litigation, he has waived his privilege, and either his attorney or the attorney representing the defendant may want to find out what the psychologist knows about the patient's history of depression. The psychologist can, as a treating expert, answer questions about his treatment. He can state that his patient displayed symptoms of depression and some impairment. The psychologist can say that the patient presented as depressed and identified the traffic accident as the cause of the depression. He can also state that as the treating psychologist, it was not his role to determine the accuracy of the patient's narrative. The psychologist can state that nothing he observed or heard was inconsistent with the patient's narrative. (3.5.5)

However, the patient's attorney may want to persuade the psychologist to opine as to whether the accident caused the depression. The psychologist cannot give an opinion on that question; he cannot state that the accident caused the patient's depression or whether the patient suffered from depression prior to the accident because he did not know the patient prior to the accident.

In addition, the defense attorney will want to question the psychologist about the patient's history in hopes that he will prove that the patient was already depressed at the time of the accident. The psychologist will have to answer honestly based on his interviews of the patient or past medical records, if he has reviewed them. However, the psychologist cannot be asked to review the records and opine as to whether the depression was a preexisting condition. He can only provide data that he was given and state how he used those data to diagnose and treat the patient.

Often attorneys will try to manipulate a treating expert into providing opinions that go beyond the diagnostic and prognostic judgments. The attorney may be unfamiliar with the differences or may try to manipulate you to assist his or her client. The attorney for your patient/litigant will often be willing to brief you prior to your testimony, but the attorney's primary purpose will be to assist his or her client, not to protect your interests. If you raise issues with your attorney about protecting your interest, the advice likely will be that you need to retain your own attorney to advise you. Hiring an attorney is often very expensive, so to avoid that expense, you need to be aware of the types of questions that are appropriate for you to answer and what types are not appropriate. This is particularly important if you are participating in a deposition and there is no judge to appeal to if lawyers raise questions that you have doubts about answering. In many cases, if you make a good faith attempt to stay within the appropriate role, the consequences of going beyond the role will not have serious disciplinary consequences. One exception occurs in child custody proceedings in which you are at risk for a licensing board complaint if you provide opinions that could be construed as recommendations on custody or visitation.

COOPERATING WITH ATTORNEYS

At times the attorney for a current or former patient may contact you for your records. Assuming that a proper release is obtained, you can legally send the information to that attorney. Sometimes you may be aware of the litigation and understand the general nature of the issues involved. At other times, you may not know why the patient or former patient wants the records sent to an attorney. If you believe that the material might be clinically or legally damaging, contact the patient to discuss the situation.

If you are required to testify as a witness for a current patient, there is a significant possibility that the treatment relationship may be damaged. To a certain extent, all successful treatment depends on the projective idealization by the patient, and that is difficult to sustain when an attorney is trying to discredit you on the witness stand. Your patient will want you to be the advocate, when your responsibility as a witness is to tell the truth. Your patient will want you to be strong and competent, while you may be anxious and uncertain. This should be discussed in advance to prepare the patient for the potential downsides of your testimony.

If you learn that the patient is in litigation and you suspect that you may be called to testify or release records, then it is prudent to discuss this situation with your patient and perhaps the patient's attorney ahead of time. There is a danger if the nature of your testimony will vary from what the patient would want you to say. Also, it is desirable to clarify payment arrangements with the patient ahead of time if you do not already have a payment agreement with your patient for the time you will spend on the legal case.

Some psychologists may advise patients that the content of their records will hurt them in court or that the content of the records is not appropriate for admission into court. However, if you make such comments, you risk giving patients bad legal advice. If you believe that the admission of the records will hurt the patient's case in court, the best advice is to discuss what is in your record with your patients so that they can consult with their attorney on the matter or discuss it with both the attorney and patient.

GETTING PAID FOR YOUR TIME

It is often the case that your participation in a court proceeding is initiated by the party who has brought a lawsuit against your patient. You will discover this when you are served with a subpoena for your testimony or records. In this situation, the subpoenaing party is not obligated to pay professional rates for the considerable time you are required to spend in order to comply. All states have laws that set a nominal statutory witness fee for fact witnesses; treating experts are usually considered fact witnesses with regard to compensation. California is the only state that statutorily recognizes the special nature of the treating expert witness role. Court decisions in many jurisdictions have awarded expert witness fees to treating experts. If you are subpoenaed by opposing counsel, you can petition the court to require payment of professional fees, but this usually requires the assistance of counsel and the expenses involved often exceed what you could reasonably expect to recover.

Even though your participation is initiated by the opposing party, your involvement is an indirect result of your provision of professional services to your patient, and it is perfectly appropriate to bill your patient for your professional time, providing that the patient has agreed to be responsible for payment. This requires that you include a provision in the initial treatment contract signed by the patient that states something like "You understand that if I am subpoenaed or otherwise required to participate in a legal proceeding as a result of providing professional services to you, you will be responsible for paying for all time expended on preparation, transportation, and testimony." Many psychologists charge more than their regular clinical fee for forensic participation because of the extra stress incurred. This must also be agreed to in writing as part of the initial contract.

TESTIFYING IN COURT

Many times you will be asked to participate in a deposition. A deposition is part of the discovery process. In order to make a proceeding as fair as possible, each side is allowed to discover what evidence the other side will be presenting in order to be better able to prepare for or refute it. When you are deposed, you are part of the discovery process. The lawyer for the person opposing your patient wants to find out what you are going to say if you are called to testify in court. A deposition is taken outside the presence of a judge. With no judge around, some lawyers will take liberties in their questioning and comments that they would not take in a trial. They may be unusually aggressive or offensive to discern how far they can push you. Your patient's lawyer will be present but will usually remain silent. He or she will save questions for the trial so as not to expose his or her strategy in advance. A deposition can be the most difficult part of a psychologist's participation in the legal process. It can be damaging to the treatment relationship. In many situations, after consultation with their attorneys, we have advised psychologists to avoid these negative impacts by encouraging their patients not to attend the depositions.

We recommend that you include a provision in your informed consent agreement that the patient is required to pay the full professional fee for all services provided, including fees for work on legal issues. As a general rule in everyday practice we recommend being generous with your time and refraining from nickel-and-diming patients for all kinds of incidental charges. However, for both personal and clinical reasons, we recommend being very strict when it comes to charging for all forensic time. The charges could include, for example, talking to the patient between sessions, talking to the patient's attorney between sessions, retrieving and reviewing records from other sources, reviewing the patient's chart, preparing for testimony, travel to and from the court room or deposition, long distance phone charges, parking costs, waiting to be called to testify, and so on. For personal reasons, you need to appreciate that the time commitment may be very substantial. Although the patient or the patient's attorney may frame the request in terms of "taking a morning off," in reality the preparation and travel time could easily escalate into dozens of hours with no guarantee that the hearing might not be postponed or that you might not be asked to return on another day. Furthermore, it may be desirable to spend time reviewing the general nature of your testimony or conclusions with the patient's attorney and the patient ahead of time for clinical reasons.

If you do not bill for your time, you may not be as committed to putting in the necessary time to ensure that you are well prepared for the deposition. However, testifying without preparation can engender substantial risks. You may confuse the patient with someone else, misstate an important point, or otherwise fail to represent yourself clearly or accurately. You need to address the issues before the court, which may include justifying the content of your notes, identifying your treatment or diagnostic hypotheses, and presenting the data to substantiate them.

Anytime you testify you also run the risk of saying something that would offend your patient and harm the treatment relationship. If the patient's case depends on demonstrating the extent of psychopathology or impairment, you could offend the patient by emphasizing the degree of the impairment. Conversely, if you fail to describe the impairment as sufficiently severe you may offend the patient as well. Therefore, you might consider debriefing the patient after your testimony or requesting that the patient refrain from attending the deposition.

For clinical reasons it is important for patients and their attorneys to appreciate the importance of your time. They will be less likely to involve you in frivolous requests for assistance if they know that they will be paying for your services.

You should not accept contingency fees; such fees are considered a conflict of interest. When on the stand, your primary obligation is to speak the truth. Any contingency fee would give a financial incentive for you to weigh the testimony in a manner consistent with your financial interests rather than the truth.

Generally, in preparation for testifying, you do not need to hire your own attorney. Sometimes the experience is unpleasant, but it does not typically generate legal risks. Here are some general suggestions about how to testify.

Get a briefing from the patient's attorney prior to your deposition or testimony. Understand relevant information about the case. Understand the attorney's strategy and where your testimony fits. Do not rely on the patient's attorney as the only source of information concerning your court involvement. Be aware of the conflicts between roles of experts and advocates. From the beginning and throughout the process, clarify your role with attorneys retaining your services.

Review your records carefully and review and know the literature concerning the services you provided. Rehearse your testimony.

Beware of manipulation by the opposing attorney. Your patient's attorney may provide assistance regarding the opposing counsel's strategy.

Limit testimony to matters that you can address in a meaningful manner. Do not assume that you know more than the attorneys about the legal system. Expect your testimony to be challenged, sometimes vigorously.

When you are on the stand, listen to the questions and respond carefully. Understand the questions and reflect on them before you testify. If you do not understand a question ask the attorney to repeat it. An excellent response to a confusing question is, "I don't understand the question; could you rephrase it?" If you don't know the answer to a question, acknowledge that fact. Do not be afraid to say, "I don't know."

Limit testimony to data regarding your own patient and opinions related to the services you provided. Do not comment on family members or others whom you have not evaluated. If you must answer a question for which you have little information or data, qualify your answers and note your bias (Standard 9.02b, 9.02c, Use of Assessments).

Do not allow yourself to get baited by the opposing attorney into responding emotionally. Explain, but do not argue. Give a competent, confident response in a neutral, nonemotional tone. Avoid hyperbole and avoid being defensive.

This can be a high-stress experience because you lack control over the process and may feel that the questions are unfair or highly biased. If you are at a deposition with no judge to monitor the process, you may encounter an attorney who wants to bait you to measure your responses in order to determine if you will be a good witness in court. After the deposition, you have a right to review your transcript; do not be afraid to make amendments. You do not have to pay for the transcript of a deposition.

TAKING FORENSIC CASES

Some psychologists enjoy forensic work; they may work with attorneys to evaluate a defendant for an insanity defense, do neuropsychological testing for a case involving a head injury, be involved in child custody cases, or otherwise provide expert opinions related to psychology/legal issues. Indeed forensic psychology is a rapidly expanding area of practice.

Those of you who do forensic work can make your experience less stressful by trying to be very clear with the referring attorney on the issues as soon as you are first contacted. You may, for example, need to clarify at the first contact, or as soon as possible, as many details as possible. Who is the client? Where is he or she? What role does the attorney want you to fill? Will you need to see or test the client personally or is this a record review? What type of services and skills are needed (and do you have those skills)? What are the legal issues to be considered? Does the attorney want a written report? Will testimony be required? What is the time frame? Who are the opposing attorney and judge (if you do much forensic work you may need to screen for potential multiple relationships)? How will you be paid? (Hays, 1990; Hess, 1998).

Some psychologists find the experience of being an expert witness exciting and rewarding (albeit at times frustrating). They may see themselves as public servants whose goal is to provide information to empower the juries to make better decisions (Brown, 2000). They may also have a good sense of themselves and their roles and have confidence (but not too much confidence) in their abilities. They do not view themselves as "opinions for hire" in which they will delete, overemphasize, or shade the evidence to support the position of the attorney who hired them. Instead, they view themselves as committed to being honest and accurate in all of their representations.

Seven Essential Points to Remember

1. Psychologists who perform forensic roles need to have a reasonable familiarity with their roles, including the procedures followed in the justice system.

2. The roles and functions of fact, expert, and treating expert witnesses vary.

3. When working as an expert witness, clarify your role with the attorney who has hired you.

4. Informed consent and documentation are especially important when working with clients in the legal system.

5. The hybrid role of treating expert presents unique ethical and legal demands that require consideration of your roles and obligations.

6. Psychologists will be able to withstand the stress of testifying if they understand some basic rules about the process and proper decorum.

7. A prime risk management rule is always treat judges with high respect.

Chapter 6: PSYCHOLOGICAL ASSESSMENT AND TESTING

Psychological assessment is a broad term. For our purposes here, it refers to the integration of a wide range of information into a comprehensive report. That information may be obtained from an interview, review of archival records, collateral contacts, questionnaires, checklists, standardized psychological tests, behavioral observations, or other sources. Psychological testing is a narrower term that refers to the use of standardized stimuli or procedures to gather information. Although some legal risks can come from psychological assessments, on the whole many of the criticisms of psychological assessments come from the manner in which psychological tests are selected, administered, scored, and interpreted. Consequently, in this chapter, we give a disproportionate amount of attention to psychological testing.

Psychological testing may be used for vocational, educational, or health care purposes. Tests are frequently used to measure academic progress, predict academic achievement, determine vocational interest, assist in career planning, identify psychopathology for health care purposes, or assist in employee selection or promotion. The use of psychological testing to plan for mental health treatment has declined substantially over the years. However, as we describe below, there has been a substantial and rapid increase in the use of psychological testing at the request of third parties. This is often called "testing with third-party consequences" or "testing with external consequences." Of course, any testing, even for planning mental health treatment, can have ramifications beyond its immediate purpose. The possibility always exists that some third party at some time or under some circumstances could get access to the testing done for treatment planning and use it for another purpose.

TESTING FOR TREATMENT PLANNING

Testing patients for the purpose of treatment planning carries some legal risk. However, such complaints are relatively rare. First, the lack of payment for such tests by third-party payors makes the overall use of psychological testing for treatment purposes less common. Second, psychologists tend to have good relationships with their therapy patients, and these relationships tend to discourage patients from filing complaints. There is a good general principle here, of course, namely, that patients who experience good relationships with their psychologists, even when the focus is on assessment, are less likely to initiate complaints. So, a good risk management strategy with assessment is to develop a collaborative relationship with patients and pay careful attention to informed consent principles.

There is a movement within psychology called "consumer focused" assessment or a similar term (Brenner, 2003; Finn & Tonsager, 1997; Fischer, 2004). No one fixed set of strategies defines this perspective on assessment. Instead it is a series of strategies that attempts to maximize patient involvement in the assessment process as much as is clinically indicated. Some of the activities could include involving patients in the phrasing of the referral question, selection of the tests to be given, wording in the social history, or phrasing of the conclusions in the final report.

This perspective on assessment has risk management advantages and disadvantages, depending on how and under what circumstances it is used. On the one hand, it could increase the legal risks to psychologists if it compromised the accuracy, reliability, or validity of the report. This could occur, for example, if the testing involved unjustified deviations from standardized test administration procedures or interpretation or the deletion of clinically relevant information from the social history.

On the other hand, it could decrease legal risk to the psychologist if it increased the accuracy, reliability, validity, or usefulness of the report and increased the extent to which patients felt invested in and confident in the assessment process. For example, a discussion of the referral question or the wording of the report may lead to the clarification of an important point that the psychologist had originally misunderstood or may lead to the phrasing of a sensitive topic in a manner that avoids unnecessary embarrassment to the patient.

GIVING A DIAGNOSIS

When assessing a patient and determining a diagnosis, the psychologist may be confronted with difficult issues. On the surface, it would appear straightforward; you give the patient whatever diagnosis is warranted by the facts. However, the issues are more complex, especially if the diagnosis may have an unintended negative consequence, such as making it more difficult for patients to qualify for life insurance, negatively biasing any future but unanticipated legal action involving the patients in which the legal action has no connection to the patients' current or past level of functioning, or stigmatizing the patients when they seek treatment from subsequent health care professionals.

It would, for example, be appropriate to give a patient a diagnosis of borderline personality disorder if the facts warranted the diagnosis, if it were the focus of treatment, or if the Axis II diagnosis were integrally involved in the Axis I diagnosis that was the focus of treatment. However, it need not be given if it is not the focus of treatment. Indeed some insurers, such as Medicare, do not pay for the treatment of personality disorders, and any Axis II diagnosis would be meaningless from the standpoint of insurance reimbursement. If the information were to be shared with another service provider, then it would be important to give comprehensive and accurate information. Again, accuracy is paramount. However, if there is uncertainty, it may be prudent to give the diagnosis in terms of ruling out certain disorders.

ACCOMMODATING CULTURAL AND LINGUISTIC DIFFERENCES

Most psychological tests have been normed with European Americans and may not be appropriate for use with individuals who do not have English as a primary language or who are from other cultural backgrounds. The optimal response to this dilemma may not be to eschew psychological tests entirely but to select, administer, and interpret the tests with caution. Many of these decisions rest, in part, on the degree of acculturation of patients or their proficiency in English. Unless the test is designed to measure English-speaking ability, consideration should be given to using a translated test. Even then, be sure that the translated test has been assessed for equivalency. Some psychological constructs that are meaningful to European Americans are not relevant to members of other cultures. Similarly, members of some cultural groups are not accustomed to sharing their problems with strangers, especially in an objective test format. In such instances, formal testing may be inappropriate or the psychologist may need to spend additional time with the patient to establish a more trusting and supportive relationship. Regardless, whenever you decide to use a test for which there are no standardized norms for the target population, you should always acknowledge that fact in your report and be cautious in presenting the results.

Sometimes, it may be necessary to modify the administration or interpretation of a test to account for the cultural or linguistic background of the patient. Any change in standardized administration or interpretation should have a professional basis and should be noted in the test report. More information on working with diverse populations is found in Section 3, chapter 8, Other Areas for Psychologists.

TESTING WITH EXTERNAL CONSEQUENCES

Most complaints about psychological assessments or testing occur when the assessment is requested by third parties. We refer to these assessments as testing with external consequences because the test results may have significant implications for the person being tested. This can occur, for example, when you test an applicant for an executive position or promotion in a corporation, for the legal right to use lethal weapons as a security guard, for eligibility as a law enforcement officer, or for entrance into a religious denomination; when you conduct an evaluation with health consequences, such as eligibility for bariatric surgery or organ transplants; when you evaluate a child for placement into a special education or gifted program; or when you conduct a child custody evaluation (special issues related to custody evaluations were covered in Section 3, chap. 3, Working With Couples, Families, and Children). You may also be asked to evaluate sexual offenders, juvenile delinquents, or others to make determinations of public risk. While all testing should have consequences, we are discussing here the instances in which testing can be expected to have significant consequences outside of treatment planning and psychotherapy.

These types of assessments have increased substantially in recent years, and we expect the demand for testing with consequences to increase. For example, we have seen a very rapid increase in morbid obesity in the United States and an increase in bariatric surgery to address that problem. The standards of bariatric surgeons require psychological or psychiatric assessment before they can perform surgery on such persons. Similarly, recent scandals have led many religious denominations to require psychological testing before individuals can enter religious training or be employed by a religious denomination. Courts have increasingly relied on psychologists to provide information on the risks of releasing individuals convicted of sexual offenses or violent crimes. Many school districts will not allow a child who has threatened violence back into school unless that child has undergone a psychological evaluation.

Consequently, assessments of this type have major consequences for the persons being examined; the results may help determine whether persons will get the surgery or transplant that they believe is necessary to save their lives, whether individuals will be incarcerated for a longer period of time, and more. In some of these circumstances, your test results or conclusions may be unwelcome by the person being tested (or the parents). Given the seriousness of negative consequences, the client may be more than willing to call your professional competence into question and to file a complaint.

To reduce your legal risk, you need to know basic information about psychological testing, specific information about the domain of assessment in which you are engaging, and the application of specific information about risk management procedures.

BASIC INFORMATION ABOUT PSYCHOLOGICAL TESTING

Here are some general rules about testing that require special vigilance. Some of these comments may appear especially elementary. Nonetheless, your report may be challenged on these elementary or basic points. Familiarize yourself with the standards of the American Psychological Association's "Ethical Principles of Psychologists and Code of Conduct" (APA Ethics Code) that deal with assessments along with other relevant documents such as *The Standards for Educational and Psychological Testing* (American Educational Research Association, American Psychological Association, & National Council on Measurement in Education, 1999). Fortunately, some quality comprehensive reviews concerning competence in psychological testing have appeared recently (Krishnamurthy et al., 2004; Moreland, Eyde, Robertson, Primoff, & Most, 1995; Turner, DeMers, Fox, & Reed, 2001)

When testing for consequences, you should be able to defend why each test was selected and was appropriate for the referral question. We recommend that you defer heavily to the test manual or professional literature for guidance on this question. Ask yourself: Has the test been validated for this purpose? Were the tests appropriate to the patient in terms of reading level, language skills, or cultural background? Most psychological tests require at least a fifth-grade reading level. If the client does not have the necessary reading skills, it may be necessary to give the test orally and note the modification in the administration in the report.

The test must be administered and monitored according to standardized procedures (or deviations from standard procedures must be noted). Factors influencing the test findings should be noted in the report and accounted for in the test interpretation. Other sources of measurement error should be noted.

Double-check for scoring errors. Even minor or inconsequential errors in administration and scoring may lead your critics to view your entire testing process with suspicion. Remember, when test results are challenged, another psychologist will review your procedures, scoring, and interpretation with a magnifying glass.

> A psychologist made several minor scoring errors in an intelligence test. None of these scoring errors altered his basic conclusions. Nonetheless, an opposing attorney emphasized these scoring errors and suggested that they represented an overall pattern of sloppiness. (3.6.1)

Include the sources of data on which conclusions are based (i.e., test data, past reports, and interview data). Did you integrate the test data with other sources of information? Is your written report understandable and free of unnecessary jargon? A general rule is, when doing an evaluation with consequences, it is essential to have a strong professional rationale for anything you do that is unusual.

> A psychologist administered the short form of the *MMPI* in a forensic case. The results were clear-cut and consistent with other sources of data. Nonetheless, the fact that she used the short form was criticized by the opposing attorney, who suggested that she was using "shortcuts" in her assessment. (3.6.2)

Nothing is wrong with using computerized test interpretations appropriately. In fact, computerized tests can help reduce hand-scoring errors. However, computer-generated interpretations only present hypotheses for you to consider and cannot usurp your judgment in reaching your own conclusions. You retain the ultimate responsibility for writing the report and supporting the conclusions.

> A psychologist used a quote from the computer-generated test to represent his conclusion. Although the quotation represented his professional opinion, the way it was presented gave an impression that he was blindly following the computerized printout. (3.6.3)

OBSOLETE TESTS

You should not use tests that are obsolete for the purposes of the assessment. Although typically you should use the latest version of a test, this may not always be clinically indicated.

> A licensing board complaint was filed against a psychologist, alleging that he violated professional standards by administering the *MMPI* to a patient, instead of the *MMPI-2*. The psychologist responded by noting that the patient had taken the *MMPI* 15 years earlier, and he believed that comparative results would be helpful in treatment planning. A consultant for the licensing board reviewed the response of the psychologist and recommended that the case be dismissed. (3.6.4)

While some might argue that the psychologist would have gotten more useful data from the *MMPI-2,* his decision to use the *MMPI* was based on sound clinical reasoning. If a licensing board were to review the decision, it could look to the test manual to determine how the test developers intended the test to be used, or it could look at whether the psychologist could provide a sound justification for his decision.

DOMAIN SPECIFIC KNOWLEDGE

Each of the areas of testing for external consequences requires detailed information about a specific area of psychology (specialized information on child custody evaluations is provided in Section 3, chap. 3, Working With Couples, Families, and Children).

Bariatric surgery assessments. Psychologists who test for bariatric surgery need to know about assessments for medical referrals and about morbid obesity (see, e.g., Buchwald et al., 2004; Greenberg, 2003). What are the surgeons looking for when they make the referral? What are your obligations to the individual being tested in terms of feedback? What special mental health needs commonly occur among morbidly obese persons? Are the applicants likely to follow the stringent life and dietary changes required following surgery? How do these features commonly show themselves in psychological test results? Are you aware that applicants for bariatric surgery often perceive themselves as desperate for this treatment and will commonly show high rates of defensiveness and denial of problems on standardized psychological tests? Do you know how to reduce this defensiveness or to account for it in your testing results? Do these features vary according to the race or linguistic background of the applicant?

Essential questions that bariatric surgeons want to know are whether the applicant for surgery will be able to follow through with the necessary stringent life change and dietary requirements following surgery and whether the patient evidences significant mental health distress beyond that related to weight management such that the surgery should be postponed.

Screening for religious occupations. When you test applicants for religious occupations, you must understand the criteria the denomination has established for entrance. While it may be obvious that the denomination may want to screen individuals who have pedophiliac inclinations or serious and pervasive mental disorders, questions sometimes arise concerning the goals of the denomination when application is made by persons with personality disorders or traits that may interfere with their job perform-ance. There is no substitute for clear and frank discussions with the refer-ral source concerning the nature and scope of the inquiry.

> A middle-aged minister had shown commendable service to her denomination for many years but then displayed substan-tial problems getting along with parishioners and was seen drinking heavily in public on several occasions. The denomi-nation ordered the minister to undergo a psychological evalu-ation as a condition of retaining her ordination. The denomi-nation used the report and other sources of data to develop a program designed to rehabilitate her. (3.6.5)

> A psychologist routinely did psychological testing for a local theological seminary. As part of her assessment protocol, she ensured that she was given the opportunity for a feedback ses-sion with each applicant. Although almost all of the applicants passed the screening, she wanted the opportunity to give them useful feedback on how they might capitalize on their person-ality strengths and compensate for their personality weakness-es to make their religious career more rewarding. (3.6.6)

Testing for educational placement. The educational testing of children can be quite controversial. Some parents have a great personal investment in whether their children will be placed in the district's gifted program. Other parents are quite concerned that their children with special needs receive the optimal school placement. When testing such children, you can be of more service to the parents if you understand the entitlements grant-ed children under state and federal law.

> One neuropsychologist in independent practice opined that a child he tested needed special accommodation in school. Another psychologist who worked for the school did not believe that the educational placement recommendations found in the report were in the best interest of the child. The two psychologists and parents met, discussed the needs of the child, and agreed on an educational program. Although the assessment of the neuropsychologist in independent practice was valuable, the school psychologist knew more about the local resources of the school. (3.6.7)

Risk assessments for sexual offenders. When psychologists test sexual offenders, they need to know the literature on such work.[1] Fortunately, a number of screening instruments have been developed for this purpose. Some test developers also conveniently provide guidance on how to place individuals into dichotomous categories such as high risk or low risk for reoffending. Unfortunately, the applicability of these screening instruments

---

[1] Portions from "Ethical and Professional Issues in Assessing Sexual Offenders," by B. Mapes and S. Knapp, 2005, *The Pennsylvania Psychologist, 65,* 3-4. Copyright 2005 by the Pennsylvania Psychological Association. Adapted with permission of the authors.

varies enormously. A screening instrument for pedophilia, for example, may have little usefulness for other forms of sexual offenses. Often the instruments have only been used with reoffenders and have not been studied with first-time offenders. Often the criteria used in the normative study were weak. For example, a study that used rearrest records for sexual offenders is likely to underestimate the extent to which the individuals will reoffend because most sex crimes are never reported, and some that are reported do not result in arrests. There is no substitute for knowing the normative data and other psychometric properties of the test used.

You need to know the criterion variables used for predicting risks. If it is arrest records, then it can be assumed that the criterion is substantially underestimated, since only a fraction of actual offenses result in arrests. Gender, age, ethnic, and linguistic factors may also influence the applicability and interpretation of the test data.

Failure to indicate these and other limitations increases the risk that you will provide the court misleading or inaccurate information. The purpose of noting these limitations is not to bog the court down in psychometric details but to help the court understand the complexities and uncertainties involved in predicting future behaviors.

For example, one set of test materials reported that individuals who fell into the low-risk range had only a 2% chance of reoffending, whereas individuals who fell into the high-risk range had a 50% chance of reoffending. However, we need to go beyond that basic statistic and ask, "Although Mr. Jones fell into the group that had a 2% chance of reoffending, is he one of those 2% who will reoffend?" Then we can describe why Mr. Jones's chances of reoffending are higher or lower than the 2% figure indicated by the test score. A common error is to misinterpret group data as applied to individual cases. In the case above, the fact that 2% of the persons who obtained a certain score reoffended does not necessarily mean that Mr. Jones has a 2% chance of reoffending. Reports should carefully explain how that 2% figure should be interpreted.

Often we are asked to predict the likelihood that a prisoner will be a risk to the community if released. At one time it was the conventional wisdom that predictions of dangerousness by mental health professionals were no more accurate than "flipping coins" (Monahan, 1981). However, subsequent research has suggested that psychologists can exercise greater skills in predicting violence, although these predictions can best be compared to meteorological (weather) forecasts in which the likelihood of violence has to be represented in terms of probability as opposed to absolute chances (Monahan & Steadman, 1996).

Several screening or predictive instruments for violence have been developed, but they have the same limitations as screening instruments for sexual offenders. Violence is a relatively infrequent event; it is often not reported to authorities; predictive scales may be limited to certain populations such as former prisoners or former mental patients; and these scales may have a high rate of false positives (Norko & Baranoski, 2005). There is a dearth of psychometrically validated assessment instruments to determine the risk of violence among children and adolescents.

These comments are not designed to denigrate the use of these scales. Indeed, they are generally far more effective than clinical intuition alone.

However, these cautions speak to the importance of clearly clarifying the basis of your judgment to the decision maker. Psychologists who fail to delineate the limitations of their assessment instruments risk an allegation of incompetent practice or incorrect diagnosis.

Preemployment testing and the Americans with Disabilities Act. Many psychologists perform screening for employers who are interested in hiring or promoting the most qualified applicants. As with any testing for external consequences situations, you should be aware of and trained in the unique domain of knowledge necessary for effective functioning in the position. Preemployment testing may, under some circumstances, involve not so much the use of psychological tests that have been standardized with normative populations but the development and validation of specific tests based on a job analysis unique to that work setting. Training as a clinical psychologist usually is not sufficient to qualify you to do preemployment testing.

In addition, psychologists who do preemployment testing need to pay special attention to the Americans with Disabilities Act (ADA, 1990), which prohibits discrimination in hiring and employment screening for persons with physical and mental disabilities. Factors used in determining whether a person is disabled include whether he or she "has a physical or mental impairment that substantially limits one or more major life activities, has a record of such an impairment, or is regarded as having such an impairment" (U.S. Equal Employment Opportunity Commission & U.S. Department of Justice Civil Rights Division, 2002, p. 2).

Of course, employers are allowed to select the most qualified applicant for a position, and the ADA does not require employers to hire otherwise unqualified persons. But employers must offer a position to a qualified individual with a disability if he or she can perform the essential functions of the position with or without reasonable accommodations. A reasonable accommodation "is any modification or adjustment to a job or the work environment that will enable a qualified applicant or employee with a disability to...perform essential job functions" (U.S. Equal Employment Opportunity Commission & U.S. Department of Justice Civil Rights Division, 2002, p. 5).

During the preemployment selection process, you may not ask about the presence of a mental disability, and using a test that is commonly used to diagnose mental illnesses (even if you do not actually intend to use it to give a diagnosis) is problematic. In *Karraker v. Rent-a-Center* (2005), for example, the 7th U.S. Circuit Court of Appeals (Chicago) ruled that an employer violated the ADA by using the *MMPI* as a preemployment screening instrument. The court noted that the *MMPI* is administered and interpreted by a health care professional, was designed to reveal a mental impairment, and is normally given in health care settings. Also, some specific disorders, such as most sexual disorders, gambling, or kleptomania, are not covered by the ADA. Substance abuse is covered by the ADA, although the employer may prohibit the use of alcohol on the premises and may dismiss employees if their job performance falls below acceptable standards. Also, employers may refuse to hire (or may fire) anyone who presents a threat to the safety of the workplace.

The preemployment screening may take into consideration personality traits related to the job under consideration. For example, chronic lateness, poor attendance, and rudeness are personality traits that may be relevant to the job. However, in and of themselves, they are not indications of mental illness, and therefore, may be considered in the employment decision.

RISK MANAGEMENT STRATEGIES

It is time to recall the three risk management poultices, *informed consent, documentation, and consultation*. Although the person being assessed is not likely to be the "client" when the assessment is at the request of the third party, it is still important to treat such persons with as much respect and courtesy as if they were the client.

> A psychologist who did employment testing always included comments about the strengths of the applicants at or near the beginning of her report. She did so because she believed that this accurate information presented a more balanced view of the applicant for the employer. Also, she reasoned, even if the applicant did not get the job and eventually saw the report (perhaps as part of discovery in a lawsuit), any personal injury to the applicant would be reduced by reading these positive statements. Finally, from a risk management perspective, it would show that she was trying to be fair and balanced in her assessment of the applicant. (3.6.8)

Always have a written *informed consent* agreement when doing evaluations with external consequences. Go over the informed consent agreement with the person ahead of time. You should clarify who is requesting the evaluation, who is paying for it, the general nature of the evaluation, the right of access to records, the potential consequences of the evaluation, and other topics. Obtain the person's signature. If the person refuses to sign, then you may want to terminate the testing.

According to the Health Insurance Portability and Accountability Act (HIPAA) Privacy Rule, patients have access to test reports and test data (their own answers and or productions). More information on access to testing information is provided in Section 3, chapter 4, Privacy, Confidentiality, and Privileged Communications, in the discussion of the HIPAA. However, in some evaluations, such as when evaluating religious professionals, Malony (2000) recommended that psychologists ensure the option of a feedback session with the individual being tested. That way, you can have assurance that the individual will have the option of getting clinically useful information.

Documentation is very important. When testing for external consequences, it is important to document the basis for your conclusions. Ideally, for every conclusion or recommendation you make for a client or patient you will be able to identify sources in the test or your interview notes to substantiate that conclusion. Keep copies of the raw notes you take during the interview. If a case goes to court, you should assume that all of your notes will be subject to discovery by the other side.

Seek clinical *consultation* as indicated. You should not assume that you will know everything about every clinical situation that arises.

> A psychologist routinely did lethal weapons assessments for individuals applying to be security guards. However, one applicant showed soft signs of a neuropsychological impairment. The psychologist spoke to a neuropsychologist about this applicant before he completed his evaluation. (3.6.9)

This psychologist was working at Bloom's higher levels of professional development and understood that consultations can take different forms and be done for different purposes. Sometimes the consultations focus on the clinical features of the patient, the context of professional services, the items in the psychologist's skill inventory, the disciplinary consequences, or more than one factor in the risk management formula. In this case, the neuropsychological signs were irrelevant to the question that the third party wanted to have addressed. However, the psychologist did receive permission from the third party to review the implications of the soft signs and encouraged the applicant to receive a more specialized evaluation from a neuropsychologist or neurologist. This consultation was easily defended in that it helped improve the quality of services provided, and it constituted an additional "system of protections" by which the psychologist could provide better services.

Seven Essential Points to Remember

1. Legal risks are more likely to occur when you are engaging in testing with external consequences.

2. When testing patients for treatment planning, be certain that you make accommodation for the cultural or linguistic background of the patient.

3. You will become a target for criticisms if you make rudimentary errors in psychological testing, such as making scoring errors, or if you are unable to justify your choice of tests.

4. When testing for external consequences, it is important to have a clinical rationale for any procedures that deviate from usual or customary practice.

5. When testing for external consequences, consider the psychometric properties of the test in interpreting the test results.

6. When testing for external consequences, you should emphasize the informed consent process and documentation.

7. When testing for external consequences, be certain that you have specialized knowledge about the area in which you are providing an opinion.

Chapter 7: **ASSESSING AND TREATING PATIENTS
WHO ARE POTENTIALLY SUICIDAL
OR DANGEROUS TO OTHERS**

Patient emergencies are a stressful part of being a psychologist. The most frequent mental health emergency is the threat of suicide. However, most psychologists will also experience the stress of dealing with patients who threaten to harm third parties (Kleespies & Dettmer, 2000). Psychologists should know their legal obligations and mandatory reporting requirements when evaluating or treating high-risk patients such as those who have HIV/AIDS or other infectious diseases and present a risk to identifiable third parties, children who are being abused, older adults who are being abused, or drivers who are impaired.

ASSESSING AND TREATING PATIENTS
WHO HAVE A RISK OF SUICIDE

Suicide is the 10th leading cause of death in the United States. The odds for losing a patient to suicide are 1 in 2 for psychiatrists, 1 in 5 for psychologists (Chemtob, Bauer, Hamada, Pelowski, & Muraoka, 1989), and 1 in 9 for psychology trainees (Kleespies, Penk, & Forsyth, 1993). Simon (2000) has commented that "there are only two kinds of clinical psychiatrists—those who have had patients commit suicide and those who will" (p. 399). Suicides take an emotional toll on treating professionals as well as their families. Chemtob et al. reported that therapists experienced high rates of psychological distress following a patient suicide.

In addition, patient suicides or attempted suicides are a frequent cause of malpractice suits (5.4% of all malpractice suits for psychologists and 17% for psychiatrists; Bender, 2005). The most recent data from the Trust-Sponsored Professional Liability Program indicate that the frequency of malpractice suits for suicide has dropped to 4%. Suicide occurs more frequently in inpatient settings. Of the few outpatient suicide malpractice cases, most result in settlements because insurance companies are afraid of emotional jury verdicts. In such situations psychologists have only a limited ability to resist the demands of the insurance company to settle (see Section 3, chap. 11, Professional Liability Insurance—Don't Practice Without It).

It is difficult to get reliable data on suicide. It is an infrequent event for the population in general; there is a tendency to underreport suicides; and the samples used for research might not necessarily generalize to the population as a whole. Nonetheless, on the National Comorbidity Survey (a study of the prevalence of mental disorders), 13.5% of the respondents reported suicidal ideation; 3.9% had a plan; and 4.6% had made an attempt sometime during their lives (Kessler, Borges, & Walters, 1999).

Although females attempt suicide more often than males, males are three times more likely to commit suicide. Most, but not all, persons who commit suicide have communicated their intent in advance, primarily to family or significant others. Multiple attempters represent a clinically more severely troubled group with an elevated risk of suicide compared to those who report just suicide ideation or a single attempt (Rudd, Joiner, & Rajab, 1996).

STRENGTHENING YOUR INDIVIDUAL THERAPIST FACTORS

You will be better prepared to deal with patients who have a risk of suicide if you have thought through your own feelings about the possibility of suicide and prepared for the eventuality of having a patient with a high risk of suicide on your caseload. Among other things, it is essential to understand how to diagnose and treat potentially suicidal patients. In addition, it is desirable if you know the involuntary hospitalization or civil commitment laws in your state; know the local crisis intervention program, if any; and have connections with an inpatient unit. If it is necessary to hospitalize a patient, the process will be easier if you already have a relationship with the hospital staff, know the admission procedures, and discuss the procedures with the patient ahead of time.

When treating patients who have a risk of suicide, it is important to have a basic knowledge of psychopharmacology so that you can understand the anticipated benefits of medications and the extent to which the patient is responding as intended. Whenever possible it is important that the psychologist obtain permission to consult with the prescriber. The psychologist should strive to develop a good working relationship and open communication with the prescriber to discuss the patient's response to the medication and report any unusual mental or physical side effects the patient has experienced as a result of the medication.

If a patient is not compliant with medication recommendations, it should be a subject of immediate concern and discussion in therapy. Some patients are reluctant to take psychotropic medications because of the unpleasant side effects of the medications. These side effects may be temporary or there may be other medications that are tolerated better by the patient. Ongoing consultation with the prescriber can be very beneficial in such situations. Regardless, problems with medications should be addressed as part of the therapy. In the rare case it may be appropriate to properly terminate treatment or refer the patient to another therapist if noncompliance with medications becomes an issue that cannot be resolved therapeutically and the psychologist believes that the medications are essential to the patients treatment and welfare. In such cases the treatment might be terminated for "failure to follow appropriate clinical advice." A proper referral should also be part of the termination process.

ASSESSING PATIENTS WHO HAVE A RISK OF SUICIDE

Of course, psychologists should ask every patient during the first session about present and past suicide ideation or attempts. No patient is too healthy to be asked.

We review here salient issues in the assessment and treatment of patients who have a risk of suicide. However, prudent psychologists go beyond what is written here and seek quality resources to guide their assessment and treatment of such patients. Excellent resources that cover the assessment and treatment of patients with a risk of suicide include Bongar (2002), the *Air Force Guide for Managing Suicidal Behavior* (U.S. Air Force, n.d.), Oordt et al. (2005), the *Practice Guidelines for the Assessment and Treatment of Patients with Suicidal Behavior* (American Psychiatric Association, 2003), and any of the works by Rudd and Joiner that are cited below.

No mental health professional can be expected to predict or prevent all patient suicides. Because suicide is such an infrequent event, sufficient professional and scientific literature does not exist to predict suicides with a high degree of accuracy. Current prediction methods produce a high number of false positives and false negatives (Rudd & Joiner, 1999). Suicide prediction is complicated by the difficulty of research in this area and the inconsistency in defining suicidal behavior and risk by different researchers. Furthermore, patients with chronic suicidal ideation represent a subset of patients with unique treatment needs.

RUDD AND JOINER'S TAXONOMY

No completely reliable algorithm based on demographic or clinical data will be of determinative value for any individual patient so psychologists must use their best judgment, informed by the professional literature, to determine the relative risk of suicidal behaviors and to modify treatment procedures to account for an increase in suicidal risk. Below we present one useful system developed by Rudd and Joiner (1999). Any psychologist who uses their system can be assured that it is a systematic and comprehensive approach, although other methods may reach the same result.

Rudd and Joiner (1999) have recommended classifying suicidality into a continuum of five categories (nonexistent, mild, moderate, severe, and extreme) based on the evaluation of eight factors (see Table 3.7.A). Using the continuum of suicidality should bring order and organized thinking to your conceptualization of suicide assessment and management. Furthermore, the fact that you used a well-recognized system will demonstrate to critics that you followed an appropriate standard of care in assessing suicidal behavior and tailoring an appropriate intervention.

All of the factors must be seen in the context of the patient's life and treatment relationship, and no simple hierarchy of factors can be used to predict suicidal risk. Any of these factors or even chance and unpredictable events (such as a job layoff) may precipitate a serious suicide attempt. Nor is the list of factors exhaustive.

TABLE 3.7.A
Continuum of Suicidality

Factor	Suicidality			
	Mild	Moderate	Severe	Extreme
Predisposition	low	moderate	high	high
Precipitants	few or none	few, handled well	multiple	multiple
Symptomatic presentation	low	moderate	high	high
Hopelessness	no	no	yes	intense
Nature of suicidal thinking	low	moderate	more intense, frequent	more intense, frequent, longer lasting
Previous suicidal behavior	no	few	multiple, low lethality	multiple, serious
Impulsivity	low	low	high	high
Protective factors	present	present	few	none

Note. From "Assessment of Suicidality in Outpatient Practice," by M. D. Rudd and T. Joiner, 1999, in L. VandeCreek and T. Jackson (Eds.), *Innovations in Clinical Practice* (pp. 101–117). Copyright 1999 by Professional Resource Press. Adapted with permission of the authors.

The *eight factors used to classify suicidality* are *predisposition to suicidal behaviors, precipitators or stressors, symptomatic presentation, hopelessness, nature of suicidal thinking, previous suicidal behavior, impulsivity (or self-control), and protective factors.* We review each of these below. As can be seen, these factors overlap to some degree.

Predisposition to suicidal behaviors is determined by looking at historical factors such as previous history of psychiatric diagnoses, history of suicidal behavior, history of being abused, and presence of family violence or very punitive parenting in the family of origin.

When asking about the family of origin, it may be prudent to start with general questions (e.g., "Tell me about your childhood. What were your parents like? What were your brothers and sisters like?"). Then go into increasingly more detail about how the family handled conflicts and the presence of arguing, verbal threats, pushing, hitting, and more.

We also suggest that you can consider other demographic and clinical risk factors for suicide. Those who are at a higher risk of suicide are older, European American, unmarried (especially widowed or divorced), male, adolescents or young adults, or members of sexual minorities.

> A psychologist did an intake interview on an older white man who was a widower, had recently been diagnosed with a serious medical condition, and hunted for recreation. Although the psychologist routinely assessed all new patients for suicide, he knew that the demographics of this individual made him a high risk for suicide. (3.7.1)

Precipitators or stressors refer to significant life events or daily hassles. Precipitants could include exit events from the patient's social field, such as the loss of a romantic relationship, loss of a job, involvement with the criminal justice system (e.g., being a victim of crime, being sent to jail, or being involved in a legal case), or a decline in health. Daily stressors refer to day-to-day inconveniences that in isolation are not particularly stressful but that have a cumulative impact. They could include an unpleasant work environment, chronic problems with a spouse or child, or ongoing financial problems.

> A psychologist interviewed a woman whose husband had just left her after he announced he was having an affair and would be leaving her for another woman. The separation forced her to move to a less desirable area of town. She was temporarily sharing custody of her children and missed having them around all of the time. She felt humiliated by the actions of her husband. She had been close to her husband's family and missed the contact with her mother-in-law. The psychologist appropriately understood that one event (the separation from her husband) had multiple implications for the patient. (3.7.2)

Yen et al. (2005) found that negative life events in the areas of criminal or legal involvement or love and marriage were related to an increased risk of suicide for patients with Cluster B personality disorders (antisocial, borderline, narcissistic, and paranoid). Of course, the same objective life event may have different implications for different individuals. The loss of a romantic relationship for one person may involve significant loss or humiliation, but for another person it may be experienced as a welcome relief. You should look at the meaning of the event for your patients and its subjective impact on them.

Symptoms refer to *Diagnostic and Statistical Manual of Mental Disorders* (*DSM-IV*; American Psychiatric Association, 1994) diagnoses and comorbidity. Although suicidal behavior is often linked to major depression, it can occur in patients with other diagnoses as well. Kessler, Berglund, Borges, Nock, and Wang (2005) found that suicidal ideation occurred across a wide range of *DSM-IV* diagnoses. For example, a patient with a generalized anxiety disorder had almost the same likelihood of attempting suicide as a patient with major depressive disorder. In fact, the diagnoses most linked to suicidal behavior were not major depression but obsessive-compulsive disorder (OCD) and substance abuse disorders (albeit with the possibility that there was a secondary diagnosis of depression or depressive features). Methodological issues in this study, such as the use of lay interviewers following a structured interview scale to determine diagnosis, raise some questions about the findings. It is possible that other diagnostic techniques may have identified a higher rate of depression among persons who attempted suicide or that a secondary diagnosis of depression could have been identified. Nonetheless, the general finding is consistent with other research in this area. In addition to the presence of a *DSM-IV* diagnosis, it may also be helpful to ascertain the presence of certain key symptoms such as anger, agitation, or a sense of urgency and the means used to reduce that agitation, such as the use of alcohol or other drugs, medication, self-mutilation, and more.

Hopelessness may be gauged, for example, by asking patients to rate themselves on a scale of 1 to 10 on how hopeless they feel (with 1 being optimistic and 10 being utterly hopeless).

The **nature of suicidal thinking** refers to the current frequency, intensity, and duration of suicidal thoughts, specificity of plans, availability of means, and explicitness of intent. When interviewing all patients, it may be prudent to include several depression- or suicide-related questions, such as "Have you ever wished that you were dead?" "Did you ever feel that life was not worth living?" or "Did you ever wish you could go to sleep and never wake up?" Depending on the responses to these questions, it may be prudent to follow up with more detailed questions concerning suicidal ideation. The Practice Guidelines of the American Psychiatric Association (2003) include many other useful questions that you can ask to assess suicidal risk.

Discussions of intent and means should be candid. You should not only ask about the contemplated means of attempting suicide but also about details of where the individual would get the pills, gun, poison, or other means to complete the suicide and where or when he or she intends to do it. Also ask about back-up plans for suicide. The frequency, intensity, and duration of these thoughts should be considered.

Coryell and Young (2005) found that for patients with a major depressive disorder, the single best predictor of a suicide attempt was how they rated the intensity of their suicidal ideation in the last week on a 7-point scale from "absent" to "very extreme." Patients who rated themselves above 5 on this scale were significantly more likely to attempt suicide.

Nonetheless, Busch, Fawcett, and Jacobs (2003) found that approximately three fourths of patients who committed suicide while hospitalized or shortly after being discharged had denied suicidal ideation when they were last questioned. How do these apparently contradictory findings concerning the predictability of self-reported suicidal intent influence the manner in which we evaluate suicidal ideation?

First no one clinical predictor of suicide will ever approach the sensitivity or specificity found in most medical laboratory tests (Coryell & Young, 2005). Also, some patients may have been sincere in their report that they did not have current suicidal ideation but experienced a sudden increase in suicidal ideation after the last interview. Others may have experienced a significant stressor or precipitant between the time they were asked about suicide and the time that they completed it. Still others might have had poor impulse control or might have been giving a false report of their suicidal ideation. Nonetheless, we can conclude that intent is an important predictor but other factors need to be considered as well, and intent can vary considerably even within a relatively short period of time. Furthermore, the accuracy of measuring intent can be improved by using redundant measures.

Previous suicidal behavior includes the frequency and method, perceived lethality and outcome, and opportunity for rescue. Part of the reason for suicidal failures is that some patients miscalculate the lethality of their suicidal attempt. This may, in part, explain why physicians have a higher rate of successful suicides than members of the population in general (Schernhammer, 2005).

Impulsivity and self-control include an evaluation of overall impulsivity, regardless of its cause. The therapist might ask the patient about feelings of being out of control or have the patient rate his or her overall degree of control on a scale of 1 to 10. The link between alcohol and suicide may be explained, in part, by the fact that alcohol reduces inhibitions and self-control. Substance abuse or significant loss may also lead otherwise well-controlled individuals to lose self-control temporarily.

Suicidal behavior has a low but significant correlation with aggressive behavior. Consequently, patients who are suicidal should be screened for aggression. Equally, patients who are aggressive or homicidal should be screened for suicidal ideation.

Protective factors refer to social support, problem-solving skills, and active treatment. The factors that mitigate against a suicide attempt include marriage, having dependent children, an appreciation that the suicide would cause pain to relatives or friends, facing a future event of importance such as a wedding, anniversary, high school or college reunion, holding religious convictions, having a useful social network, or possessing good problem-solving abilities. Having a strong therapeutic working relationship can also be a protective factor.

> A psychologist interviewed a woman who demonstrated a very elevated risk of suicide. However, this woman also had very strong religious beliefs and stated that those beliefs forbade her from committing suicide. (3.7.3)

> Another psychologist interviewed a man who demonstrated a very elevated risk of suicide. Because of a terminal medical condition he was strongly tempted to commit suicide. However, he stated that such an action might have a serious negative impact on his grandchildren whom he loved dearly. He said, "I could never do that to them." (3.7.4)

REDUNDANT SYSTEMS OF PROTECTION IN ASSESSING SUICIDAL BEHAVIORS

As noted in Section 3, chapter 1, Competence, you can reduce the likelihood of a serious professional error if you have a redundant system of protection. In a hospital, nurses, pharmacists, colleagues, and other medical personnel will ideally be a second "set of eyes" for the attending physician or psychologist to catch any glaring errors in the orders or prescriptions. Similarly, psychologists in outpatient practice can create a redundant system to act as a second source of data.

In outpatient settings, the sources of data include other health care professionals (such as a prescribing psychopharmacologist) and family members who can, if clinically indicated, monitor the patient and assist in treatment. We described in Section 3, chapter 1, Competence, how consultation and documentation can also act as important sources of data.

Psychologists can also use screening instruments that will act as a second source of information on a patient who has a risk of attempting suicide. These instruments do not replace clinical judgment but can be used to check the perceptions of the interviewing psychologist. Often screening instruments, such as the Scale for Suicide Ideation (Beck, Kovacs, & Weissman, 1979), the Beck Hopelessness Scale (Beck, Weissman, Lester, & Trexler, 1974), or a similar scale that takes about 10 minutes to administer can be used to supplement, not replace, the clinical assessment.

> A psychologist interviewed a patient who claimed that his suicidal ideation was almost entirely gone and that the risk of suicide was now over. However, the psychologist suspected that the risk of suicide was higher than the patient acknowledged. Consequently, he had the patient complete a Beck inventory; the patient acknowledged the presence of suicidal ideation. The psychologist used this information to justify the continued emphasis on suicidal prevention. (3.7.5)

TREATMENT PLANNING BASED ON RISK ASSESSMENT

According to Rudd and Joiner (1999) the degree of suicide risk can be used to determine the optimal treatment plan. The treatment plan should not just focus on the *DSM-IV* diagnosis and assume that through treatment of that particular diagnosis (e.g., depression), the suicidal ideation will go away. Instead, there is a need for specific interventions to control the suicidal impulses as well as treatments designed for the *DSM-IV* diagnosis itself. The schema suggested by Rudd and Joiner is shown in Table 3.7.A (p. 158). We provide below additional comments on the types of interventions.

MANAGING AND TREATING PATIENTS WHO HAVE A RISK OF SUICIDE (CONTEXT OF TREATMENT)

The management and treatment of suicidal behavior can be guided by the outcome of the detailed assessment shown in Table 3.7.B. As a general rule, the suicidal precautions should increase as the patient moves up the suicidal risk continuum. Even at the mild level of suicide risk, however, you should periodically check on the strength of the suicidal risk factors.

SUICIDE-SPECIFIC INTERVENTIONS FOR PATIENTS WITH SEVERE OR EXTREME RISKS

The safest treatment options include hospitalization because of the increased opportunity for continual monitoring for the patient's safety and response to medications. If hospitalization is not possible because the

TABLE 3.7.B
Recommended Interventions for Patients at Risk of Suicide

Risk	Intervention
Severe or extreme	Evaluate for psychiatric hospitalization
	Ensure that patient is accompanied or monitored at all times
Moderate	Consider these options:
	Evaluate for psychiatric hospitalization
	Increase frequency or duration of outpatient treatment
	Involve family, friends, or support systems if clinically indicated for support or monitoring, such as through a suicide watch
	Evaluate symptoms and goals frequently
	Ensure 24/7 availability of emergency contacts
	Consider medication
	Use telephone contacts for monitoring
	Implement a safety agreement if ego-syntonic and clinically indicated
	Consult
Nonexistent or mild	Reevaluate risk if circumstances of patient deteriorate substantially

patient does not agree or qualify for a civil or involuntary commitment, then provide as many of the options in the moderate-risk category as possible. Safety is the almost sole focus of treatment. For example, remove lethal agents and be alert to sudden changes in behavior. Increase the frequency of sessions if possible; maximize involvement of significant others when they are nontoxic; involve others in monitoring the patient; ensure that you are available for emergencies; consider between-session telephone monitoring; develop a safety agreement if it is clinically indicated and therapeutic; and keep the patient informed about all you are doing.

SUICIDE-SPECIFIC INTERVENTIONS FOR PATIENTS WITH MODERATE RISK

With moderate-risk patients you should consider implementing specific safety features if clinically indicated. However, below we suggest modifications in these interventions when working with patients who have serious personality disorders and a moderate risk of suicide. Nonetheless, with most patients, as much as possible and when clinically indicated, involve them in the decisions about the suicide intervention strategies. You may, for example, ask patients if they would like to come in for an extra session this week or have you call them at home during the week or both. It is very important that you fully document any interventions you make and the rationale for the interventions as well as interventions you considered but decided not to use along with your rationale for not using them.

> A psychologist was treating a man with strong suicidal ideation. The psychologist knew that the patient needed increased monitoring at home at least until a psychiatric evaluation could be arranged. He told the man, "Your wife needs to know how badly you are doing. I know she is in the waiting room and I am going to bring her into the office. Would you like me to tell her how badly you are doing or would you like to tell her yourself." (3.7.6)

Psychotherapy treatment strategies. Techniques for reducing depression are well known to psychologists and include cognitive reconstruction, improvement of daily functioning, improving social relationships, understanding of personal dynamics, and more. Of course, the psychologist should continue to treat the primary *DSM-IV* diagnosis. However, when treating patients at risk to attempt suicide, it is generally indicated to include suicide-specific interventions as well. In therapy you should work on reducing symptomatic variables such as hopelessness, depression, severe anxiety, impulsiveness, and anger management. Work on individual characteristics that increase risk, such as attributional style, cognitive rigidity, and problem-solving ability and have patients take responsibility for their own actions. Address suicidogenic beliefs such as "suicide is the only way to solve my problems"; "my sins are so great than only my death can atone for what I have done"; or similar beliefs.

Generating social support. Inform the patient and the patient's family (if indicated) of your responsibility to protect the patient's life. "If I believe that you are at a risk of killing yourself, from both a therapeutic and humane perspective, my most important treatment goal is going to be to keep you safe and alive."

When possible and appropriate, significant others should be included as part of the patient's treatment. Pros and cons of involving third parties vary from patient to patient and from time to time over the course of treatment. Assess whether the family can be an ally in the treatment process. It is particularly important in outpatient treatment that others are available to help the patient be safe between sessions. Document when such situations are clinically contraindicated. When family is not available, consider other sources of support including clergy, friends, and coworkers.

In some rare occasions, if it is clinically indicated, you may inform third parties of the suicidal risk posed by your patients without their consent. In these situations your moral obligations to beneficence (promoting the welfare of your patient) temporarily trump your usual respect for patient autonomy. Of course, whenever one moral principle is trumped by another, you should make reasonable efforts to minimize the harm to the offended moral principle. For example, if you have patients who present a high risk of suicide and it is absolutely necessary to inform family members to ensure their safety, you can give the patients a choice as to whether they can call the family with you on the extension or whether you should make the call (with them in the room and ready to get on the phone if needed).

Medication. Does the patient hold false beliefs about medications that reduce his or her ability to make informed decisions about their use (Newman, 2005) such as the belief that the patient will become addicted to drugs or that medications are only for "crazy" people? Patients from cultural minorities may be more suspicious of the motives for medication and believe that they are being used as "guinea pigs" for studies designed to improve the welfare of European Americans

Do not make taking medication a condition of treatment unless medication is necessary for effective functioning. For patients with chronic personality disorders, medication may be helpful in some contexts and minimally helpful in others. Do not assume that the refusal to take medication is always a symptom of pathology or transference. When in doubt, consider the importance of the therapeutic relationship and do not force the medication issue unless it is clearly important.

Safety agreements. Many psychologists use safety agreements (also called no-harm contracts or safety contracts). However, you should only use them if you believe that they have clinical value for a particular patient.

These contracts are more effective when they

1. include as many affirmative statements as possible (Newman, 2005; e.g., "I recognize that I have considerable resources to battle this depression");
2. are created collaboratively with the patient and tailored to unique life circumstances and perspectives; boiler plate contracts are suspect;
3. identify a stimulus cue such as the feeling that the impulse of suicidality is overwhelming; and
4. identify responsibilities and options of patients to follow when urges become strong.

From a risk reduction perspective, the only value of safety agreements is whether they facilitate the treatment process. In and of themselves, safety agreements have no legal value and certainly will not serve as a significant protection in a licensing board complaint or malpractice suit. The content of the agreement and process of getting the agreement signed should reflect underlying treatment and moral values. They should reflect the wishes of the patient (respect their autonomy), promote patient welfare (beneficence), and not be acquired through bullying or harping (nonmaleficence). If safety agreements are not done with these caveats in mind, then the agreement is clinically useless and may be harmful.

Safety agreements can be clinically contraindicated if they are used only to reduce clinician anxiety or lead to reduced vigilance or a power struggle between psychologist and patient. Remember that we listed the advice to "always get a patient with suicidal ideation to sign a safety contract" as an example of a false risk management principle.

> A psychologist was treating a patient with pervasive and long-standing relationship issues. One day the patient announced that she was revoking the safety agreement. Instead of focusing on the safety agreement the psychologist focused on the patient's current functioning and ways to decrease her dysphoria and reduce impulsivity. Given the unique characteristics of this patient, the psychologist believed it would be

> clinically contraindicated to push the acceptance of the safety agreement. At the end of the session the patient stated that she intended to follow the safety agreement, although the psychologist was well prepared to have the patient leave without mentioning the safety agreement again. (3.7.7)

TREATING PATIENTS WHO HAVE A CHRONIC RISK OF SUICIDE AND A SERIOUS PERSONALITY DISORDER

Here are some examples of troubling patient behaviors that may demonstrate a serious personality disorder or other pathology in the context of suicidality.

1. Sometimes patients will discontinue medication abruptly or discontinue taking it as prescribed. Past experience may suggest that the patient will deteriorate substantially. At other times, the medication is of marginal value and it is not worth the power struggle to get the patient back on medications.
2. The patient may revoke a release of information form with the treating psychiatrist or psychopharmacologist.
3. A patient may decide to discontinue the safety agreement, announcing that he or she no longer feels that it can be honored.
4 A patient may announce that he intends to commit suicide if a certain event occurs, such as if his ex-wife ever gets married (which may or may not be imminent), if he loses a particular court case, if he does not get accepted to graduate school, or if he fails to achieve some other personal goal.
5. A patient announces she will kill herself if the therapist ever terminates treatment. Therefore, the psychologist who might otherwise be thinking that the patient might do better elsewhere is suddenly faced with increased fear of liability if the treatment were to be terminated.
6. The patient refuses to pay for therapy or refuses to consider a referral to a more appropriate treatment modality, even if it is a supplemental treatment, such as a time-limited dialectical behavior therapy (DBT) group.

A few patients have serious personality disorders characterized by chronic suicidal risk or what has been called a "suicidal career" (Maris, 1981). Usually they have Cluster B personality disorders (e.g., borderline). Ordinarily the treatment of patients at risk to attempt suicide requires a focus on their primary diagnosis and specific strategies designed to reduce the suicidal ideation or impulses. However, focusing on suicidal ideation or impulses may inadvertently reinforce those ideas or impulses and be clinically contraindicated.

Patients with serious personality disorders typically will not benefit from hospitalizations unless there are coexisting symptoms of serious depression or psychosis or unless they move into the areas of severe and extreme suicidality. Consequently, their treatment usually requires that the outpatient therapist tolerate a long period of chronic suicidality. In fact, the hospitalization of these patients may, at times, be clinically contraindicated.

Of course, some patients with chronic suicidality and personality disorders experience periods of acute suicidality. So we have acute risk, chronic high risk, and chronic high risk with exacerbation (see Table 3.7.C, p. 173). Nonetheless, even patients with chronic risks of suicide and serious personality disorders may have acute exacerbation of their suicidal ideation or impulses and will move into the high-risk category with the same requirement for an emphasis on protection and suicide prevention. Thus, we have the following categories of suicidal behavior and corresponding philosophies of treatment.

Often these patients have the diagnoses of bipolar disorder (BPD), PTSD complex, or chronic mental disorder with persistent pain. They pose the most frequent psychological high-risk management problems.

Patients with serious personality disorders often have chronic thoughts of suicide and frequently mutilate themselves or have suicide gestures or attempts. About 1 in 10 will successfully complete suicide, which is a rate similar to patients with schizophrenia and major mood disorders (Paris, 2002). Most of the patients in this category are women, and some may complete suicide after multiple attempts. A comorbid diagnosis of substance abuse and major depression increases the risk of suicide.

These patients are extraordinarily hard to treat. The possibility of a suicide is often an important part of the defensive structure as the only means of escaping intractable psychic pain. Gestures are often the means of secondary gain for acting out rage. Often these patients present with a long history of numerous psychiatric hospitalizations, suicide attempts, self-mutilation, and treatment failures. "An excessive focus on suicide prevention with these patients can prevent therapists from doing their job" (Paris, 2002, p. 741). The treatment process becomes derailed when therapists spend too much of their time on suicidal behaviors. It may be preferable to deal with the underlying causes, such as the inability to regulate emotional states.

> Given the chronicity and severity of the behaviors engaged in by clients diagnosed with BPD, therapists treating these patients are prone to make some common mistakes. They may become emotionally over involved, engaging in heroic efforts to save their patient's lives, only to pull back abruptly when they run out of ways to save the patient or the patient fails to be sufficiently grateful. Therapists may become demoralized by the patient's lack of progress and frightened, in particular, by the patient's ongoing urges to die. Or, they may get angry and punitive toward the patient, blaming the patient for not getting better more quickly. (Sanderson, 2002, pp. 36-37)

It is highly recommended that therapists have training and experience in treatments specifically designed for such persons, such as DBT (Manning, 2005; Sanderson, 2002), which involves a balancing of acceptance of the patient's current struggles and problem-solving strategies. The same dialectic of "empathic understanding and striving for therapeutic change" (Newman, 2005, p. 77) appears in the treatment of individuals with bipolar and other serious mental disorders.

When treating patients with serious personality disorders who have chronic suicidal ideation, you should get regular consultation. Be certain that you have the emotional resources for this work because these situations create high stress and require enormous clinical and personal resources. Avoid treatment of such patients when you question your expertise. A referral to a therapist with more expertise will most likely be appreciated by the patient. Don't let your savior fantasies get in the way of your better judgment. Be alert to countertransference issues, feelings of personal responsibility, rage, and burnout. Often DBT is best done with consultation teams. Regular attendance is expected. "A current maxim is that therapists cannot say that they are doing DBT unless they attend a consultation team regularly" (Sanderson, 2002, p. 37).

However, patients with BPD often benefit more from day hospital or intensive outpatient treatments. Involving family members in treatment may be clinically indicated. The goal of involving the family is to inform them of the nature of treatment, the reasons for it, and how they can cooperate with the treatment goals and assist recovery.

RISK MANAGEMENT WITH PATIENTS WHO HAVE A RISK OF SUICIDE

It is important to recall the risk management formula,

$$\text{Clinical risk} = \frac{(P \times C \times D)}{TF}$$

In this formula, P = patient risk characteristics; C = context; D = disciplinary consequences; and TF = therapist factors.

Risk in these situations is increased by certain patient factors, contexts of treatment, and our individual therapist factors.

Good risk management with patients at risk to attempt suicide focuses on the triad of risk management: informed consent, consultations, and documentation. As much as possible, patients should be informed of the general nature of your treatment plans, including your need to communicate with any prescribers, family members, or significant others (if clinically indicated), and their need to generally cooperate with treatment.

When creating records for patients at risk for suicide, we recommend that you follow the analogy of the ninth-grade algebra teachers who give credit to students for showing the steps of their problem solving even if the final answer is not completely correct. Good records are a must for both clinical and risk management reasons. Future clinicians and members of a review team or jury should be able to read your records and develop a general understanding of what you did, why you did it, what you did not do, and why you did not do it. Such careful records may discourage future potential lawsuits. Or, if a lawsuit occurs, those good records will assist in your defense, may help with a positive jury verdict, or may reduce settlement costs.

Not only do good records include the minimum required by state law, they also detail why you made important treatment decisions. For example, if you decided not to hospitalize a patient, then it would be prudent to describe in detail the reasons why you made that decision.

A psychologist was treating a man who was in the moderate range of suicide risk. Ordinarily it would have been appropriate

> to contact the man's family about his clinical condition and solicit their involvement, monitoring him and assisting in furthering the goals of treatment. However, there were unusual clinical features that strongly argued against this approach. Consequently, the psychologist documented why she made the decision not to inform the patient's family. Fortunately, the course of treatment was successful. However, if a tragedy had occurred and the conduct of the psychologist had been called into question, she could have provided sound clinical reasons why she did not solicit the family's involvement. (3.7.8)

This example provides another illustration of several points we have raised throughout this book. First, good risk management principles should be consistent with good patient care. It would have been poor practice (and poor risk management) to have contacted the family without considering the impact on this particular patient. Second, it illustrates that whatever general rules may apply in treatment, ultimately you have to make decisions based on sound clinical judgment for the particular patient. The practice of psychology cannot be performed by rote or by following predetermined algorithms. Instead, it requires you to use informed clinical judgment.

Finally, this example shows how documentation, if done properly at the highest level of Bloom's taxonomy, reflects your careful thought as an integral part of good patient care. Recall that at the lower levels of Bloom's taxonomy, you would only document the minimum required by law. At the higher levels, however, your notes would demonstrate your thinking process; reflect careful considerations for the quality of care; and justify your actions on clinical, ethical, and legal grounds.

Always document your consultations. Discuss a variety of strategies with other involved professionals or consultants on a regular basis. Consult with the patient's family if appropriate. Consult with managed care representatives or case managers about alternative resources. If you are supervising others, make certain your supervisees consult with you.

PATIENTS AT RISK FOR SUICIDE IN INSTITUTIONAL SETTINGS

Institutions such as psychiatric hospitals, jails, juvenile detention facilities, or half-way houses have greater obligations to prevent suicides because they have a greater degree of control over the patients, inmates, or residents. When liability occurs in such settings, it can be for failure to diagnose suicidal impulses or failure to adequately plan for the treatment. However, liability can also occur for failure to communicate the risk (e.g., a patient tells a nurse she is suicidal, but the nurse does not tell anyone else or document the statement), failure to order adequate precautions (e.g., a patient is noted as more suicidal in the record, but the institution fails to order an increase in precautions), failure to implement orders to increase precautions (e.g., the health professional in charge of treatment orders increased precautions, but they are not implemented as ordered), or failure to reevaluate the suicidal individual at crucial time periods (e.g., before a discharge or transfer).

Documentation is essential to note what was done or not done and why.

> A psychologist worked in a prison that had the philosophy that "suicide is everyone's business." Guards were instructed to report all threats of suicide immediately, whereupon a predetermined suicide assessment and prevention procedure was put into place. The facility has not had a suicide in more than 20 years. (3.7.9)

POSTVENTIONS

The loss of a patient by suicide is a very upsetting experience for mental health professionals. Many psychologists experience great grief or even become depressed following the suicide of a patient. The death of a patient needs to be processed. If necessary, it is safer to do this in your own personal therapeutic relationship, which is confidential. Be careful not to engage in self-recrimination in a nonconfidential relationship. Telling a colleague "I should have seen it coming" could be used against you in the event that the case ever came before a disciplinary body. The suicide of a patient is an occupational hazard of being a psychologist. Show concern for your colleagues when you learn that one of their patients has committed suicide. Even a brief phone call or a tactful note can do much for a colleague in distress.

These experiences can be especially difficult for interns and beginning psychologists. Perhaps they do not have the confidence that develops with years of experience and cannot place the event into perspective.

Fortunately, many institutions now consider the suicide or attempted suicide of a patient to be a sentinel event and will do a root cause analysis of what led to the suicide. Ideally, there will be no presumption that any professional made an error. However, the institution may review its internal procedures to determine if more could have been done to prevent the suicide. If this review is done as part of the institution's peer review process, the information and findings may be confidential under the laws of the state.

Also, it may be clinically indicated to respond to an outreach from the family of the patient. In most states a family member is the legal executor, sometimes referred to as the personal representative, who has the authority to waive the confidentiality of the psychologist-patient relationship. However, you need to check the law in your state for the exact rules. When permitted by state law, you may discuss some of the general therapeutic issues with the patient's family, share your condolences, and try to give the family a sense of closure. Not only is this a humane thing to do, it also reduces your risk of being sued if you are open, caring, and forthright with the family. At times, families have found it healing to have the psychologist attend the funeral of the loved one.

Your actions should be governed by whether or how you can be of benefit to the family. If you are extremely distraught yourself, you may want to delay the meeting until you have better control over your own feelings.

Tact and therapeutic discretion are important when a patient has committed suicide. A psychologist accurately noted in his records that the patient engaged in a vitriolic diatribe against his wife in the last session. After the suicide, the widow insisted on receiving a copy of her husband's records, and under the laws of that state, she was entitled to see them. The psychologist turned over the records in his office but initiated the meeting by describing how anger is a common manifestation of depression, and the anger is usually directed against persons whom the individual loves the most. The comments of the psychologist and his detailed discussion afterward helped the widow to place the comments of her late husband into perspective. (3.7.10)

ASSESSING AND TREATING PATIENTS WHO POSE A RISK OF HARMING OTHERS

When psychologists think of violence toward others, they often think of the duty-to-warn or duty-to-protect standards that resulted from the well-known case, *Tarasoff v. Regents of the University of California et al.* (1976). However, the most common situation involving violence that psychologists can expect to encounter is that of domestic abuse, although it does not present a high risk to the psychologist from a disciplinary perspective. There is typically no duty to warn or protect in cases of domestic violence because the spouse already knows that she has been harmed or threatened (we are using the feminine pronoun to refer to the victim because the large majority of victims of domestic violence are female). Also, psychologists may encounter children who are endangered by their caregivers or other situations in which patients or others are at risk of harm.

DUTY TO WARN OR PROTECT

From a risk management perspective, the duty to warn or protect is a low-frequency, high-impact event. Some duty-to-warn cases have been highly publicized, but they are relatively rare in occurrence. Since *Tarasoff*, many state courts or state legislatures have established some form of the duty. There is no substitute for knowing the law in your states. Most states establish a duty to warn or protect; some states specify how that duty is to be discharged; some states provide immunity to mental health professionals who make a good faith effort to notify or protect identifiable third parties; and a few states specifically do not permit a breach of confidentiality even to protect an identifiable third party who may be harmed by your patient.

In the original *Tarasoff* case a psychologist was treating a patient who made a serious threat to kill an identifiable third party. The psychologist took the threat seriously and attempted to commit the patient to a psychiatric hospital. The commitment attempt failed; the patient dropped out of treatment; and the supervisors of the psychologist forbade him from taking any more steps to protect the identified victim. Less than three months

Application of Suicidal Assessment and Treatment Recommendations to the Detailed Case Example

The treating psychologist would be wise to review the suicidal risk for the patient in the detailed case example in Section 1. Table 3.7.C provides an evaluation of the case on the eight factors previously identified as relevant to the assessment of suicidal risk.

At this time, the psychologist does not know enough about the patient to make an accurate assessment. Depending on the results of further inquiry, the patient may fall into the moderate or perhaps severe or extreme range of suicidality. The example presents the woman as a chronic patient and hints at a serious personality disorder. Consequently, it is not clear whether she should be receiving suicide-focused or diagnosis-focused treatment (see Table 3.7.D). If she falls into the severe or extreme range of suicidality, she should not be terminated at this time.

after the aborted commitment attempt, the ex-patient killed his intended victim.

The parents of the victim sued, and in 1974, the California Supreme Court ruled that the psychologist had a duty to warn the identified victim. The decision was followed by extensive criticism from both legal and mental health experts. The California Supreme Court then took the unusual step of rehearing its own case. In the second *Tarasoff* decision in 1976, the California Supreme Court ruled that the psychologist had a duty to protect the identified victim. According to that decision, a mental health professional may discharge the duty to protect through steps designed to diffuse the danger, such as implementing a psychiatric hospitalization, other than just notifying the intended victim.

The treatment of patients who present an imminent threat to third parties requires three steps: assessment, development of an appropriate treatment plan, and implementation of the treatment plan (Appelbaum, 1985). The assessment of danger usually means more than just having a patient utter a verbal threat of harm to an identifiable third party.

Typically, you do not need to issue a warning or take protective measures simply because a patient has issued a verbal threat. Instead, the verbal warning or threat is only one of several factors (albeit a serious one) to consider when assessing the dangerousness of a patient. Other factors to consider include the context in which the threat was made, the intent, and the availability of opportunity. The likelihood of acting on threats is increased if the patient abuses alcohol or other drugs, has a background of violence, or lives in a subculture in which violence is accepted or endorsed.

It is common for patients to express an attempt to harm, or at least extreme anger at, an identifiable individual. However, in most instances, when patients express anger against a third party, the therapist can address this issue in therapy or modify the focus or frequency of therapy, and this may be a sufficient means of providing protection for the third party. Notifying a third party of potential danger is a fairly rare event. However, whenever a patient makes such a threat, it is important to document your decision making concerning the threat. Even if you decide not to warn or

TABLE 3.7.C
Factors Relevant to the Assessment of Suicidal Risk
Applied to the Detailed Case Example

Factor	Evaluation
Predisposition	Need to know about the patient's family of origin and the possibility of abuse or overly punitive parenting
Precipitants	Few or none, although termination of treatment should probably be considered one
Symptomatic presentation	High at this time; in the recent past, moderate
Hopelessness	Not reported in the case example
Nature of suicidal thinking	Need to assess in terms of frequency, intensity, and duration
Previous suicidal behavior	Some attempts, lethality not specified
Impulsivity	High during periods of stress, although there is no report of the patient's using recreational drugs
Protective factors	Few social supports, family relationships strained

TABLE 3.7.D
Philosophy of Treatment for Patients With Acute
and Chronic Risk of Suicide

Risk	Philosophy of treatment
Acutely suicidal	suicide focused
Chronically suicidal with personality disorders	diagnosis focused
Chronically suicidal with personality disorders with acute exacerbation	suicide focused

act to protect an identified victim, it is still prudent to describe your decision making in detail. Even if the anger appears to be dissipating, it is good practice to revisit the issue of harming the third party regularly throughout therapy.

Violence assessment instruments may be used as a redundant measure. However, as was noted in chapter 6, Psychological Assessment and Testing, these instruments have many limitations that must be factored into your decision making.

Finally, it is good practice to *assess for suicidal intentions* whenever an individual expresses a strong intention to harm a third party. There is a significant correlation between homicidal and suicidal behaviors, especially for persons with impulse control problems.

If the determination is made that the individual does present an imminent danger of harming an identifiable third party, then *the second step is to develop an intervention plan* that is likely to diffuse the danger. Unless mandated by state law, warning the intended victim should be only one of several possible interventions. Other interventions include a psychiatric hospitalization, a referral for medication, a shift to family therapy (to strengthen the monitoring by other family members or to reduce intrafamily conflict), a request to remove lethal weapons, increasing the frequency of therapeutic contact through increased sessions, between-session telephone monitoring, or other interventions. As with other patients, it is important to focus on the therapeutic relationship. Sometimes psychologists feel so bothered by the threat of violence that it impedes their ability to form a productive working relationship.

As much as possible, involve the patient in these decisions. If patients have informed you of their impulses to harm an identifiable third person, they may still have some ambivalence about harming that individual. You should be able to harness that healthy ambivalence to motivate them to participate in actions to diffuse the danger. Often family members or friends can be part of the intervention and may act as a redundant system of protection. For example, a family member may agree to be caretaker for the guns until the situation becomes diffused.

The third step is to implement the treatment plan. Although this step may seem self-evident, it should be remembered that in the original *Tarasoff* decision, the treating psychologist decided to reduce the danger to the identifiable third party by hospitalizing his patient. However, the police failed to implement the involuntary hospitalization; the patient dropped out of treatment; no further attempts were made to protect the identified victim; and she was subsequently murdered.

If the decision is made to hospitalize the patient, then it is essential that the admitting physician understand the severity of the patient's threat. If the decision is made to increase the frequency of outpatient contacts, then it is essential that the patient keep those appointments. Failure to do so requires a reconsideration of the treatment plan (VandeCreek & Knapp, 2001). The psychologist must be fully familiar with the various state statutes regarding admission and discharge of patients in mental health facilities or psychiatric hospitals, including the requirements for voluntary and involuntary hospitalization.

These three steps are not always sequential. It is necessary to continually reevaluate the degree of dangerousness throughout the course of therapy and to modify the treatment plan as conditions change.

Informed consent is important throughout this process. You will reduce the potential sense of betrayal if you have notified your patient at the start of therapy, either directly or through the Privacy Notice, of your obligations to protect when patients present an imminent danger to harm an identifiable third party. If such a threat occurs and you live in a state that has a duty to warn or protect or provides immunity if you warn an intended victim, then it may be necessary to reiterate your obligations to the patient. Also, the informed consent process involves more than just notifying the patient of your legal obligations and can also include an active effort to involve the patient in the treatment and safety planning. Of course, whenever a *patient makes a halfway credible threat against an identifiable third party,* it is desirable to rely on *consultation* and *careful* documentation.

OTHER DANGEROUS SITUATIONS

Psychologists can expect to encounter patients who are HIV positive or who carry hepatitis or other sexually transmitted diseases. Sometimes these patients engage in indiscriminate behavior that risks infecting others. State laws vary considerably in identifying legal obligations in these situations, and it is important to have current knowledge of the specific requirements in your state.

Our recommendation is to think clinically in these situations even if you do not have an obligation to warn or protect. Strive to understand the reasons for a patient's nondisclosure of HIV status. The patient may be dealing with fear of domestic abuse, fear of being abandoned (and having one's children abandoned by the primary wage earner as well), or other relationship issues. Fortunately, a wealth of clinical information has emerged that can guide psychologists who are treating patients who have HIV/AIDS or other diseases (see, e.g., Anderson & Barret, 2001).

Every state requires psychologists to report suspected child abuse. The criteria for reporting vary from state to state; there is no substitute for knowing the law in your state. Typically the statutes require that you must be treating the abused child for the requirement to apply, although in some states you are mandated to report if you learn of the abuse through any professional contact. The standard for reporting is set deliberately low; often a reason to suspect the abuse is sufficient to trigger the reporting requirement. The state agency, not you, must make the determination whether to investigate the abuse. Again, there is no substitute for knowing the exact law in your state. The Child Welfare Information Gateway provides electronic access to each state's statutes on child abuse and neglect at http://www.childwelfare.gov/.

Some states have reporting laws for elder abuse, impaired automobile drivers, treating patients who have had sexual contact with a psychotherapist, or encountering medical errors. The focus and requirements of these reporting laws vary substantially. Sometimes they are mandatory; sometimes they are discretionary. Sometimes they require the permission of the patient; sometimes they do not. There is no substitute for knowing the exact law in your state.

DOMESTIC VIOLENCE

Between 15% and 20% of women experience violence from a spouse or intimate partner each year (Harway & Hansen, 2004), although physical abuse also occurs in dating relationships and same-sex relationships. Sometimes the injuries can be quite severe or result in death. Although lower income patients are more likely to come to battered women's shelters, do not assume that domestic abuse is unlikely to occur among higher income persons. Domestic abuse occurs across income, racial, and religious groups. Many senior citizens have been abused for years without publicly acknowledging it. The frequency of female abuse against men is increasing, although the large number of victims continues to be women.

Anytime you take a marital case or see one member in a marital relationship you should screen for domestic violence. The conversation can start with general questions such as "What do you disagree about and how do you express your disagreements?" followed by more specific questions such as "Do you ever shout, yell, feel afraid, place hands on each other?" Sometimes victims will deny or minimize the consequences of domestic violence if asked directly or attribute their injuries to accidents (e.g., black eye from running into a door, sprained ankles from falling down several steps). Also, about 20% of the American population (including many women) believes that domestic violence is justified.

The treatment of domestic abuse often requires special skills and access to alternative services to ensure that the abuse is stopped and to determine if and how the relationship can be saved. Treatment may require an extensive network such as a victims support group, legal services, and housing or shelter options.

Seven Essential Points to Remember

1. Suicide is the most prevalent mental health emergency for psychologists.

2. Psychologists should have a systematic method for assessing suicide and developing a treatment plan.

3. Patients who have a risk for suicide along with a serious personality disorder may require treatment procedures different from those for patients who have a risk for suicide and no serious personality disorder.

4. You should know the specific procedures needed to reduce the likelihood of suicidal behavior and how to integrate them into the overall treatment of the patient.

5. You should know the law in your state concerning the duty to warn or protect, how to hospitalize patients in psychiatric facilities, how to assess the potential for violence, and how to develop and implement treatment plans to reduce the likelihood that violence will occur.

6. You should know the mandated reporting laws in your state.

7. Screen all marital couples for domestic violence.

Chapter 8: **CONSULTANT OR SUPERVISOR,
DIVERSITY ISSUES, CONFLICTS IN
INSTITUTIONAL SETTINGS, AND
TERMINATION OR ABANDONMENT**

In this chapter, we review several areas of concern for psychologists including the roles of consultants and supervisors, ways to be of assistance to persons from culturally diverse backgrounds, unique issues that arise when working in institutions, and issues surrounding termination and abandonment.

PSYCHOLOGIST AS CONSULTANT

Sometimes psychologists use the term *supervisor* to refer to any activity when two or more psychologists talk about a case. However, this is an inaccurate use of language. Supervision occurs when you are overseeing those who cannot legally do what they are doing without your oversight. When supervising others, you have legal responsibility for their actions. Everything else is consultation and should be labeled as such.

In Section 2 we discussed the risk management benefit of getting consultation as a way to determine your risk by better understanding patient, contextual, and individual therapist factors. Here, we discuss the legal risks when you act as a consultant, which are very low except when the case is controversial or when it takes on the aspects of a supervisory relationship. In consultation the person seeking the consultation retains the responsibility to accept or reject whatever advice is received. Consultants have no assurance that the information provided by the consultee is accurate or comprehensive, and they have no control over the behavior of the consultee.

ENSURING EFFECTIVE CONSULTATION

One might argue that a spouse or close friend (assuming they are mental health professionals) could be very helpful if they have a good appreciation of your clinical skills and your personal therapist factors. They may be able to discern when you are being overly confident or hypercritical. On the other hand, a spouse or close friend may be reluctant to be critical of you and therefore be of no consultive value, especially if you both have a subclinical folie à deux in which you reinforce each other's clinical idiosyncrasies. At the other extreme, impartial experts theoretically have no secondary relationship with you that would contaminate their comments. When it comes to getting objective information about your techniques or a particular diagnosis, arms-length consultants are often best.

> A husband and wife therapy team (who were eventually disciplined by their licensing board) typically had their patients engage in unusual practices, such as stripping naked during therapy. Although they participated in a consultation group with other mental health professionals, they never shared their "idiosyncratic" (and iatrogenic) method of doing therapy with the group. They self-validated the technique by talking only with each other. (3.8.1)

If you are approached for a consultation, try to specify the goals of the consultee. Do you have expertise in the area in which consultation is requested? Is the request for a consultation on a specific case or for ongoing feedback? Sometimes you may want to see patients directly, although usually you will review the clinical details, the chart, or the report with the consultee. You should obtain the necessary level of detail needed to provide a useful opinion. Effective consultation may focus on the therapeutic process as well as case-specific facts. Consultation will help identify the pros and cons of different options or present the devil's advocate perspective, thus challenging the consultee's assumptions and requiring him or her to consider other options.

> A psychologist acquired a local reputation as being "the" expert on dissociative identity disorder (DID). Often local psychologists contacted her for a detailed consultation when they encountered a patient who appeared to have this diagnosis. In reality, she was somewhat of a DID skeptic and typically challenged the mental health professionals to rethink their diagnosis. (3.8.2)

> A psychologist started a group for practitioners who used eye movement desensitization and reprocessing. This time-limited consultation and education group met for 2 hours a week for 15 weeks. She used a format that combined lecture and case discussion. Each participant was guaranteed an equal amount of time to discuss cases. (3.8.3)

A key element in this group is that all of the participants are licensed mental health professionals who retain the final decision-making authority and may accept or reject the recommendations of the group leader as they see fit. A prudent group leader would clarify the nature of the consulting relationship, preferably in writing, before the group began. However, if the group leader accepted unlicensed individuals into the group, did not clarify the consultive nature of the group (or referred to it as peer supervision), or allowed her name to be used on external communications about patients, then the relationship was becoming more and more like supervision.

Over the years each of the authors has sought consultation for professional services both as practicing psychologists and as risk management consultants. Personally we have found that our most helpful consultants have been excellent listeners, helped us solve problems, challenged us with relevant questions, and of course, provided expert information if needed.

When we have acted as consultants ourselves, we have found that almost all consultees are forthright about their issues and are receptive to and appreciative of feedback. On rare occasions, a consultee appears to have desired a predetermined answer and selectively presented information to support the position he or she had already reached. In such a situation, you may well be surprised at the advice you have supposedly given! You should be aware of this possibility and ensure that you are listening to the consultee carefully and taking enough time to understand the issues clearly. At times you may question your consultee about the information being provided or ask him or her to repeat back the recommendation you have made. It is best to follow up on the consultation and document what was recommended and what was ultimately done by the consultee. Although you may not be legally liable for consultees' gross distortions or for opinions based on their selective reporting of facts, you nonetheless want to be as useful as possible to your consultees.

Consultation Applied to the Detailed Case Example

We would recommend that the psychologist treating the patient in the detailed case example provided in Section 1 seek consultation. The patient presents several high-risk factors: She is suicidal and has difficulty maintaining relationships, and her mother and the attorney may be assumed to have some interest in litigation. Her family may not be wealthy, but they most likely earn a very good income.

The individual therapist factors might not be adequate to address her needs. She would benefit from, among other things, more supportive family involvement, a relationship with a more skilled psychopharmacologist (preferably a psychiatrist or a prescribing psychologist), and a supplemental dialectical behavior therapy group. Furthermore, the treating psychologist is beginning to feel emotionally strained by the demands on her time and frustrated by the failure of the patient to adhere to the treatment protocol.

The consultation that the treating psychologist should seek could involve one of several questions. It could involve, for example, "Should I terminate with this patient?" "Could I get a sense of refreshment so that I can continue with this patient?" and if so, "What can I do differently from a therapeutic perspective to mobilize her to adhere more conscientiously to the treatment recommendations?"

PSYCHOLOGIST AS SUPERVISOR

In contrast to the role of consultant, psychologists who serve as supervisors have elevated legal risks. They are responsible for the work product of their supervisees who legally become the "hands and legs" of the supervisor. Effective supervisors can reduce their legal risks by prudent hiring and monitoring practices. Supervision occurs most frequently in graduate school training; in practicum and residency training programs; in postdoctoral internships; in the required one year of supervised practice prior to licensure; and when the psychologist is responsible for the treatment provided by others in institutional settings, such as hospitals, schools, prisons, or mental health centers.

SELECTING AND HIRING YOUR SUPERVISEES/EMPLOYEES

The time you put in up front in selecting supervisees may save you a lot of trouble later. Have a comprehensive application and interview form that goes back to the time the individual graduated from college. Ask applicants why they left previous jobs. Ask about any gaps in their employment history. Check references and be cautious if the past employer will only give the dates of employment without comment or uses code words such as "he left by mutual decision" or "we had to agree to disagree on certain issues." Verify all licenses and the existence of any complaints against the potential supervisee. Some states will do background checks for reports of founded child abuse. Require and review those background reports. Look at their resume or CV.

Check their ability to get along with others, to accommodate themselves to your rules, and to contribute to your practice in terms of technical skills and personality. You do not want to hire the "walking lawsuit" or individuals who believe that they are entitled to certain unrealistic benefits or individuals who perceive that they are continually the victim of unfair practices.

Ask the prospects what they want from this job or training program. Clarify their expectations and yours. You do not want to hire someone who cannot work overtime if overtime is frequently required. You do not want to hire someone who needs 2 hours of personal supervision a week to get licensed if you are unable to provide such supervision.

Develop an employment agreement that among other things requires the prospect to follow the American Psychological Association's "Ethical Principles of Psychologists and Code of Conduct" (APA Ethics Code) and applicable state and federal laws. Failure to follow these rules should be grounds for employment termination.

Check to ensure that your professional liability policy covers you for your supervisory activities. The policy will probably not provide coverage for the supervisee unless he or she is your employee, in which case an additional premium will be charged for the supervisee.

MONITORING YOUR SUPERVISEES

As a supervisor, you assume full responsibility for the work product of your supervisees. You should not undertake supervision without the expectation that you will take full legal responsibility for the services delivered. To their credit, most psychologists tend to be democratic in nature and are reluctant to tell people, "Just do it because I told you so." They believe in the value of educating and empowering employees and trainees, treating them with respect, and encouraging independent thought. However, legally, the supervisory relationship is a hierarchal one. As the supervisor, you are responsible if your supervisee makes mistakes. You are responsible if your supervisee decides to do massage therapy with the patient with a serious personality disorder, gives the patient a ride home, and gives the patient his or her private phone number. You are responsible if your intern fails to read the patient intake sheet in which the patient writes in large bold letters "HELP ME! I THINK I WILL KILL MYSELF," fails to address suicide in the intake session, and the patient subsequently attempts suicide. You are responsible when your supervisee writes a letter to an attorney stating that the child she is treating would be better off living with the mother or father, even though she has not conducted a custody evaluation and has never even seen one of the parents. You are responsible when your practicum student diagnoses every child she sees as reactive attachment disorder, regardless of the symptom presentation.

Of course, most supervisees will not make such glaring errors of judgment. However, some with the best of motives will make these or similar errors; after all, that is why they are called supervisees. The general rule is that you are responsible for these errors, although courts may make an exception if the supervisee deliberately withheld information from you or directly violated your instructions. Nonetheless, if you failed to meet with your supervisee on a regular basis, failed to correct ongoing problems that had been identified, ignored his or her requests for help, disregarded his or her concerns, in other ways provided poor supervision, or did not keep good supervision notes, your legal exposure will be substantially increased.

> A practicum student was cautioned to be very careful of the boundaries she maintained with one of her patients. Against the knowledge and advice of the supervising psychologist, the practicum student developed a social relationship with this patient that soon went sour. When responding to the investigator from the licensing board, the supervisor was able to produce notes relevant to this particular patient that documented her explicit instructions to avoid any boundary crossings. (3.8.4)

You should take supervision seriously because of the risks that it creates for you. Let your supervisees know the standards and procedures you will use for evaluating them. Devise a method of assessment appropriate to the individual and his or her needs and level of training. When possible, use direct observation or audio- or videotapes in addition, review all reports, participate in cotherapy, and review self-reports of the supervisee. It is mandatory to give your supervisees routine and timely feedback; it is equally important to follow up on implementation of the feedback and evaluate them on the basis of their performance. You should have clear performance criteria (preferably written) and objective performance measures that are applied in a timely manner. Do not be lulled into thinking that your supervisees can handle everything that comes up.

Ensure that patients know the supervised status of their therapist (Standard 10.01c, Informed Consent to Therapy) and that they know how to contact you directly if problems arise. This means that you do not permit supervisees to market your practice as if it were their practice, collect fees for themselves, or otherwise act as if they were practicing independently. When patients consent to receive care from a trainee or supervisee, they do not consent to receive substandard care. If such a patient sues, the trainee or supervisee, the supervisor, the agency, and the educational institution may all be defendants.

> An enthusiastic unlicensed postdoctoral fellow had, without the knowledge of his supervisor, arranged to have some patients receive therapy privately from him at his home. Upon learning of this arrangement the supervisor confronted the postdoctoral fellow and noted that his employment contract required that he follow the APA Ethics Code and state law that among other things prohibited postdoctoral fellows from practicing psychology independently. (3.8.5)

You must ensure that your supervisees are competent to perform all of the activities that you assign to them (Standard 2.05, Delegation of Work to Others). For example, only assign neuropsychological assessments to trainees if you are qualified to perform them yourself. Do not assign patients with substance abuse to your supervisee, unless you can work with these patients. Your supervisees should be able to perform all of the activities that you assign to them; that is the purpose of supervision. A supervisee is held to the same standard of care as a licensed professional. You should intervene when your supervisee does not provide adequate care. Also, you need to ensure that your supervisee is free of any contraindicated multiple relationships or conflicts of interests with patients (Standard 2.05).

> A postdoctoral fellow expressed an interest in learning more about neuropsychology. However, his supervisor had limited knowledge in that area of practice. The supervisor, however, arranged for the fellow to receive supervision from a neuropsychologist who had the experience and skills necessary to provide the supervision. (3.8.6)

Ideally you should have training as a supervisor. You are not qualified to be a clinical supervisor merely because you were once supervised. Most important, supervision is not therapy, and therapy is no substitution for supervision. Developing skills as a supervisor parallels the development of other professional skills; it improves with education, self-reflection, and experience. If you are asked by a training program to supervise students and you have not received any training to carry out this role, ask the training program for assistance or secure training on your own. Some doctoral training programs now consider supervision a core competency in professional practice and include training in supervision in doctoral work, although that has not always been the case.

Document your supervisory work. Make notes for each patient discussed in supervision. You should know enough about each patient to develop and monitor a treatment plan and to intervene when necessary. Some states require supervisory notes. Good supervisory notes can protect you if you or your supervisee is charged with misconduct.

PROMOTING THE WELFARE OF YOUR SUPERVISEES

The APA Ethics Code states that

psychologists do not harm, exploit, or have sex with their supervisees. (Standards 3.04, Avoiding Harm; 3.08, Exploitative Relationships; and 7.07, Sexual Relationships With Students and Supervisees).

However, you will want to do more than just avoid harming your supervisees. Actively strive to create a pleasant work environment for your employees and supervisees. Not only are such environments intrinsically desirable but they also improve morale and set a positive tone that may be reflected in the quality of patient care.

Think about Bloom's taxonomy on competence and how you can help your supervisees move to the highest level. Teach them what you know about risk management in your supervisory sessions and in the general manner in which you run your practice.

From a practical perspective, the legal liability of supervisors increases when supervisees are less than forthright about their dilemmas or clinical problems. Supervisors are in a unique role in which they should be both supportive and nurturing of their supervisees, particularly because they also have an evaluative function.

The nature of the supervisory relationship tends to reinforce the supervisee for "looking good" and avoiding self-disclosure of ignorance or shortcomings. The supervisor needs to facilitate a climate in which honesty and healthy self-reflection occur. Such conduct is more likely to occur when supervisors invest themselves in the supervisory relationship, search out ways to be positive and reinforcing, and give helpful information. Suggest strategies to help supervisees in their clinical work; directly observe the supervisees' interactions with patients; and give frequent, concrete, and helpful feedback on performance. Just as a strong relationship is essential for a good outcome with patients, a strong relationship is essential for good supervisory work.

One way to meet the obligations of supervisors is to consider communitarian Amitai Etzioni's (1996) reformulation of the Golden Rule: "respect and uphold society's moral order as you would have society respect and uphold your autonomy" (p. xviii). That is, the best way to promote the welfare of supervisees may be to help them promote the welfare of their patients. Good supervisors will treat supervisees with respect and also encourage them to treat their patients with the same respect (Knapp & VandeCreek, 2005).

> A psychologist in charge of the university training clinic took his job very seriously. He was quite explicit about the high standards of conduct he expected from practicum students. Yet, he was very generous with praise when it was deserved. His feedback was useful, specific, and frequent. Despite the inherent stress of working in a university clinic, he made certain that the work place was as pleasant and relaxing as possible. (3.8.7)

SUPERVISION OF NONPROFESSIONAL EMPLOYEES

Many of the principles applicable to professional supervisees and employees apply to nonprofessional employees as well. Care should be taken in recruiting them, defining their responsibilities, giving them feedback on their performance, and creating a pleasant work environment. Draft a written contract or letter of agreement. All employees need to be trained on confidentiality requirements even if you are not a covered entity under the Health Insurance Portability and Accountability Act (HIPAA). The extent of the training varies according to the job responsibilities of the employee.

Many successful psychologists claim that their support personnel are a major reason for their success. They pay these individuals well, try to make working conditions pleasant, and treat them with great respect. They purchase up-to-date computer equipment, provide continuing education opportunities, and have regular staff meetings. In return, they expect their employees to interact professionally with patients, show initiative, troubleshoot, and ensure the smooth and efficient running of the practice. One psychologist commented that he would rather spend his time treating patients than cleaning up billing problems.

DIVERSITY

Diversity issues are addressed throughout this book (see, e.g., Section 3, chap. 1, Competence, and Section 3, chap. 6, Psychological Assessment and Testing) but deserve to be emphasized again here. From a risk management perspective, the diagnosis and treatment of individuals from diverse backgrounds has not, as yet, become a major source of disciplinary actions for psychologists. Indeed the literature on therapy outcomes with persons of diverse linguistic or cultural backgrounds has not yet shown that matching the cultural background of the therapist and client is a necessary condition for effective outcomes. Nonetheless, research in psychotherapy with culturally diverse groups is replete with methodological issues, such as the degree of acculturation of the patient; the possibility of a bicultural identity; and the interaction of cultural background with gender, sexual orientation, disability, or other factors (Lam & Sue, 2001).

Anecdotal information is gathering concerning misdiagnoses of patients because of the failure to understand their cultural background or treatment failures because the mental health professional did not make accommodations for the cultural background of the patient. In consideration of this emerging body of information we present a series of questions that you need to ask yourself concerning your ability to provide services to individuals from backgrounds that are diverse in terms of language, ethnicity, culture, or race.

Are you trained to work with patients from diverse backgrounds? Do you refrain from treating persons from diverse backgrounds if you lack the information or skills essential for the effective delivery of services (Standard 2.01b, Boundaries of Competence)? You may treat patients without the necessary skills in an emergency or if you are delivering services in an area of the country where other qualified persons are not available (Standards 2.01d, Boundaries of Competence, and 2.02, Providing Services in an

Emergency). Even so, do you seek to acquire the necessary skills through consultation, reading, study, or supervision? Are you aware of how patients from diverse backgrounds can express their distress or how they may react to psychological treatment? Do you learn from your patients about the special cultural expressions that may interact with your mental health services? Do you invite patients from diverse backgrounds to share their perspectives and collaborate with you in understanding their needs? Are you aware of how different cultures prefer to involve the extended family in therapy?

> A psychologist had an initial interview with a young woman from India who was seriously depressed and had suicidal ideation. The psychologist knew enough about Indian culture to understand that her patient's older brother, who lived in the same city, was presumed by the family to be responsible for her welfare. With the permission of her patient, the psychologist contacted the older brother and asked him to participate as a collateral contact in therapy. (3.8.8)

When using interpreters, do you educate them on the need for confidentiality? Do you obtain the informed consent of patients before seeing them (Standard 9.03c, Informed Consent in Assessments)? Do you avoid using interpreters if they have a clinically contraindicated multiple relationship with the patient (Standard 2.05, Delegation of Work to Others)?

> A psychologist at a mental health clinic did an intake interview with a man of Chinese descent who was born and raised in Vietnam and who spoke little English. He had an unusual Chinese dialect and no appropriate interpreter could be found. Consequently, his adult children were used as interpreters. This was not an ideal situation, but it appeared to be the only way to ensure that services could be provided. (3.8.9)

Do you use assessment instruments appropriate for the population tested, and if appropriate tests are not available, do you note the limitations in your test interpretations (Standard 9.02b, Use of Assessments)? Do you make adaptations of psychological tests from a sound knowledge base? Unless done for testing linguistic ability, is the test administered in the primary language of the patient? If not, is this noted in the psychological report? Do your interpretations consider the situational, personal, linguistic, and cultural differences and how they may influence the testing results (Standard 9.06, Interpreting Assessment Results)?

You should be aware that diversity issues can also apply to individuals with physical or mental disabilities, including deafness and hearing impairments. You should be familiar with the provisions of the Americans with Disabilities Act (ADA) and its implications for your services. For example, you should be aware of your obligation to provide reasonable accommodations for individuals with disabilities. This may mean, for example, hiring an interpreter when treating a deaf patient or ensuring you can make arrangements to see a patient who needs a handicapped accessible office. (More information on the ADA can be found in Section 3, chap. 6, Psychological Assessment and Testing.)

Furthermore, diversity issues may also apply to individuals who are lesbian, gay, transgendered, or confused about their sexual orientation. As with other individuals you should treat them only if you can provide the necessary services, if it is an emergency, if you are working in an underserved area, if other qualified professionals cannot be located, and if you undertake the necessary activities to acquire competence. Diversity issues should always be considered with respect to patient characteristics (P) and therapist factors (TF) when utilizing the risk management formula to assess risk.

CONFLICTS IN INSTITUTIONAL SETTINGS

Some psychologists work in institutions that provide less than optimal services to patients or work for employers who do things that appear contrary to the APA Ethics Code or patient welfare. Consider these examples that are based on real cases.

> A psychologist working in a prison was given a caseload of hundreds of inmates, many of whom were suicidal or had serious mental disorders. There was inadequate medical backup. The psychologist was justified in his fear that one or more of the inmates would "hang up" (commit suicide) and worried about the extensive unmet needs among the prisoners. (3.8.10)

> A psychologist working in a hospital warned that a particular patient still harbored strongly homicidal thoughts toward an identified third party. Nonetheless, the supervising psychiatrist ordered the release of this patient and instructed the staff that they were to make no effort to warn or protect the identified victims, even though the person lived in a state that had a duty-to-warn or duty-to-protect statute. The psychiatrist dismissed the concerns of the psychologist. (3.8.11)

> A psychologist worked for a community agency that was having a difficult time meeting its budget. In order to draw more medical assistance funds, the director instructed staff to start seeing more patients but only for 30 minutes instead of 45 minutes, with the expectation that they could bill more per hour by billing two half-hour sessions instead of one 1-hour session. The director also instructed the staff to double book patients. (3.8.12)

Among their other concerns, psychologists working in these settings worried about their legal liability. Could the psychologist in the prison be held liable for the suicide of one of the prisoners? Could the psychologist in the hospital be held liable if the patient harmed the identifiable third party? Could the psychologist in the community agency be held liable for harm that comes from delivering second-rate care?

Again it is appropriate to consider the risk management formula,

$$\text{Clinical risk} = \frac{(P \times C \times D)}{TF}$$

In this formula, P = patient risk characteristics; C = context;
D = disciplinary consequences; and TF = therapist factors.

In these situations, the issue is whether the context created by the institution, combined with the patient factors and individual therapist factors, will lead to unacceptable risks.

In each of these cases the psychologists are at an increased risk for disciplinary actions as the institutional demands increase the risk that patients or third parties will be harmed. However, if you find yourself in similar situations you can take certain steps to reduce your liability. Your obligations are to try to protect the welfare of the patients as much as possible and to bring the problems to the attention of the administrative personnel.

It is impossible to identify a certain number of steps that qualify as adequate measures in each of these examples. Much depends on the specific circumstances, the politics of the agencies, and the personalities of the individuals involved. Administrators are not always heartless bean counters. Often they are aware of the problems (or wish to become aware of the problems) in the delivery of services. However, funding shortfalls or other pressures may call for compromises for what is perceived as the greater good. Generally it is better to start with the assumption that the directors are well intentioned. Try to understand their perspective on why these decisions were made. On the other hand, be assertive about the impact of the decisions on your patients, on the welfare of the institution, and on you personally. You might request that the agency agree in writing to indemnify you for any harm that results from the agency's policies.

Be tactful and use your skills as a psychologist as much as possible to resolve these problems. If an educational approach fails to resolve the situation, you may decide to escalate the tactics, be more confrontational, or go over the head of the administrator. Even if you are more confrontational, you should avoid personalizing the issue whenever possible. Focus on the policy or the action, not on the character or competence of the individuals involved, unless there is clear incompetence at the base of the problem that those responsible for governance of the institution need to address

Document the means you used to correct the situation, protect patient welfare, and bring the problems to the attention of the administrators. In the worse case scenario when a tragedy occurs, you will have documented that you tried to address the issue ahead of time and took reasonable steps considering the circumstances.

> A prison warden was sympathetic to the mental health needs of the inmates, made an effort to secure additional services, and was very clear that other prison staff were to cooperate with the psychologist as much as possible. In the meantime, the psychologist gave priority to prisoners who had a risk to attempt suicide until more resources could be devoted to prisoner care. (3.8.13)

> After the attending psychiatrist refused to discuss the psychologist's recommendations that the patient was not ready for discharge, the psychologist documented her concerns and forwarded them to the medical director. The relationship between the psychiatrist and psychologist became so strained that the psychologist left her job in the hospital. The discharged patient who was the subject of the conflict between the psychologist and psychiatrist was subsequently arrested on an assault charge (not against the identified victim) and sent to prison. (3.8.14)

> The treating psychologist objected to the assembly line method of treating patients. However, his concerns soon become moot as the community agency was unable to meet its financial obligations and closed. (3.8.15)

Sometimes problems can be worked out. Sometimes they cannot. It may be useful to remember that someday you may be an administrator and have to instruct staff to do things that they do not want to do or that they believe are unethical. Ask yourself how you would like them to approach those problems with you.

> A psychologist was supervising an intern at a residential facility. The intern claimed that she received information from a child she was interviewing that mandated a report to the child protective services agency. However, the psychologist knew that child protective services would not become involved because the child had reached the age of 18 and therefore did not qualify for protective services. The intern took a self-righteous and confrontational attitude, insisted that the psychologist was wrong, threatened to file a formal complaint against the psychologist, and went ahead and filed the report with the child protective services anyway (neglecting to mention the age of the child). Needless to say, child protective services was not pleased when staff went out to investigate a report that, because of the age of the child, should never have been filed. (3.8.16)

The supervising psychologist noted that zealousness in protecting abused children is commendable, but it can become a problem unless it is tempered by perspective, prudence, and good judgment. Given the extreme initial reaction of the intern and the fact that she threatened to file a licensing board complaint against the psychologist, the supervising psychologist sought consultation to determine whether she should continue to supervise this intern.

TERMINATION AND ABANDONMENT

Usually the decision to end treatment is made jointly between you and your patient. Sometimes termination may occur because the therapist is moving, has a serious illness, or because of another major life change that prohibits the treatment from continuing. In some instances, however, your patient will terminate unilaterally either by canceling the last appointment, failing to reschedule, or otherwise discontinuing appointments. At other times, however, you may want to terminate against the wishes of your patient. In those circumstances you may worry that you will be abandoning your patient. Abandonment refers to termination of therapy when you know or should have known that the patient needed more therapy and you did not provide a referral.

The APA Ethics Code provides general rules about terminating patients without their consent. Standard 10.10a, Terminating Therapy, states,

> Psychologists terminate therapy when it becomes reasonably clear that the client/patient no longer needs the service, is not likely to benefit, or is being harmed by continued service.

Standard 10.10c states

> Except where precluded by the actions of clients/patients or third-party payors, prior to termination psychologists provide pretermination counseling and suggest alternative service providers as appropriate.

The general risk management rule is not to terminate against the wishes of patients if they are in life-endangering crises. If therapists decide to terminate the treatment, they should give adequate notice and provide referrals for other treatment opportunities if more treatment is needed. Referrals have to be appropriate, not perfect. These rules will be explained in more detail below and exceptions and qualifiers noted.

FINANCIAL REASONS

Perhaps you wish to terminate because the patient lacks financial resources to pay for treatment. The insurance for the patient may have been exhausted, or the patient has had a sudden decline in income through a job loss. Perhaps the patient says that he or she will no longer make payments because other expenses are a higher priority. At times, it may be obvious that patients are struggling to make necessary payments for food, mortgage, and other essentials. At other times, patients may appear insensitive to their obligations to pay you and give a higher priority to other expenses (such as a costly vacation, new computers, or a wide-screen HDTV set) that are discretionary.

Some of these problems can be avoided by being very clear in the informed consent process at the start of therapy. Standard 10.01a, Informed Consent to Therapy, of the Ethics Code requires psychologists to inform patients about the anticipated course of therapy and fees.

Problems arise if you allow patients to accumulate debts without addressing the issue forthrightly. If patients are having problems paying for services, then it is better to deal with the issue early rather than allowing debts to accumulate. It is not in your interest, nor in the interest of the patient, for you to passively allow the patient to take advantage of your kind nature. Perhaps the patients are in denial and are avoiding looking at finances objectively or are insensitive to financial obligations to others. In either case, they are manifesting an unhealthy trait that should not be reinforced.

> A patient pleaded that he was unable to pay for services and had not paid the psychologist in months, but later the psychologist learned that the patient had insurance, submitted bills to the insurance company, collected the payments, and pocketed the money. (3.8.17)

Of course it is preferable to prevent these nonpayment problems as much as possible. Anticipate financial limitations ahead of time. If patients are unable to meet your expectations for payment, don't take them on as patients. It is unfortunate but true that the risk of a complaint before a licensing board increases dramatically when a psychologist files a collection action against a former patient for an outstanding bill. The time, effort, money, and other resources rarely justify the amount of money that may be collected by filing a collection suit (see Section 3, chap. 9, The Reluctant Business Person).

To reduce nonpayment problems many psychologists adopt a pay-as-you-go approach and require payment at the time of service, much as many physicians and dentists do. If the patient cannot afford services, you can consider other options in addition to terminating the patient, such as reducing the fee, having the patient attend sessions every other week (if clinically indicated), moving the patient to group therapy, referring the patient to a free or low-fee outpatient clinic, or some combination of these arrangements. However, make these arrangements specific; don't just let your financial problems go unaddressed.

The Ethics Code requires that you discuss the termination or transfer of services early in treatment if limitations in services because of finances can be anticipated (Standard 6.04d, Fees and Financial Arrangements). It is preferable not to "skim the cream" of insurance reimbursement. That is, you should be very reluctant to accept long-term patients with the goal of using their insurance and then referring them when the insurance reimbursement ends. The criteria for accepting patients should include the ability to be of professional benefit to them and should not be based solely on their financial status. Just as you would not accept patients who have problems outside of your area of competence with the intent of referring them out, you should not accept patients for whom financial limitations will cause a potentially painful and clinically contraindicated termination.

Of course you cannot always predict the length of treatment when you first accept a patient. The degree of pathology might not be obvious until the patient has been seen in treatment for several weeks or even months. Or the patient may deteriorate substantially over time as a result of unpredictable life circumstances. Nonetheless, to the best of your ability, you should try to anticipate the length of treatment and the financial resources of the patient ahead of time.

THE PATIENTS NO LONGER BENEFIT FROM OR ARE HARMED BY THERAPY

Sometimes you may want to terminate treatment because it has become obvious that your ability to treat the patient effectively has been compromised. Perhaps your inability to help the patient was not obvious until you had seen the patient for several sessions, or perhaps the needs of the patient changed over time. For example, a patient may benefit from your treatment of his depression but then express an interest in improving his parenting ability, which may or may not be an area of your expertise.

At other times, therapy may reach a stalemate because of the actions or inactions of the patient or because the patient has reached a plateau in therapy. Perhaps the patient is noncompliant with treatment, is resistive to further treatment suggestions, refuses to follow through with a recommendation to consult a physician, or misses too many sessions despite repeated efforts on your part to motivate the patient to comply. Some patients use the sessions unproductively and discuss superficial issues that are more appropriate for chitchat than therapy. Other patients may repeatedly arrive late for appointments without justification and with such frequency that the quality of therapy is compromised. While each of these examples may be evidence of resistance by the patient in psychodynamic treatment, each may also indicate that the treatment has taken a lower level of priority for the patient whose pain may have been significantly diminished.

You can and should terminate a patient if you are unable to provide a reasonable level of quality of care (Standard 10.10a, Terminating Therapy). The patient does not have to agree to the termination. However, it is in these situations that it is necessary to bolster your decision with the risk management poultices: informed consent, documentation, and consultation.

If you are considering terminating a patient, it is important to clarify your reasons with the patient as soon as possible and to give the patient the opportunity to provide feedback on your decision. Perhaps the therapy can be modified and become helpful for the patient. In any event, you need to prepare the patient for the possibility of termination. If you do decide to terminate the patient, it is important to document that you discussed the clinical reasons for the termination and involved the patient in the decision as much as was clinically indicated. When patients are terminated against their wishes, you create a situation in which one moral principle such as beneficence (the desire to promote the patient's welfare) or nonmaleficence (the desire to avoid harming the patient) temporarily trumps another moral principle (respect for patient autonomy). Whenever one moral principle is used to trump another, it is desirable to minimize the impact on the offended moral principle. In this case, that might mean making an effort to give the patient as much autonomy as clinically indicated in determining the nature of the termination. You might say, for example, "As we have discussed, I will no longer be seeing you after June 1. Do you want to have any more weekly sessions with me until then?"

Many psychologists will not terminate patients against their wishes unless they receive a professional consultation first. This decision, which may be clinically justified and necessary at times, nonetheless involves an increase in risks for the psychologist.

If the patient needs more treatment, but you are unable or unwilling to provide it because of your lack of expertise or the patient's lack of progress, then it is preferable to give the patient the option of at least three names of mental health professionals or agencies that can be of help. How much more you should do becomes a clinical decision. You may make the appointments for some patients, attend the first session with their new therapist, or make yourself available for a limited period of time until they have their first session with the new therapist. For other patients such extra steps would be clinically contraindicated.

Some patients may feel intense anger at you for terminating treatment despite great efforts on your part to explain the reasons for the termination and despite your efforts to seek a transfer to another therapist. If you decide that further contact would be clinically contraindicated, then stick to that decision. That is, you should not respond to crisis phone calls after the termination date, respond to letters urging you to resume therapeutic contact, or talk to intermediaries who will plead the case for the patient. At times, ex-patients have gone to extremes and filed complaints against their former therapists for the purpose of being able to see them (and talk to them) at the hearing. Responding to any outreach after termination may result in intermittent reinforcement of unwanted behaviors.

> A patient was highly resistive to treatment, missed many appointments, called the emergency service for relatively minor complaints, discontinued medications against medical advice, stopped paying for services, and tried to argue with the therapist over innocuous comments. After repeated efforts to motivate the patient and cautions that continued noncompliance would result in termination, the psychologist eventually terminated the patient. At their last session the patient refused to leave the office, but after 2 hours was cajoled into leaving. The patient continued to call the emergency service, refused to follow up with any recommendations for referrals, and appeared at the psychologist's office unannounced and told the patients in the waiting room that this psychologist had "ruined her life." (3.8.18)

Appropriately, after termination the psychologist refused to return emergency phone calls and had office staff handle the ex-patients' uninvited entrance into the office. The psychologist understood that contact with the ex-patient would result in intermittent reinforcement of intrusive behavior.

This psychologist knew the importance of establishing firm boundaries. Earlier in her career she knew an unfortunate colleague who, when faced with a similar situation, refunded fees to the patient in an effort to appease her. Unfortunately, the patient construed this as an admission of guilt and filed a malpractice suit.

The general rule is not to terminate or transfer patients who are in a crisis. However, the transfer of some patients who have a low level of chronic suicidality becomes a problem, especially if the termination temporarily increases suicidal ideation. The psychologist needs to carefully balance the long-term interests of the patient versus the short-term risks and recognize that in rare circumstances it may be necessary to terminate with patients who have a moderate risk of suicide. You should be reluctant to transfer a patient if the suicidal risk is severe or extreme. One psychologist reported that he continued to see a patient with a moderate risk of suicide for 3 months after informing the patient of the necessity to terminate. In this case the psychologist believed it was important for him to get a clearer baseline for the functioning of the patient and the immediacy of the risk of suicide. Also, this psychologist designated a fixed date for the termination. That firm date removed any ambiguity about the end of the relationship.

SUBTLE TERMINATIONS

At times, psychologists encounter patients who are ambivalent about treatment and give subtle or not so subtle indications that they intend to terminate treatment. The question arises as to how much energy the psychologist should put into persuading them to continue with treatment.

Much of the decision is context dependent. For a patient with a more transient disorder and substantial emotional and social (but not financial) resources, it would most likely be clinically indicated and sufficient to review the likely nature and course of therapy and feel confident that the patient can balance the advantages and costs of therapy without substantial harm.

On the other hand, some patients may have more serious disorders or evidence serious suicidal ideation. For these patients it may be clinically indicated and necessary to expend more effort. For example, you may make a phone call to check on how they are doing or send an encouraging reminder letter. You need to use your clinical judgment. The specific type of outreach varies from patient to patient, and for some patients, such an outreach may be interpreted as "ambulance chasing" or otherwise be clinically contraindicated.

> A psychologist was treating a seriously disturbed patient who displayed highly offensive behavior in the therapy sessions. It would have been the dream of the psychologist for her to go away and never come back, and he was aware that he might, without attempting to do so, discourage her from returning through nonverbal or other subtle responses. The psychologist was aware of this propensity on his part and did what he could to confront the problematic behaviors, address her presenting problems, and avoid creating an unpleasant therapeutic atmosphere that would encourage the patient to terminate. (3.8.19)

UNAVOIDABLE TERMINATIONS

Some involuntary terminations are unavoidable. Perhaps you are moving away or retiring. Or perhaps you have a physical illness that requires you to reduce the level of your workload. Perhaps you have a personal problem that impairs your ability to provide the necessary service (Standard 2.06b, Personal Problems and Conflicts). Perhaps you are pregnant and plan to take a maternity leave. Perhaps you are employed by a third party or as an independent contractor on a time-limited assignment.

From a clinical perspective, the unavoidable termination of a patient through retirement or the psychologist's pregnancy requires tact and sensitivity in introducing the topic to the patient and handling emotional reactions to it.

> A psychologist with a chronic health condition was required to undergo surgery that necessitated a long absence from her professional obligations. She had to balance the need to give an honest explanation to her patients about why she was withdrawing professional services temporarily (and would be back on only a limited basis afterward) with the need to protect her privacy. She was also concerned that in the small town where she lived, some patients might hear about her surgery from other persons in town. Consequently, she mailed a general letter to all of her current patients at the same time, briefly noting the changes in her professional service caused by her health condition and stating that they could discuss the issue in more detail at their next therapy session. (3.8.20)

This type of termination involves little risk of disciplinary actions, assuming that you have informed the patient in a reasonable period of time and have made reasonable efforts to facilitate the transfer of services (Standard 3.12, Interruption of Psychological Services).

If you are employed by or are participating in a contract relationship with a third party, you should

> *make reasonable efforts to provide for orderly and appropriate resolution of responsibility for client/patient care in the event that the employment or contractual relationship ends, with paramount consideration given to the welfare of the client/patient" (Standard 10.09, Interruption of Therapy).*

You may terminate a patient when the patient or a close friend or relative of a patient threatens you (Standard 10.10b, Termination Therapy).

OTHER UNCOVERED ABSENCES

It can be considered abandonment if you are unable to respond to patients' crises because of lack of an adequate on-call system or lack of adequate coverage when you are on vacation or because you are otherwise unavailable and fail to ensure that the patients understand the coverage arrangements. There are no absolute standards for coverage after hours or when you are on vacation that are appropriate for all psychologists. The exact nature of your after-hours or vacation coverage may vary according to the needs of your caseload. However, you should not take patients with certain serious diagnoses who are likely to need emergency services without making adequate provisions to be available to them.

> One psychologist saw clients primarily for career counseling or personal coaching, although she sometimes had patients with somewhat more serious mental health needs. Given her caseload, the likelihood of after-hours emergencies was quite low. (3.8.21)

> Another psychologist had a heavy caseload and often was unable to schedule patients for 2 or 3 weeks after their last appointment. His reduced availability for routine appointments greatly increased the likelihood that patients would use the after-hours emergency services. Both for risk management and clinical care reasons, this psychologist sought ways to reduce his caseload. (3.8.22)

Of course, psychologists should arrange for coverage when they are out of town or otherwise unavailable. The nature of the substitute coverage should be explained to patients at the beginning of treatment as part of the informed consent process. You should also reiterate your procedures for coverage to your patients before you leave town.

> A patient became outraged when she called the answering service of her therapist and received a return phone call from another therapist who was covering for her. The patient filed a complaint with the licensing board alleging a breach of confidentiality. Fortunately, the treating psychologist could produce an informed consent document signed by the patient informing her that the psychologist shared after-hours coverage with several other psychologists when she went out of town. Although the psychologist was exonerated from any wrongdoing, the whole episode might have been avoided if the psychologist had reminded the patient of this policy. (3.8.23)

Application of Risk Management Procedures to the Detailed Case Example

The clinical situation described in the detailed case example presented in Section 1 illustrates some of the important considerations when deciding to terminate patients against their will.

As noted in Section 3, chapter 7, Assessing and Treating Patients Who Are Potentially Suicidal or Dangerous to Others, it is not clear if this patient is in the moderate or severe range of suicidal risk. Because this patient may present a high risk, you should get more information and seek consultation before concluding that you should terminate the patient. The focus of the consultation should be on the suicidal risk of the patient, whether you can be of benefit to this patient, whether the service is iatrogenic, and what options could be available for this patient.

If you decide to terminate, you should document that you discussed the termination with your patient and gave her reasons why you decided to terminate. The documentation should be detailed and include clinical reasons why treatment is no longer in her best interest. Your treatment notes provide an opportunity to present your reasoning including the pros and cons of continuing treatment. Be certain to give her referral information for further treatment. If permitted by the patient and clinically indicated, communicate to the parents why the decision was made to terminate treatment.

Be prepared to receive substantial hostility from the patient if you decide to terminate against the patient's wishes. After the termination date, be prepared for a barrage of phone calls, e-mails, and other communications. Responding to these advances may reinforce the patient and encourage her to make further attempts to contact you.

Seven Essential Points to Remember

1. A consulting relationship is between legal equals.

2. Except in narrow circumstances, supervisors are legally responsible for the actions of their supervisees.

3. Supervisors can greatly reduce legal risks by carefully selecting and monitoring their supervisees.

4. Psychologists who are insensitive to the unique needs of diverse populations risk providing a substandard quality of care.

5. You may terminate patients if they do not pay for services or are not benefiting from services. Do not terminate patients who are in a crisis.

6. Work hard to ensure that you and your patients agree on the need to terminate. If you must terminate a patient, be sure that you thoroughly explain the reasons to your patient, document the discussion, and if the patient needs more treatment, provide referrals.

7. Address problems with employers with tact and sensitivity. Be prepared to be assertive if the employer is showing disregard for public welfare or safety.

Chapter 9: **THE RELUCTANT BUSINESS PERSON**

Many psychologists are reluctant business persons. They entered the field to deliver health care services and do not wish to be bothered with the business aspects of practice such as advertising, collecting and paying bills, following up on insurance claims, and pursuing unpaid debts. Nonetheless, psychological practice is a business, and the manner in which psychologists conduct their business can have a substantial impact on the quality of their careers. Tasteful advertising and efficient billing practices can give patients a favorable impression. Fee disputes can spill over into the clinical area and dissatisfaction with clinical services can be reflected in nonpayment of fees. Misunderstandings or disagreements about fees often precipitate charges of professional misconduct from disgruntled patients.

While it is not illegal to run an inefficient or disorganized business, those distractions may prevent you from attending to your professional responsibilities. Because you are responsible, both ethically and legally, for the actions that others take on your behalf, you should choose all employees carefully, including those who provide support services such as accounting, answering services, and other psychology-related services (see Section 3, chap. 8 on supervision concerning procedures for hiring and supervising employees).

RISK MANAGEMENT FORMULA

When we think of the risk management formula,

$$\text{Clinical risk} = \frac{(P \times C \times D)}{TF}$$

In this formula, P = patient risk characteristics; C = context; D = disciplinary consequences; and TF = therapist factors.

we can see business issues have an impact on several levels.

Misunderstandings about the nature of services or the fee arrangement can cause some patients to be more hostile or suspicious of the psychologist. An office that has a clearly written and defined set of office policies sets a professional context for treatment. Furthermore, a psychologist who produces distasteful or misleading advertising or who is unclear or inconsistent about billing and fees can create a poor impression or engender discontent and a sense of betrayal among patients.

FINDING PATIENTS THROUGH MARKETING YOUR SERVICES

The first impression that patients may have of you is through your marketing, a general term that includes all activities by which you let others know about your services. Marketing includes word of mouth, professional business cards, advertising in yellow pages and magazines, online services, and more. Although you want your advertising to attract patients, it is important to consider your advertising carefully so that you convey accurate information in a tasteful manner. Of course, you must avoid advertising that is false, deceptive, or misleading. Try to be scrupulously accurate in what you put in your advertisements. Avoid vanity credentials (see Section 3, chap. 1, Competence). Include only those degrees that are from regionally accredited universities or that were the basis on which you became licensed.

> A psychologist developed an extensive practice in sports psychology. It appeared to be a natural extension of her earlier career as a health education teacher. Her advertisement represented her credentials as "M. Brown, Psy.D., licensed psychologist, Ph.D. in *physical education.*" That way potential clients would more clearly understand her training and credentials. (3.9.1)

Make certain that brochures or business cards are of good quality and tastefully done. Some psychologists claim so many areas of expertise on their professional business cards that one, at first, would question their integrity. It is increasingly common for psychologists to have professional Web sites. Often these contain articles on a particular topic designed to attract interested persons to the psychologists' Web sites. Great effort should be put into advertorials to ensure that they are accurate, up-to-date, and helpful.

> A psychologist with a specialty in anxiety disorders had a well-developed Web site that included links to the Anxiety Disorders Association of America and other specialty organizations. He included several reviews he had written on contemporary books on the treatment of anxiety disorders and other brief but useful articles. Among other things, he gave a fair and balanced review of the relative roles of the nonpharmacological and pharmacological options for treatment. (3.9.2)

However, marketing your services will involve more than just advertising. Psychologists also market their practices through speaking engagements. One psychologist gave a series of lectures on autism at a local bookstore. Another psychologist gave a grand rounds lecture at the local hospital on psychological aspects of fertility. Another psychologist spoke to local churches on the psychological aspects of international and interracial adoptions.

> A psychologist who had been a well-known local athlete acquired a doctorate in psychology and then returned to practice in the town where he attended undergraduate school. He lectured on the problems associated with head trauma in sports and developed a head trauma protocol for student athletes. Several high schools adopted his protocol when a high school athlete died after returning to practice prematurely from a head injury. (3.9.3)

Do not minimize the social value of your work. Of course, psychologists need to be appropriately humble. Psycholgists do not have the knowledge or skills to help all persons. But they do have considerable knowledge and skills that can substantially improve the lives of their patients. In public presentations you should put your best foot forward. Ensure that your information is accurate and up-to-date. Don't be afraid to say "I don't know." Don't be flustered by questions and rude behavior.

> Once while giving a presentation a psychologist was interrupted by a member of the audience who claimed that psychologists were people who weren't good enough to get into med school; psychology was a pseudoscience; and chemists and physicists were the real scientists. The psychologist responded tactfully and patiently to these comments. After the presentation the commentator said privately "I was just testing you." (3.9.4)

Get involved with your community not only through local events but also through your local or state psychological association. Serve on committees and do not hold yourself above doing "grunt work" if it needs to be done. In addition to contributing to the profession and probably learning some things of value, professional associations are an important source for professional contacts (Wunsch, 2005).

LOOK AT YOUR WHOLE PRACTICE

Attending carefully to the details of your practice can ensure the overall quality of your work experience. For example, many psychologists take special steps to incorporate a sense of beauty into their offices. They may select wall paintings that are especially meaningful for them. One psychologist had a stunning painting given to him by a former patient who had made significant progress following a severe brain trauma. It reminded him of the human determination to thrive despite adversity. Another psychologist decorated her office beautifully and always had classical music playing in the office. Psychologists should ensure that their office furniture is comfortable, thus conveying their sense to their patients that they are important and valued.

Details such as the availability of parking, lighting of the street outside of the office, cleanliness of rest rooms, tidiness of the waiting area, and sound control within the office area can influence overall patient satisfaction with your services.

BILLING AND BILL COLLECTION

Billing issues should be considered from the very first contact with prospective patients. It is prudent to establish the patient's ability to pay before services begin. You should not accept patients into your practice who cannot pay for services unless you are willing to accept them at a reduced rate consistent with their ability to pay. You can minimize patient dissatisfaction by clearly explaining policies on fees ahead of time. It is desirable to inform patients of the fee, what services are billed, when payment is due, use of credit cards, and other aspects of billing. Give patients a written policy when they begin therapy (see the American Psychological Association Insurance Trust's [the Trust] sample Psychologist-Patient Agreement at www.apait.org).

Explaining the billing procedures clearly helps patients to make an informed decision about whether they want to pursue treatment with you. Try to ensure that they clearly understand relevant billing practices. True informed consent means more than just getting the patient's signature on an informed consent form. Although the patient's signature may ensure your right to pursue collection of disputed fees, when patients do not pay their bills you have an area of contention that may impede the quality of the treatment relationship. Also, from a risk management perspective, you have a disgruntled patient who may look for other grounds on which to formally complain about you.

The office practices of psychologists vary considerably with regard to insurance payments. Some psychologists bill the insurance company themselves; others accept only payment directly from the patient. Many psychologists contract directly with insurers or managed care companies. Unless specified otherwise in a contract between the psychologist and an insurer or managed care company, the professional relationship exists between the psychologist and the patient, not between the psychologist and the insurance company. Regardless of payment arrangements, the services provided will be judged according to the accepted ethical standards and practice guidelines governing the profession. The standards that apply to treatment of paying patients apply equally to pro bono or volunteer services.

Psychologists vary on how they handle insurance billing for couples. The relevant questions are Who is the identified patient? Does this individual have a disorder covered by the insurance policy? Is the treatment directed toward relieving this disorder? If so, a chart can be opened on that patient and the insurance company can be billed. Of course, the spouse may attend the sessions as a collateral contact. Most insurance companies do not pay for marital enrichment alone. If a patient lacks a diagnosis from the most recent manual for mental disorders, then most insurers will not pay for the services.

> A psychologist accepted a young man into treatment for his anxiety that was, among other things, creating strains in his marriage. His wife attended several sessions as a collateral contact. The psychologist billed the insurance company for treating the man. (3.9.5)

The psychologist was acting appropriately. The patient had a diagnosis; the treatment was directed toward alleviating the diagnosis; and the wife attended therapy in a clearly collateral context.

> A psychologist accepted both members of a couple who were having marital problems into treatment. Although the wife was in substantial distress, the husband was not. The psychologist saw them together and directed therapy at alleviating the distress of the wife, with the husband acting in a supportive role. The psychologist billed several sessions under the wife's name and then several sessions under the husband's name. He gave the husband the diagnosis of adjustment disorder, even though it could not be justified on the basis of the clinical presentation. (3.9.6)

This psychologist's procedures were problematic. He should not have given the husband a diagnosis that was not justified, even if it was necessary to secure additional insurance reimbursement. In contrast to the first psychologist, the psychologist gave a diagnosis that was not warranted, could not be justified by the treatment notes, and did not guide treatment.

The routine practice of giving unwarranted diagnoses or otherwise systematically misrepresenting services is an example of insurance fraud, which is the systematic misrepresentation of billing information for personal gain (Kalb, 1999). Even the most honest health care providers sometimes make a billing error or misunderstand an ambiguous billing procedure. Of course, all psychologists should try to bill as accurately as possible. However, conscientious psychologists should not become unduly concerned about being charged with fraud. On the other hand, those psychologists who routinely misrepresent information to insurance companies could be charged with fraud. In the example above, the actions of the second psychologist could be interpreted as fraud.

Waive copayments only on a case-by-case basis and only if permitted by the insurer and state or federal law. Some psychologists establish sliding fee scales. Although we appreciate the attempt to make services affordable to persons who otherwise cannot afford services, such arrangements may create problems. It is hard to be entirely fair in establishing sliding scales. Patients may learn that others are paying less for services than they are; there is the potential that some patients may abuse the sliding fee scale; and you need to ensure that the sliding scale does not put you in violation of insurance contracts you have signed. Some psychologists have stopped using sliding scales but will waive a portion of the fee on a case-by-case basis as needed. We are aware of instances in which the misuse of sliding scales has resulted in charges of insurance fraud.

Some psychologists barter on occasion. At times it can be a mutually rewarding experience. However, you need to use caution and refrain from bartering when it is exploitative or clinically contraindicated. One suggestion is to barter only when the value of bartered objects is agreed on in advance. Bartering for services creates a greater possibility of misunderstanding or ill feelings and may create problems with the IRS. Bartering should rarely, if ever, be used. There are far better ways to receive payment for services than barter.

> A psychologist allowed a patient to pay off part of his debt by providing lawn care to her home and office building. The patient dutifully spent three hours mowing the lawn, but he did not trim the grass along the sidewalk nor did he sweep the grass clippings off the sidewalk. The psychologist felt she was

> getting second-rate service. When she confronted her patient on the quality of his service, he was indignant, noting that the $40 she paid him was far below average payment for equivalent services. Both parties believed they had been short-changed in the deal. (3.9.7)

It is commendable for psychologists to have a sense of fairness in all business practices.

> A psychologist had a private practice and worked as a school psychologist in a local school district. He was approached by parents who requested that he conduct a psychological evaluation on their child. The psychologist listened to their concerns but then suggested that they contact the school where the testing could be done for free. (3.9.8)

This psychologist understood the potential conflict of interest and showed consideration for the welfare of the family. He genuinely saw himself as a person who wanted to promote the interests of his patients. He also understood that the parents might feel betrayed if they later learned that the school district would have done the same testing without charge.

However, there is a difference between being compassionate and being a doormat. Avoid allowing a patient's bills to accumulate. If patients are unable to pay, you can make special payment arrangements; the patient can use credit cards; or the patient can take out a loan to make payments. Many patients go into debt for something they perceive as valuable, such as a new TV set, and the same rules should apply to therapy if they perceive it as valuable. However, it is unwise to let unpaid bills accumulate without addressing the issues directly with your patients. Unfortunately, some patients have a sense of entitlement and will take advantage of you.

> Whenever he did psychological testing, a psychologist always ensured that the patients paid for the entire testing ahead of time. Parents or patients may sometimes complete the testing and then refuse to pay, especially if they are not totally satisfied with the results. However, once the testing is completed, the patents have a right to the test report because it is part of the protected health information under the Health Insurance Portability and Accountability Act (HIPAA). (3.9.9)

> Another psychologist took an imprint of the patient's credit card with the intention of billing for any services that were unpaid at the end of the month. While this is not inherently unethical, it would be preferable to have the patients pay at the time of each service. (3.9.10)

As long as you have informed patients ahead of time, you may charge them for any professional services you provide. While we would not recommend nickel-and-diming patients for brief phone calls, brief notes to other professionals, or other de minimus services, we would recommend that you inform them of the cost of performing professional services of substance, such as a detailed consultation with an attorney or a detailed letter that takes considerable time to produce.

Of course, you may terminate patients because they have not paid for services. However, do so cautiously. Ascertain why they have not paid for service, and if possible, negotiate a payment plan or discuss other payment arrangements. If patients must be terminated for nonpayment of services, refer them for any needed services (see Section 3, chap. 8 on termination and abandonment).

Use bill collection agencies with discretion or not at all. Never use a collection agency "on principle" or to "teach the patient a lesson." The use of collection agencies is a billing and risk management decision, and any sense of betrayal or anger should not be a factor in your decision. Some patients fail to pay their bills because they are inconsiderate or insensitive to their obligations to others. They may have had no intention of making payment in the first place and have no intention of doing so now. Using collection agencies or attempting to collect an outstanding balance can precipitate an allegation of misconduct against you, especially if the patients thought the services they received were unsatisfactory or unhelpful

Select and use collection agencies carefully because they are acting on your behalf, and you are ultimately responsible for their actions. If they are abusive or unprofessional, it will reflect poorly on you. If you use a collection agency, provide no more information than necessary (e.g., amount owed) to protect the patient's right to privacy (Standard 4.04, Minimizing Intrusions on Privacy). Alert patients before turning over the account for collection, and give them an opportunity to make payment arrangements.

DEALING WITH INSURANCE COMPANIES AND MANAGED CARE ORGANIZATIONS

Absent a contract specifying otherwise, ensure that your patients know that they, not the insurance company, are ultimately responsible for payment of services. If you are operating under a managed care organization's (MCO) contract, be scrupulous about recording and following the billing procedures of the insurer. You must fully understand the specific provisions of each MCO contact that you have entered and be able to interpret the requirements of each contract to your patients covered under that contract.

Clarify session limits with the patient as early in the treatment as possible. In doing so, you will be heading off allegations of abandonment, which is the abrupt ending of services during a time of need. Discuss with your patients the treatment options that will be available should more care be needed than the contract will provide. Options may include referral to a low-cost center and shifting to a fee-for-service system with you at full or reduced rates (Acuff et al., 1999). Read your contracts carefully to determine if they permit you to enter into private fee arrangements with patients for covered or noncovered services.

The risk management features we discussed in Section 2 have relevance for this topic. Informed consent is important for informing patients about fees in that it reduces the likelihood of a sense of betrayal. Also, documentation is important in that it provides evidence that the patient agreed to the billing and fee arrangements.

RUNNING A PROFESSIONAL OFFICE

Psychologists vary in the business arrangements of their practices. Some operate sole proprietorships, while others have professional corporations, partnerships, or other business arrangements. Consult with professionals before deciding which business arrangement is best for you.

It is common for psychologists to share office arrangements or services in a way that gives an appearance of a group practice. They may have a central reception or waiting area, share secretarial services, have a common phone number or letterhead, share advertising in the yellow pages or local newspapers, or otherwise give an impression that they are a professional group. There is nothing wrong with such arrangements. Indeed, they can be convenient in that they reduce overhead for each practitioner involved. However, such loosely organized groups have special risk management implications. If one partner is sued, the other parties may be implicated in the suit on the basis of their public appearance as members of a group practice. You can take measures to limit such impressions by using a disclaimer, indicating the separateness of the professionals in your privacy notice, or having public notices that you are not affiliated. Check with your attorney for advice regarding the risk involved with loosely associated group practices. Check with your malpractice carrier about your coverage if you are named as a defendant when allegations are made against your colleague. Most malpractice carriers will provide coverage for this risk for a modest premium.

If you provide services in an unusual setting or under unusual circumstances (e.g., in the residence of a patient or group therapy in your living room), do your patients understand that the setting is incidental to your role as a professional? Clearly establish the ground rules to help maintain the professional relationship.

Make certain you have office and professional liability insurance and know the extent of your coverage. Get the appropriate business associate agreements signed as required by HIPAA.

WHEN EMPLOYEES LEAVE

One major source of ill feelings may be the departure of directors, officers, or employees from group practices. When someone leaves a group practice, the individual often wants to take his or her patients and patient records with him or her. Although it is not a major source of professional liability complaints for psychologists, it often leads to ill feelings that could have been avoided if problems had been anticipated and discussed ahead of time. It is best to develop a written agreement that clarifies the parameters of leaving the practice. The terms of the agreement should give the highest priority to the welfare of the patients.

Sometimes employers have restrictive covenants that prohibit employees from practicing within a certain mile radius or for a certain period of time after leaving the practice. For example, a restrictive covenant might prohibit a former employee from practicing within 5 miles of the group practice for 1 year after leaving. Some courts have overturned these types of noncompete agreements because they are too restrictive. It is also problematic for patients if such noncompete clauses are enforced because the restrictions reduce the choices of the patient who may want to continue with the departing employee.

Seven Essential Points to Remember

1. Be tasteful and accurate in marketing your services. Claiming too much expertise in too many areas of practice diminishes your credibility.

2. Informed consent and documentation are very important in reducing patient dissatisfaction about fees or billing policies.

3. Do not let debts accumulate. Be aware of the risks involved in using bill collection agencies and small claims courts.

4. Invest time and effort in ensuring the professionalism of your support staff.

5. Clarify employment agreements ahead of time.

6. If you hire professional employees, establish a policy ahead of time concerning the disposition of cases and patient records in the event that your employees leave your practice.

7. Although loosely organized groups may have financial advantages, you may need to take special steps to reduce your liability for the actions of other members of the group.

Section 3:
APPLICATIONS OF THE RISK MANAGEMENT MODEL

Chapter 10: **CLOSING A PRACTICE AND RETIREMENT**

Retire: To withdraw from one's occupation, business, or office; to stop working

INTRODUCTION

Retirement from practice is an issue that eventually must be addressed by all psychologists. Retirement can come about in many ways; a systematically planned cessation of practice; death or disability; an externally imposed change in lifestyle; a decision to change careers, or a necessary relocation, to name a few. Like taxes, retirement is inevitable and it is highly advisable for all psychologists to have a plan to address the numerous issues they will face when the golden years approach.

The purpose of this chapter is to identify the major issues involved and to provide some guidance on managing risk during this phase of life. Much of the following advice and many of the examples we use apply to psychologists who provide psychotherapeutic or counseling services. We must keep in mind, however, that, in addition to psychologists who provide direct health care services, retirement will impact all psychologists, including those who are primarily engaged in teaching, research, industrial organizational consultation, or evaluative or forensic services. Psychologists in these various areas of practice will face unique challenges when retirement is reached.

WHEN IS RETIREMENT, RETIREMENT?

One of the wonderful things about the profession of psychology is that there is no mandatory retirement age. If you love your work and can continue to provide services competently, age may not be a determinant in the retirement equation. Psychologists in good health can continue to be engaged in the practice of psychology long after they close their full-time practice. Part-time teaching, consultation, supervision, and pro bono work opportunities are readily available for senior citizen psychologists, especially those well known in their community. It is a wise person who remains active during retirement years. Former APA President Dr. Diane Halpern strongly advised psychologists to engage in volunteer work during retirement (2004). Psychologists who follow this advice should remember that they are still providing psychological services. The liabilities and risks associated with providing health care services, teaching, consultation, supervisions, testing, and a myriad other activities, whether for a fee or pro bono, remain the same as during preretirement years.

PART-TIME PRACTICE AND PRACTICE DURING RETIREMENT

Many psychologists retire from practice and then provide voluntary or pro bono services to organizations or agencies. This can take the form of consulting, seeing the occasional patient, teaching, or supervising staff. Some believe they are retired when they stop providing psychotherapeutic services even though they continue to provide other psychological services pro bono. In a sense they have retired from their major area of practice but, from a risk management perspective, they are still providing professional services and could be held liable for mistakes or bad outcomes.

For many psychologists retirement is viewed more as a transition to a different level or kind of work than a termination of all professional activities. Many psychologists who retire continue their same line of work, although at a lower frequency. Others take part-time jobs in related fields or volunteer their services. A survey of APA members showed that 64% of psychologists who planned to retire expected to continue working part-time as psychologists (Chamberlain, 2004).

One retired psychologist took an adjunct faculty position at a nearby university. Another psychologist continued to see patients part-time through a local group practice, although she was careful not to see the more difficult cases. Another psychologist volunteered as a supervisor for a local shelter for abused women, while another retired clinician provided evaluations of students in a local private school.

The good Samaritan aspects of these commendable contributions should not override the risk management concerns. The same issues concerning risk management apply here as in other professional services. In such situations it is important to restrict your services to areas of competence and keep up-to-date with the literature. Unfortunately, some perhaps not-so-well-meaning and litigious patients may seek disciplinary actions against psychologists for what they perceive as incompetence or misconduct, even though these psychologists are volunteering or working for nonprofit organizations for a minimal or token salary. Even if you continue to provide a reduced level of professional services post retirement, whether for a small fee or pro bono, you should maintain your professional liability insurance to protect you from any risks associated with those services during the period of part-time retirement.

Well-meaning leaders of charitable organizations may pressure you into providing or supervising clinical services. No doubt, many psychologists make valuable contributions through such services, and our comments should not be construed as trying to discourage you from contributing to worthwhile organizations or maintaining a connection with the profession you practiced for a great part of your life. However, your services can be more meaningful for both you and the organization if you conscientiously apply the risk management principles we have discussed in this book.

If you are approached to provide limited services during your retirement years, it is important to clarify exactly what is being asked of you. Are you a supervisor (where you assume full clinical responsibility for services) or a consultant (where you provide input that the agency can choose to accept or reject as it sees fit)? While functioning in the role of a consultant may reduce your exposure for damages, it does not eliminate the possibility that a suit could be filed against you. Ensure that you are competent to provide the services required, and insist that certain patient protections and risk management standards be maintained. The agency or organization may be willing to pay the cost for you to maintain your professional liability insurance as a token fee for your services.

> A retired psychologist was approached by the Chair of the Board of Directors of a local HIV/AIDS clinic to become a supervisor of counseling services. However, over time the paraprofessional counselors working at the clinic had evolved their own independent and idiosyncratic styles of intervention and strongly opposed the decision to appoint a supervisor. There was a possibility that the paraprofessional counselors might sabotage the efforts to retain the services of the supervising psychologist at the clinic. It was apparent to the psychologist that the Chair of the Board had not thought through the implications of the decision to seek these special services. Did he want to reign in the volunteers or was he looking for a figurehead consultant to add prestige to the clinic? (3.10.1)

The psychologist met with the volunteer paraprofessional counselors and demonstrated that she was going to be respectful of their perspectives. The psychologist was able to gain the trust of the volunteer paraprofessionals; they soon modified their strong stand against working with the psychologist. The psychologist also consulted with the Chair of the Board and helped him to clarify his expectations of her role.

RETIREMENT PLANNING

How you go about closing a practice depends on a variety of factors, including the nature of the practice, whether you are closing your practice temporarily (such as for parental or sick leave) or permanently, and whether you have a solo practice or work with others in a group practice or an agency setting. Sometimes the transition will be planned, welcomed, and expected. However, you also need to think about the difficult issues that your death or disability may create.[1] In any event, you should plan well ahead for retirement and consider your own needs as well of those of your patients, office partners, and other affected persons (Koocher, 2003).

The 2002 American Psychological Association's "Ethical Principles of Psychologists and Code of Conduct" (APA Ethics Code) requires that

[1] From "Some (Relatively) Simple Risk Management Strategies," by E. Harris, 2004 Spring/Summer, *MassPsych: The Journal of the Massachusetts Psychological Association, 48,* 27-28. Copyright 2004 by the Massachusetts Psychological Association. Adapted with permission of the author.

> *unless otherwise covered by contract, psychologists make reasonable efforts to plan for facilitating services in the event that psychological services are interrupted by factors such as the psychologist's illness, death, unavailability, relocation, or retirement* (Standard 3.12, Interruption of Psychological Services)

and that they

> *make plans in advance to facilitate the appropriate transfer and to protect the confidentiality of records* (Standard 6.02c, Maintenance, Dissemination, and Disposal of Confidential Records of Professional and Scientific Work).

On first appearance, it seems that your professional liability risks would end for you and your loved ones when you have retired. This is not always true.

> A psychologist in solo practice died suddenly in a car accident. His widow, who was not a trained health care provider and had no involvement in his practice, was forced to deal with the complications of closing his practice while, at the same time, trying to handle her grief and the other complications caused by his sudden death. Since she did not understand how to handle confidential records, she announced her intention to hold a "records open house" where former patients could come to the office, go to her late husband's office files, and retrieve their psychotherapy records. Local psychologists who learned of her plan intervened and suggested more appropriate ways to handle those records. (3.10.2)

Planning thoughtfully for retirement means making many decisions, including, but not limited to, when to close your office, when to stop taking new referrals, when and how to tell your patients that you are retiring, when to take down your web pages, and when to notify your referral sources. You will also need to decide to whom you will be referring current patients who will need on-going treatment after you retire, and how you will handle contractual obligations such as office leases, bank accounts, billing services, managed care organization contracts, and phone answering services. In addition, you need to be aware of the ethical and statutory requirements for keeping records after you retire, proper procedures for forwarding patient records, if requested, protocols for responding to inquiries from patients after you retire, and other practice matters.

Clinical Issues

It may be prudent to set a firm date for closing your practice well in advance and to announce this to patients and other interested parties well ahead of time. Ideally, at some predetermined time, you should simply not take on any new cases and allow for the gradual attrition of current patients. However, the therapy for some patients will have to be interrupted at the point of retirement and you will need to refer them for additional care. Some patients, especially those with chronic needs, may react with anger, loss, or a sense of abandonment upon learning of your retirement and may need more time to process the change. It is important to identify your patients who may react in this way and give them ample notice of your retirement so they have the additional time to work through these issues.

In small communities, where information travels quickly by word of mouth, you may wish to inform all your patients about your plan to close your practice at the same time. One way to guarantee consistency of information is to send all current and recently terminated patients a letter announcing your retirement and the closing of your practice. Ragusea (2002) has presented such a sample letter. There is, however, a risk with using this generic notification procedure, especially with current or former patients whose spouse or family members may not know they are in treatment with you and inadvertently intercept the letter. In some states, this technically could be a breach of confidentiality. It may be prudent to handle such situations personally by phone.

Use your discretion in deciding which former patients to notify. Some former patients will appreciate knowing your decision, and it may help them avoid inconvenience and emotional upset if they feel they need additional services and always thought that you would be available. In addition, some former patients may wish to have their records transferred to another provider.

How much information should you give to patients concerning the reason for your retirement? The decision to retire may not be entirely voluntary, and may be prompted by growing health concerns, family obligations, or other occurrences outside your control. Patients vary in the extent to which they need to know or can handle this type of information. These are individual clinical decisions that need special consideration.

Psychologists with assessment-based or consultative practices face many of the same problems therapists do when they retire. While relationship-based issues common in psychotherapeutic practices may be less important for psychologists primarily engaged in assessment or consultation, the problems with referral, maintenance, and transfer of records, and access to and the management of clinical information are much the same. All of these areas must be addressed in order to minimize risk.

Be certain that you have informed managed care companies and meaningful referral sources. If you sell your practice to another provider or wish to recommend other providers for former patients, the letter can provide the necessary information. Remember, in some states (e.g., New York) patient records may not be turned over to a purchaser or successor practitioner without a written authorization from the patient. Also, for those subject to the HIPAA Privacy Rule and who keep psychotherapy notes, it appears from a strict reading of the HIPAA regulations that, absent a properly signed authorization, those psychotherapy notes cannot be transferred *to anyone* (including practice partners, purchasers, and estate executors). This issue could be addressed in your patient consent form that is provided to all patients at the beginning of services. Keep in mind that psychotherapy notes may only be released with a patient's authorization. A sentence or two in the patient consent form describing how records and psychotherapy notes would be handled if you close your practice should suffice. You may need to indicate that a separate authorization will be required to transfer or release any psychotherapy notes. If you are selling your practice, it would be prudent to work closely with an attorney familiar with the laws and regulations regarding confidentiality, record keeping and record transfer in your state, and the requirements of the HIPAA Privacy Rule.

As noted below, from a risk management position, it is preferable to make professional referrals while you are still covered by your malpractice insurance policy rather than after you have terminated your professional liability insurance policy.

Learn your state laws concerning retirement. Some states require you to publish ads in the paper. If this is required, then you should also specify this in your advance directive or professional will.

Part of your planning may involve the development of a referral list for current and former patients. In some cases, it may be desirable to speak with the new therapist personally. You need to obtain patient consent for providing copies of your records to new therapists. However, retain the originals of all patient records for the period of time legally required by your state law, or the APA Record Keeping Guidelines if your state does not have a law on record retention.

You may consider placing your license on inactive status. Many psychologists desire to maintain their license on full active status to provide flexibility should they decide to provide services in the future. Others keep their license active in order to maintain a professional identity. If you terminate your license and continue to practice psychology, you may be subject to an investigation and fine from the licensing board for practicing without a license. In addition, if you terminate your license but maintain your professional liability insurance, any claim brought against you may not be covered by your insurance because professional liability policies generally do not cover the unlawful practice of psychology.

Of course, you need to consider the possibility that you will want to return to professional practice and the cost in terms of reactivating the license (for example, you should learn the mandatory continuing education requirements, if any, for reactivating your license). However, one fact to consider is that, if a complaint were filed against you, the Board might not allow you to surrender an active license to avoid prosecution.

Business and Practical Issues

You also need to attend to business issues. Close unnecessary bank accounts, and review and, as appropriate, terminate leases, office agreements, contracts with billing agencies, answering services, agreements for marketing and advertising your services, ads or columns in local newspapers, or other contracts with business associates. If possible, settle unpaid accounts before you retire. Inform employees, colleagues, referral sources, and others who are associated or have been associated with your practice.

INSURANCE

The best risk management advice we can give to senior citizen colleagues who are semiretired is to maintain your professional liability insurance during your retirement years if you plan to continue to provide psychological services, even if for reduced or no fees on a very part-time basis. While this advice, on first glance, could appear to favor the interests of the insurance industry, the value of this recommendation will be instantly clear if a malpractice suit or licensing board complaint is filed against a semiretired practitioner who is uninsured. A malpractice suit against an uninsured retired psychologist could potentially wipeout the entire retirement savings portfolio. In the final analysis, it is a business decision where cost is weighed against the risk of a negative outcome.

If you are providing pro bono services for an agency or clinic, you might want to negotiate with the clinic to pay the cost of your insurance or provide you with legal assurances that the clinic will indemnify you for all the services you are to perform for the clinic.

Some of the basic differences between an occurrence-based and a claims-made professional liability insurance policy become glaringly apparent at the time of retirement. An occurrence-based professional liability policy covers incidents that occurred while the policy was in force regardless of when the claim is filed. Therefore, a claim filed after an occurrence policy has been terminated will be covered but only if it relates to professional services rendered while the policy was in force. If you cancel your occurrence policy and are sued sometime in the future for something you did while the policy was in force, you will be covered for that claim, subject to the terms and conditions of the policy. If you provide any professional services after the policy has been canceled, however, you will not be covered for these additional services.

A claims-made professional liability insurance policy covers an incident that occurred and was filed while the policy was in force. Unfortunately, claims against psychologists generally take some time to be filed. A significant percentage of claims based on alleged negligence in any particular year will be filed in future years. To ensure continued coverage after a claims-made policy has been terminated, the psychologist may purchase an Extended Reporting Period endorsement, commonly referred to as "tail coverage." Some malpractice carriers, including the policy issued through the Trust-Sponsored Professional Liability Program, offer a free tail upon your complete retirement, or if you become disabled for six months and are not able to practice, or if you die. (See chap. 11 for more information on these types of coverages.)

If you cancel your claims-made insurance policy and are sued sometime in the future for something you did while the policy was in force, you will not be covered for that claim unless you have purchased the tail coverage or received a free tail upon retirement. When cancelling or nonrenewing a claims-made policy as part of your retirement planning, always be sure to request the free tail. Of equal importance, you should instruct your spouse, partner, colleague, or personal representative to request the free tail on behalf of your estate in the case of your untimely death.

Here are a few final thoughts on professional liability insurance. If you have cancelled or not renewed your professional liability insurance policy we strongly recommend that you discontinue *all* professional activity. If you had a claims-made policy, be certain to acquire unlimited tail coverage. If you are insured through the Trust-Sponsored Professional Liability Insurance Program, you may obtain a free tail upon your full retirement from all practice, but you must make this election within 60 days of the expiration of the policy. With a claims-made policy it is inadvisable to try to save a few dollars by purchasing a policy with lower limits of coverage during the year immediately proceeding retirement. If you purchase lower limits of coverage during the final year of practice, those lower limits will apply to all claims brought in the future.

THE SLIPPERY SLOPE OF PRACTICE DURING RETIREMENT

If you receive a request for records after you have cancelled your professional liability policy, it is not a good idea to respond by reevaluating the data or offering a summary rather than the record itself. Reevaluating the data for the current request or writing the summary would be considered a new professional act that may not be a covered event. The postretirement release of records that were developed and maintained during your active practice when your policy was in force is an extension of your past practice, and may possibly be covered either under a terminated occurrence policy or a claims-made policy with the appropriate tail coverage. On the other hand, the act of creating a summary of the record or assisting someone in interpreting the record is a new professional act for which you have no insurance coverage. If you must testify at a hearing or deposition pursuant to a subpoena or court order, you should not offer any professional opinions. Testifying in court or at a deposition in any role other than that of a percipient or fact witness may constitute a new professional service and any lawsuit or licensing board complaint resulting from that activity may not be covered by a terminated professional liability policy. These are complicated and tricky situations. It would be prudent to consult with legal counsel before responding to a court order or subpoena.

You should be careful when a former patient contacts you concerning a referral. Keep in mind that one of the reasons psychologists are sued is for improper referral. If a former patient requests information on where he or she should go for services, you can refer the patient to his or her family physician, the managed care company if one is involved, another provider who has agreed to assist in the referral process, or a local or state psychological association that may have a referral service. Avoid recommending a specific practitioner. If you highly recommend a specific referral source and something goes wrong with the future treatment, you increase the likelihood that you could be named as a defendant in a malpractice suit alleging "improper referral." When making postretirement referrals, it would be prudent to provide the person with three names and state that you do not have current information other than that the person is listed as licensed.

Be prudent on giving psychological advice, even in social situations. This advice is applicable both pre- and postretirement. Engaging in this type of activity after retirement is potentially more problematic, especially if you have cancelled your professional liability insurance. Well-meaning professionals, thinking they were being polite or helpful while at a social function, have been criticized (and sometimes sued) for giving professional advice. The key is whether a professional relationship has been established when giving advice in a nonprofessional setting such as a social event. A plaintiff's attorney will argue strongly that the recipient of the advice thought it was a professional service, that is, in the eye of the beholder it was a professional request and a professional service. Needless to say, this can be dangerous territory.

Be prepared to receive inquiries from former patients and third-party sources for several years after you retire. This may mean responding to requests for records or even a subpoena for your testimony on a case you evaluated several years ago.

> Three years after a forensic psychologist retired, an attorney contacted her, requesting her test results and records on one of the psychologist's former clients. The attorney suggested that the psychologist's records and testimony might be needed for a personal injury case in which her records might have had some relevance. The attorney provided a signed authorization and wanted to use the materials in a case. The psychologist sent the unaltered records in response to an appropriately signed release and informed the attorney of the charges for her services if called to testify. The psychologist was aware that testifying in court about the examination would constitute new professional services. The activities factored in the psychologist's realization that she needed to reactivate her professional liability insurance. (3.10.3)

SUDDEN CLOSURE DUE TO DEATH OR DISABILITY

All of us are at risk for sudden death or disability. In fact, at most age levels, incapacity due to disability is far more likely than death. It is best to prepare for any unforeseen traumatic event while you are healthy. Many psychologists have professional wills that instruct the personal representative on how to manage the assets of the practice upon the death of the practitioner. Ideally, the personal representative will be another psychologist or attorney with experience in such matters, although often other mental health professionals can handle the responsibilities adequately. Specific instructions should include important practice information such as the location of the appointment book and office keys, computer passwords, banking institutions and bank accounts, and other business details (Ragusea, 2002).

Instructions should be comprehensive and address all issues relevant to your specific practice. In general this would include how to contact current patients and how their records are to be handled, maintained, or disposed of, and which insurers or referral sources should be contacted. You should also leave instructions regarding record retention and document destruction. Be certain that your professional will is in compliance with statutory requirements, such as whether to announce your retirement in the paper (if your state so requires). While it is unlikely that an estate would be sued because records are missing, it can happen. Your lack of preparation may place an unusually difficult burden on your family or partners at a time when they already have enough emotional and practical issues to consider.

PSYCHOLOGICAL ASSESSMENT AND FORENSIC PRACTICE

There are special considerations for psychologists who primarily provide forensic or evaluative services such as neuropsychological evaluations; custody evaluations; evaluations of individuals who have been injured in an accident; testing for worker's compensation and social security cases; testing for school placement; or evaluations for hiring, promotion, and retention in employment settings. These services are generally characterized by short-term contact with patients or clients to provide important information for businesses, schools, or regulatory and legal systems. Treatment or the delivery of health care services is rarely part of this type of practice. Psychologists who perform these evaluative services are frequently called on to testify in court regarding the results of their evaluations. The distinguishing characteristic is that while the services are performed short term, the psychologist may be called to testify some time well into the future. Psychologists whose primary practice involves testing and assessment must plan carefully for their retirement. They may well be subject to subpoena for depositions and court testimony. In addition, their former clients may request that their records be sent to lawyers, regulatory agencies, schools, courts, or other providers of psychological services. These requests may continue well beyond the time of retirement. Remember, psychological services that are provided after the professional liability insurance is terminated will not be covered; exactly what constitutes a new psychological service could be a matter of debate.

Psychologists who provide evaluative services have several options to reduce their risk postretirement. One is to continue to purchase professional liability insurance until all cases have been completed and there are no future expectations for providing additional services. If you decide to keep your insurance in force postretirement, you may wish to purchase the Trust-Sponsored Professional Liability part-time policy with a substantial savings off the full-time policy premium. If you have had an occurrence policy, you could terminate the occurrence policy and change to a first-year step rate claims-made policy, again at the part-time rate. Another somewhat more drastic option to reduce risk that does not involve the continued purchase of professional liability insurance would be to terminate all activity at a time certain and turn over all your records to another practitioner who agrees to respond to any request for information from your files. Under this scenario you would be placed in the position with the least chance of providing future services. However, the risk of being compelled to testify in some future legal action remains, and this could easily be interpreted as the practice of psychology.

SUMMARY

One might ask: "Why spend so much time on a chapter on retirement?" There are several reasons. First, this is a topic that is rarely discussed in the literature, especially from a risk management perspective. Second, the available data regarding membership in the American Psychological Association clearly indicate that a significant portion of psychologists are nearing the retirement age. And third, there are specific issues related to retirement and insurance that need to be understood in order to make sure that you are protected from potentially devastating malpractice claims after you have closed your practice.

Most psychologists want to continue to practice, at least part-time, for many years after their "official" retirement. However, the risk management formula

$$\text{Clinical risk} = \frac{(P \times C \times D)}{TF}$$

In this formula, P = patient risk characteristics; C = context;
D = disciplinary consequences; and TF = therapist factors.

should apply even when professional services are volunteered or delivered at a greatly reduced fee. Semiretired psychologists need to consider all of the parts of the risk management formula including the potential for a decrease in their therapist factors if their energy decreases or if they fail to keep up-to-date with advances in the profession. Equally important, however, when psychologists drop their professional liability insurance the potential disciplinary consequences become so high that every professional act involves too much risk and should be avoided.

Seven Essential Points to Remember

1. Psychologists planning to retire need to give themselves plenty of time to think through and implement their decision.

2. Psychologists planning to retire need to anticipate such issues as informing their patients and referral sources, maintaining or destroying business and clinical records, and deciding whether to keep their licenses active.

3. State laws vary on what is required of psychologists who retire or discontinue practicing.

4. Psychologists need to purchase a "tail" if they have been covered by claims-made insurance.

5. Psychologists who retire and discontinue their professional liability insurance policy should refrain from engaging in any professional activities.

6. Psychologists should prepare for their sudden death or disability by creating a specific and detailed professional will.

7. Psychologists who are semiretired (and working or volunteering part-time) are held to the same standards of professional conduct as psychologists who are working full-time.

Chapter 11: PROFESSIONAL LIABILITY INSURANCE— DON'T PRACTICE WITHOUT IT[1]

There is a story of the enterprising private practitioner who found a way to save money on the cost of professional liability insurance: He didn't buy any. To protect himself from the risk of a large financial loss that might accompany a malpractice suit, he placed all of his assets, including his checking and savings accounts, his investments and certificates of deposit, his retirement fund, his car and home, and more in his spouse's name. He declared himself "suit proof," rationalizing that with nothing to collect, no lawyer would chose to sue him. There are several problems with this approach.

1. The plaintiff's lawyer would have no way to know that the practitioner had attempted to shelter his personal assets. This information would not be available until the litigation was well into discovery. Therefore, the strategy to make himself suit proof would not work.

2. In some states marital property is considered commonly held and changing the ownership or title may not have the desired effect.

3. Once the suit is filed, the named defendant must respond within a specified time period or a default judgment will be entered against him or her. Responding to a suit will require the services of an attorney unless the practitioner represents himself—in which case the practitioner has a fool for a client. The cost associated with the response to the initial filing normally would be covered by professional liability insurance. The legal expenses in a malpractice case may be quite high. Historical data indicate that for every dollar spent on a jury award or settlement of a case, almost four dollars are spent on the legal defense.

4. A judgment could be imposed by a court against the practitioner that might attach future earnings.

5. These financial arrangements will be doubly detrimental should the practitioner or his or her spouse decide to get divorced.

Another private practitioner, also relying on questionable judgment, decided to purchase the least expensive professional liability coverage available in the market. But cheap policies come at a price. The lower cost may indicate instability of the insurance company, may reflect inadequate pricing of the product to cover future claims, may reflect important restrictions on coverage, may represent an attempt by the carrier to capture a

---

[1] The authors wish to thank. Steven P. Benson, General Counsel for the Trust and partner of the Washington, DC, law firm of O'Brien, Birney & Butler for his assistance with the technical legal aspects of this article.

larger share of the marketplace by temporarily lowering the price only to increase rates in the future, or may involve combinations of the above. Rest assured, when one insurance carrier's prices are substantially out of line with the marketplace, there may be significant risks associated with the purchase of this coverage.

It is important for psychologists to realize that purchasing professional liability insurance is not like purchasing milk or other products that are used immediately. The premiums paid for professional liability coverage are an investment in the future—usually the distant future. It is not uncommon for suits to be filed several years after the alleged malpractice occurred. An insurance carrier that lowballs the price to attract insureds today may not have the financial stability to provide coverage in the distant future, or the carrier may decide to drop this particular line of coverage sometime in the future.

When contemplating professional liability insurance, the psychologist should consider the issues discussed below.

WHY PURCHASE PROFESSIONAL LIABILITY INSURANCE?

The only reason to purchase *any* type of insurance is to protect yourself from the financial consequences of a loss, including, but not limited to, losses due to injuries from an auto accident, the cost to replace stolen property or repair damage to personal property, loss of income due to disability or death, or financial losses associated with allegations of professional misconduct.

WHO NEEDS PROFESSIONAL LIABILITY INSURANCE?

Psychologists who act in their professional capacity, whether it be providing health care services, industrial or organizational services, or work in an academic setting, should have professional liability insurance to cover any claims brought against them for their services.

On the other hand, many psychologists employed in agency or institutional settings do not have their own professional liability coverage. They rely on the agency to cover any claims against them. It is questionable, however, if most agencies are able—or willing—to fully defend and indemnify the psychologist for allegations of malpractice for work performed for the employer.

The agency that is not insured would have to rely on its own resources to respond to a case against the agency and the named psychologist. While the agency may be able to retain legal counsel to represent the parties, it is possible that it may not be able to pay any damages awarded by a jury. In this situation, the psychologist could suffer significant financial losses.

Depending on the nature of the case and the charges filed against the agency and the psychologist, the agency, blaming the psychologist for the alleged malpractice, may refuse to defend or indemnify the psychologist. This is most likely to happen if the psychologist is accused of an activity that was not authorized as a part of his or her employment contract. While a charge of sexual misconduct is the most obvious example of unauthorized behavior, many other activities could potentially fall under this category, including any professional service that was not listed in the employee's job description. The decisions to defend or not defend could be made by the agency with the agency's best interest in mind and only after the suit is filed.

The psychologist employed by an agency should determine if the agency has adequate malpractice insurance to cover the activities of employees. If the agency does not have malpractice insurance covering employees, it is self-insured. In that case the psychologist should seek written contractual assurances from the proper authorities documenting the agency's ability and willingness to cover a malpractice case against an employee. The inquiry should address the agency's procedures to defend and indemnify a suit naming employees, the limits of coverage, what acts are included and excluded, and whether the agency could refuse to provide coverage against the named psychologist. Where applicable the response should be from the agency's board of directors or other legally responsible party.

A psychologist without professional liability insurance who provides professional services outside the agency setting (e.g., teaching, supervision, consultation, or a part-time private practice) will have an uninsured exposure for these services. A suit brought against the psychologist for services rendered outside the primary employment setting generally will not be covered by the employer or the employer's insurance.

As psychologists become more familiar with the types of exposure they have for the delivery of professional services, more and more are purchasing their own professional liability coverage. This includes psychologists working primarily in educational settings. There is always a risk of suit from a student who received a poor grade or for professional services related to the academician's supervisory responsibilities.

AVAILABILITY OF COVERAGE

Psychologists may select from a variety of policy types and coverage limits. They also may purchase professional liability coverage from a number of different carriers. The availability of professional liability insurance for psychologists is generally a function of the cyclical changes in the insurance industry. In a soft market, the competition for premium dollars is intense and insurance companies will increase their cash flow by offering new lines of coverage or by lowering premiums on existing products to lure customers away from another company. In this scenario, competition works to the advantage of the insured: Prices are stabilized or may be reduced and policy features and enhancements may be improved. Insurance has always run in cycles, however, and hard markets follow soft markets. In a hard market, premiums will increase dramatically; new exclusions will be added to policies in an attempt to control costs; and some companies may decide to drop certain lines of coverage. Recently, a number of carriers have dropped professional liability coverage for psychologists. Other carriers offer professional liability policies only in a limited number of states.[2]

[2] The APA Insurance Trust (the Trust) has continuously sponsored a national program with very competitive rates for more than 22 years, during both soft and hard markets. In addition, the Trust-sponsored Professional Liability Program has been the leader in introducing important enhancements and innovations in this line of coverage.

THE BASIC TYPES OF PROFESSIONAL LIABILITY COVERAGE

There are two basic types of professional liability coverage offered in the market today: occurrence and claims-made coverage. Occurrence coverage costs more, but it is generally easier to understand and administer. The premiums for claims-made coverage are lower but the coverage issues are more complicated.

From the early 1970s until the late 1980s, the vast majority of psychologists were insured under an occurrence-type policy. In 1991, the major malpractice insurance carriers, concerned about the unanticipated losses associated with claims filed many years after the alleged malpractice, moved from occurrence coverage to claims-made coverage. Today the Trust-Sponsored Professional Liability Program offers the psychologist a choice of occurrence or claims-made coverage.

Occurrence Coverage

For a claim to be covered under an occurrence policy, the alleged misconduct must occur during the policy period. The claim can be reported anytime regardless of whether the policy is in force at the time of the report. Therefore, a psychologist with occurrence insurance is covered in perpetuity for any covered incident that occurred while the policy was in force. If you are going to purchase occurrence coverage, be sure you are dealing with a carrier with significant financial resources. If a carrier goes into receivership, there may not be assets necessary to respond to a claim filed in the future.

The premiums collected for any year for an occurrence policy must be adequate to cover all potential claims that occurred during that policy year for all claims filed against the insured at any time in the future. Therefore, the premiums for an occurrence policy are substantially higher than the premiums for a claims-made policy, especially when compared with the premiums for a claims-made policy during the first years of coverage. A special feature of the occurrence coverage is that a practitioner may drop an occurrence policy at any time (e.g., as a result of retirement, a job change, a change in carriers, or a change to a claims-made policy) without fear that a suit filed in the future for alleged malpractice that occurred when the policy was in force would not be covered. Under an occurrence policy, claims are covered according to the terms and conditions of the policy in force at the time the accident occurred.

Claims-Made Coverage

For a claim to be covered under a claims-made policy, the alleged misconduct must occur during the policy period, *and* the claim must be reported during the time the policy is in force. Put differently, for a claim to be covered under a claims-made policy, the insured must have been covered under the same policy both when the covered incident occurred and when the claim was filed. All claims-made policies have a "retro date" or the date the policy was first issued. Any claim alleging malpractice that occurred prior to the retro date will not be covered under the policy.

The premium for the first year of a claims-made policy only covers claims that occurred during the first year and are filed during that year. During the second year of coverage, the premium must cover any claims from both the first and second year that are filed in the second year. Premiums for the third year must cover three years of potential claims. Therefore, premiums for claims-made policies are lower during the first years of coverage and increase as the policy continues in force. Each additional year of coverage represents a new step rate in the premium for a claims-made policy. When the policy matures (typically sometime between the 6th and 8th years), it begins to mimic the coverage offered under an occurrence policy. A mature claims-made premium will be similar to the occurrence premium.

A practitioner must take care if he or she wishes to drop a claims-made policy (e.g., as a result of retirement, a job change, a change to a different carrier, or a change to a different type of coverage). If a claims-made policy is terminated for any reason, the practitioner must purchase "tail" coverage (sometimes referred to as extended reporting period [ERP] coverage) to extend the period for reporting claims beyond the termination date. A practitioner who drops a claims-made policy should purchase the tail coverage or if purchasing a new policy, should purchase other insurance with the same retro date as the terminated policy. The practitioner who fails to exercise one of these two options will be without insurance should a suit be filed after the termination date, even though the allegations of malpractice may have occurred while the policy was in force.

The psychologist who wishes to change from claims-made coverage to occurrence coverage will need to purchase the tail coverage on the claims-made policy to close out coverage under the terminated policy and pay the current premium for the occurrence policy.

The psychologist who wishes to keep claims-made coverage but change insurance carriers should either (a) purchase the tail coverage for the terminated policy and pay the first year step rates for the new claims-made policy or (b) not purchase the tail coverage for the terminated policy but purchase coverage in the new claims-made program using the same retro date and step rate of the terminated policy (e.g., a psychologist who switches policies after the 5th year would purchase the new claims-made policy at the 6th-year step rate). All other issues being equal (e.g., viability of carrier, scope of coverage, availability of advocacy and risk management services, representation on behalf of the insured, and service), the choice is basically a financial decision. Generally, it will cost less to drop the current claims-made coverage and purchase the claims-made policy from the new carrier using the same retro date and step rate as the terminated policy. In this scenario, the total exposure for all potential past claims is shifted from the old carrier to the new carrier.

It should be obvious that the difference in price between an occurrence and a claims-made policy will be an important part of the buying decision. Claims-made coverage can save the practitioner considerable money during the first years the insurance is in force. If the policy is terminated, the practitioner may elect to purchase tail coverage for the claims-made policy. Under the Trust-Sponsored Professional Liability Program, tail coverage costs 175% of the last year's premium for an unlimited ERP.[3] The money saved during the policy's first years will generally exceed the cost of the tail coverage.[4]

---

[3] The Professional Liability Program sponsored by the Trust provides a free tail upon the death of the practitioner, upon the practitioner's permanent retirement, or if the practitioner becomes disabled and is unable to practice.
[4] Tail coverage may be purchased for 1 year or 3 years for lower rates, but this is not recommended because of the long delay in reporting claims in psychological practice.

FIGURE 3.11.1
Claims-Made Vs. Occurrence Rates

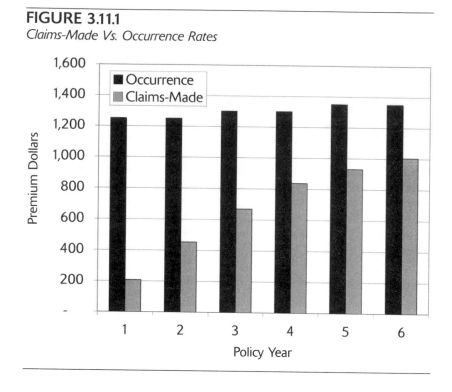

Under a claims-made policy, claims are covered according to the terms and conditions of the policy in force at the time the claim is filed.

HOW MUCH COVERAGE SHOULD YOU BUY?

The limits of liability in a professional liability policy are listed as a dollar amount for each incident and an aggregate dollar amount available during the policy period. Today most practitioners purchase $1mill/$3mill in coverage, meaning the policy would pay a maximum of $1 million for a single incident and up to $3 million in losses for the year the policy was in force. The higher aggregate level of coverage, $3 million, does not necessarily reflect increased exposures in the practice of psychology. Rather, managed care companies generally require the higher levels of coverage for membership on provider panels, and these limits also may be required by hospitals where the psychologist has a staff appointment or is a member of the hospital staff. Regardless of the level of coverage, the most important risk management decision is to purchase adequate levels of professional liability coverage to protect against potentially catastrophic financial losses.

POLICY PRICE

The price for malpractice insurance varies as a function of the type of policy, the policy limits, the scope of coverage, and the geographical location of the insured. All other things being equal, a claims-made policy is less expensive than an occurrence policy, especially during the first years of coverage. As the claims-made policy matures, however, the premiums begin to reach the same levels as premiums for occurrence coverage. As noted above, additional charges may be necessary when terminating a claims-made policy.

The higher the policy limits, the greater the premium. Today practitioners may purchase coverage limits ranging from a low of $200,000/$200,000 to a high of $2mill/$4mill. Amounts greater than $2mill/$4mill are subject to additional underwriting requirements.

Policy price is determined in part by the scope of coverage offered. Lower premiums may reflect the exclusion of specific professional activities in the policy. A carrier may decide to exclude coverage for any claims arising out of the delivery of professional services in a specific setting (e.g., correctional institutions), or the carrier may place restrictions on the delivery of specific types of professional services (e.g., working with victims of trauma, custody evaluations, or use of recovered memory techniques). The major carriers offer policies that have exclusions or limitations for claims related to sexual misconduct. The type of the exclusion or limitation will affect policy price.

An analysis of claims frequency and costs in the late 1980s demonstrated that psychologists in some of the lower risk states were subsidizing the cost of coverage for psychologists in higher risk states. A single national premium could no longer be justified, and it was necessary to charge different rates for different states. The Trust-Sponsored Professional Liability Program was divided into three regions (see Table 3.11.A), with the lowest rates in Region A and the highest rates in Region C. Table 3.11.A shows the current allocation of states to regions.

TABLE 3.11.A
Allocation of States for Insurance Rates

Region A		Region B		Region C
Alabama	Massachusetts	DC	New Hampshire	Arizona
Alaska	North Dakota	Florida	New York	California
Arkansas	Oklahoma	Georgia	North Carolina	Colorado
Connecticut	Rhode Island	Idaho	Ohio	Louisiana
Delaware	South Carolina	Illinois	Pennsylvania	Michigan
Hawaii	Utah	Kansas	South Dakota	Minnesota
Indiana	Vermont	Maryland	Tennessee	New Jersey
Iowa	West Virginia	Mississippi	Texas	New Mexico
Kentucky	Wyoming	Missouri	Virginia	Oregon
Maine		Montana	Washington	
		Nebraska	Wisconsin	
		Nevada		

Note. Rates are lowest in Region A and highest in Region C.

DEFENSE COSTS OUTSIDE POLICY LIMITS

A malpractice insurance policy is a contract between the insurance carrier and the insured. It requires the insurance carrier to *defend* and *indemnify* the psychologist for any covered wrongful act. The policy defends the psychologist by requiring the carrier to retain an attorney and pay for the legal costs involved. The policy indemnifies the psychologist by paying for damages awarded by a jury or cash settlements up to the policy limits within the contractual obligations of the policy. Because the cost to defend a malpractice action can be very high, the practitioner is advised to avoid any policy that includes the cost of defense within the policy limits. If the cost of defense is within the policy limits, any legal expenses incurred will reduce the amount of coverage available for settlement or jury awards. Policies in which the defense costs are outside the policy limits do not reduce the policy limits and are not that much more expensive.

READ YOUR POLICY

While most psychologists have some form of malpractice coverage, it is surprising how few psychologists have actually read their policy. It is extremely important that the practitioner understands what is covered and what is excluded in the policy, and what conditions, if any, must be met to keep the coverage in force. An insurance policy is a legal contract; it contains obligations that both parties must meet, including a requirement that the insured cooperate with the carrier to defend a claim against the insured. The psychologist who fails to fulfill the stated conditions may find that the carrier will exercise its option to deny coverage for a specific claim or not renew the policy, or in the extreme, the carrier may file suit against the psychologist to rescind the policy.

All insurance policies contain an "insuring agreement," which states that for the premium paid, the carrier will defend and indemnify the insured for any covered wrongful act committed during the policy period arising solely out of the performance of professional services as a psychologist. While this statement may give the appearance of broad-based coverage, all parts of the policy must be considered as a whole to fully understand how the policy works.

Malpractice insurance policies require that the insured must report all claims to the insurance carrier immediately and that the insured may not assume any obligations, incur any costs, or enter into a settlement without the company's written consent. If an insured violates any of these or other important conditions, the carrier may deny coverage for a claim reported later. The policy may also contain conditions related to how claims are settled and the responsibility of the insured and the carrier in any settlement negotiations.

All insurance contracts contain exclusions that will limit the company's liability to those events that the insurance is intended to cover. Typical exclusions include, but are not limited to, claims against the psychologist for the unlicensed practice of medicine; dishonest, criminal, fraudulent, or intentional acts; business relationships with current or former clients; and specific limitations for sexual misconduct claims. If a suit is filed against a psychologist that alleges fraudulent or intentional acts or other acts of misconduct that are excluded in the policy, the carrier may deny coverage altogether. Alternatively, the carrier could issue a *reservation-of-rights* letter stating that the company will defend the claim but will not be obligated to pay for any damages awarded based on the excluded activity. In the latter case, if a jury subsequently awards large damages for the intentional acts, the psychologist, not the carrier, would be responsible for payment. These limitations generally do not apply to claims that are settled. It should be noted that some lower priced policies contain exclusions that are considered to be a normal part of psychological practice. It is clear that the cheapest policy is not always in the practitioner's best interest.

The psychologist who has not read his or her policy may be surprised to find that some activities may be excluded. A policy that only covers claims filed by the psychologist's patient could possibly result in denial of coverage for claims filed by a third party who is not a patient of the psychologist (e.g., a known or unknown third party who was injured by the psychologist's patient). The purpose of insurance is to cover the risks associated with the delivery of professional services. A policy that limits coverage or excludes certain types of services shifts that risk back to the psychologist. Read and understand your policy.

SPECIAL PROVISIONS FOR SEXUAL MISCONDUCT

Historically, approximately 20% of all cases and 50% of all losses against psychologists have been for sexual misconduct. There is some preliminary evidence that the number of sexual misconduct claims may be decreasing in recent years, but this type of misconduct still represents the highest exposure for insurance carriers. Some carriers address the problem by excluding coverage for sexual misconduct claims. Other carriers attempt to limit losses by capping the amount of damages that a policy will pay for sexual misconduct claims. The Trust-Sponsored Professional Liability Program will defend a psychologist accused of sexual misconduct but will not pay damages. Regardless of the method used to curtail coverage, practitioners know that sexual misconduct is unethical and in some states a criminal offense. If insurance companies were to provide unrestricted coverage for sexual misconduct claims, the premiums would increase dramatically.

The coverage problem occurs when a frivolous claim for sexual misconduct is filed against the psychologist. If a policy excluded all coverage, including a legal defense, it would not be helpful. A policy that caps the amount of damages to be paid leaves the insured exposed to any judgments in excess of that amount, including cases that can be settled for an amount in excess of the cap. It is also important to know whether a policy that caps damages will provide multiple defenses for multiple claims against the practitioner.

If a psychologist is found to have engaged in sexual misconduct, the consequences to his or her career may be devastating. It is almost a given that the carrier will terminate coverage and highly unlikely that any other carrier will insure the individual, at least in the near future. Without adequate insurance, the practitioner will not be able to serve on managed care panels or find employment in certain institutional settings. In addition, allegations of sexual misconduct are frequently reported to licensing boards, which may result in additional sanctions against the practitioner.

SPECIAL PROVISIONS FOR SETTLEMENT OF A CLAIM

Most practitioners are surprised to learn that the vast majority of cases against psychologists are settled prior to going to trial. Settlement is the preferred option for the psychologist and the insurance carrier because trial is always risky; you can never predict the response of a jury. The plaintiff may wish to settle a case for the same reason. Settlement is often reached if the cost of trial and the potential damages are projected to be higher than the terms of the settlement or if the plaintiff's case is weak and the case can be settled for less than the cost of the legal defense.

Many practitioners do not believe that settling a case is in their best interest. Settlement, however, may be beneficial for the defendant because it avoids prolonged litigation, including depositions, a public hearing, and court testimony. In addition, settlement resolves a very painful situation for the practitioner, one that is frequently associated with loss of income due to the time involved in this type of litigation. And there is always the possibility that a jury will award an amount that is in excess of the practitioner's policy limits, in which case the practitioner must pay the difference. Settlement of a frivolous case generally does not have a significant negative impact on the psychologist's practice. Large settlements, however, may evidence serious misconduct and may have significant consequences.

There are three basic ways an insurance policy may address settlement: (a) The company may settle any claim against the insured without the insured's knowledge or consent; (b) the company may not settle any claim against the insured without the insured's consent; and (c) if the company is able to reach a settlement agreement with the plaintiff, the insured may refuse to consent to the settlement, but the company's liability for the case would then be capped at the amount of the proposed settlement. In this third option, the risk of not settling a case is shared with the insured.

When a financial settlement is reached, a payment will be made to the plaintiff; charges will be dropped; and generally there will be no admission of wrongdoing or guilt. The psychologist and his or her personal attorney should review any proposed settlement document carefully to be sure that the all issues are resolved.

INSURING GROUP PRACTICES

The move from the solo practice model to the group practice model has brought new challenges to the practitioner seeking to insure the group practice. Insurance carriers understand the risks associated with the independent or solo practice of psychology. In group practices, however, the risk of exposure to litigation becomes more complicated. A suit resulting from the negligence of one member of the group may well name all members as defendants as well as the corporation or partnership. Therefore, a single incident of alleged malpractice may result in multiple suits against the practitioners in the group.

Insurance carriers have struggled with the proper way to provide comprehensive coverage for group practices. Some carriers do not insure group practices. Some charge a separate premium for each owner, each employee, each independent contractor, and for the group name. Others collect a premium for each professional associated with the group but do not charge a premium for the group name. Lower premiums generally are charged for nonpsychologist professional owners or employees (e.g., social workers and counselors) working in the group. Special discounts based on group size may be available. With so many variations in pricing group policies, it is imperative that the practitioner seeking a quotation for group coverage compare apples with apples. Policy features and coverage limitations, however, are more important than price when shopping for insurance: This is especially true with group insurance.

One important feature to consider is the available aggregate limit of coverage in a group policy. If five psychologists each purchased policies for $1mill/$3mill, the total aggregate amount of insurance in force for these practitioners would be $15 million. The maximum payment for any single claim would be $1million. If these same individuals were insured under a group policy with limits of $1mill/$3mill, the group would only have $1mill/$3mill to insure all five members. The practitioner should avoid a group policy in which the aggregate limit of coverage is shared by all group members.[5] Policies are available today that provide each insured with his or her own aggregate limit of coverage. Thus, the group policy with five psychologist owners would have $1mill/$15mill coverage available.

THE BUYING DECISION: CLAIMS MADE OR OCCURRENCE

The majority of practitioners, approximately 80%, purchase the less expensive claims-made insurance. Others feel more comfortable with the more expensive occurrence policy form that is somewhat more flexible if the practitioner wishes to change insurance companies or policy types. Depending on policy features, both types of coverage will protect the practitioner from potential catastrophic financial losses due to a malpractice suit. A significant difference between the policy forms relates to how each type of policy responds to a claim.

Recall that in an occurrence policy a claim is covered according to the terms and conditions of the policy in force at the time the alleged malpractice occurred. In a claims-made policy, the claim is covered according to the terms and conditions of the policy in force at the time the claim is filed. Therefore, if new coverage features are added to a claims-made policy, these features will apply to all previous years the policy was in force because any suit would be covered according to the conditions of the policy at the time the claim was filed. Likewise, if the carrier removed certain coverage features from a claims-made policy, it would affect all previous years the policy was in force. On the other hand, new coverage features added to an occurrence policy would only apply to the policy in force when the features were upgraded. Removal of coverage features from an occurrence policy would not impact any previous occurrence policy. As long as the practitioner feels confident that coverage under the policy will

[5] Some managed care companies have refused to deal with groups with a shared aggregate limit of coverage, believing that the group is underinsured.

233

be improved, the claims-made policy may offer better coverage.

Unfortunately, the individual practitioner has no influence with the carrier regarding coverage issues. Fortunately, psychologists insured under the Trust-Sponsored Professional Liability Program are well represented for these issues with the carrier. The Trust, serving as an advocate for its insureds, negotiates both policy price and new policy features each year with the carrier.

THE IMPORTANCE OF REPRESENTATION

In addition to representing the interests of psychologists with the insurance carrier, the Trust-Sponsored Professional Liability Program provides Trust insureds with special Trust-Sponsored Risk Management Workshops and Independent Study Courses,[6] the free Advocate800 Risk Management Consultation Service, and a case review procedure in which colleagues of the insured review any negative decision made by the carrier regarding denial of coverage, termination of coverage, or problems with an attorney or case management. The Trust also produces risk management articles, videos, books, and other risk management materials to help practitioners avoid unnecessary complaints or allegations of misconduct.

In the final analysis, professional liability insurance should provide the comfort a psychologist needs to engage in his or her profession without excess worry and sleepless nights. Psychologists with questions regarding their professional liability coverage or other important insurance products may contact the Trust at 1-800-477-1200.

---

[6] Substantial premium discounts apply for psychologists who participate in these risk management activities.

Seven Essential Points to Remember

1. An agency's malpractice insurance policy is unlikely to cover activities, including professional activities, outside of the regular job responsibilities of the psychologist.

2. The two types of malpractice insurance coverage are occurrence and claims-made. A psychologist with an occurrence policy is insured in perpetuity for any covered incident that occurred while the policy was in force. A psychologist with a claims-made policy is insured if the covered incident occurred both when the insured was covered and when the claim was filed. Psychologists with claims-made insurance should purchase a "tail" when they discontinue their coverage.

3. Psychologists should read their policies carefully to ensure that they understand their obligations and rights, and those of the insurance company.

4. Malpractice insurance policies require the insured to report all claims to the carrier immediately, and prohibit the insured from entering into a settlement without the company's written consent.

5. Insurance policies typically exclude coverage for the unlicensed practice of medicine, criminal or fraudulent acts, business relationships with current or former clients, sexual misconduct, contract disputes with third parties, and fee disputes with clients.

6. The vast majority of cases against psychologists are settled out of court before going to trial.

7. In a group practice, a single incident of alleged misconduct may result in multiple suits against all of the practitioners in the group.

AFTERWORD

The primary goal of this book is to decrease the likelihood that you will be the subject of a malpractice suit or licensing board complaint. A secondary goal is damage control should a suit or complaint be filed against you. A third goal is to provide a new and innovative way to view and understand ethics and risk management in the delivery of psychological services.

This book provides more than the standard cookbook, one size fits all approach to ethics and risk management. We believe that the cookbook approach, which has been so popular for the past two decades, is no longer useful by itself. Today, the professional community is clearly more sophisticated and wants to look beyond rote learning and application of the rules. Years of experience have taught us that many situations and clinical conundrums cannot be easily resolved by strict obedience to a set of rules that may or may not apply to a specific fact situation. Practitioners want to provide the best psychological services within the context of the proper ethical and legal standards rather than have their services dictated by a set of rules that at times may seem arbitrary, if not counterproductive.

In this book, we have set forth a new approach, a new way of thinking about ethics and risk management, and a new way of applying these principles in unusual and not-so-clear-cut case scenarios. This approach goes beyond blindly applying the rules regardless of the situational factors involved. Instead, it is based on a comprehensive analysis of the situational factors, of patient or client characteristics as well as therapist factors, and of how these factors interact to increase or decrease ultimate risk factors in practice. While you should always retain a realistic understanding of potential problems that may lead to disciplinary actions, this should not intimidate or inhibit you from delivering services in an ethically and professionally sound manner.

In the Preface we noted the importance of forethought, thought, and afterthought when you practice your profession. Essential parts of your planning or forethought should include the following: use of the risk management formula

$$\text{Clinical risk} = \frac{(P \times C \times D)}{TF}$$

In this formula, P = patient risk characteristics; C = context;
D = disciplinary consequences; and TF = therapist factors.

to guide professional decisions; a reliance on the risk management strategies based on overarching ethical principles (and avoiding false risk management principles); a knowledge of when and how to use risk management strategies (informed consent, documentation, and consultation); a desire to practice at the highest level of Bloom's taxonomy; and the appropriate use of knowledge in specialized domains of practice such as testing and providing forensic services, treatment of children, or the management of patients with suicidal tendencies.

We hope that by analyzing each situation in light of the risk management formula, you will automatically use this heuristic and the suggested risk management strategies when you sense an increase in your professional risk. This book cannot protect you from all mistakes, essentially an impossible goal; however, it should help to decrease the frequency of mistakes as well as the severity of any unfortunate outcomes.

You belong to a great tradition of healers. You can be proud of what you and your profession have accomplished. The services you provide, or if you are enjoying your retirement years, have provided, have greatly benefited society. We sincerely hope that this book will assist you during your professional career and into retirement.

REFERENCES

Acuff, C., Bennett, B., Bricklin, P., Canter, M., Knapp, S., Moldawsky, S., & Phelps, R. (1999). Considerations for ethical practice in managed care. *Professional Psychology: Research and Practice, 30,* 563-575.

American Educational Research Association, American Psychological Association, National Council on Measurement in Education. (1999). *The standards for educational and psychological testing.* Washington, DC: American Educational Research Association.

American Psychiatric Association. (1994). *Diagnostic and statistical manual of mental disorders* (4th ed.). Washington, DC: Author.

American Psychiatric Association. (2003). Practice guidelines for the assessment and treatment of patients with suicidal behaviors. *American Journal of Psychiatry, 160* (Suppl. 11).

American Psychoanalytic Association. (1995). *Practice Bulletin 2: Charting psychoanalysis.* Retrieved October 10, 2005, from http://apsa.org/pubinfo/pract21.htm

American Psychological Association. (1993). Guidelines for providers of psychological services to ethnic, linguistic, and culturally diverse populations. *American Psychologist, 48,* 45-48.

American Psychological Association. (1994). Guidelines for child custody evaluations in divorce proceedings. *American Psychologist, 49,* 677-680.

American Psychological Association. (2000). Guidelines for psychotherapy with lesbian, gay, and bisexual clients. *American Psychologist, 55,* 1440-1451.

American Psychological Association. (2002). Ethical principles of psychologists and code of conduct. *American Psychologist, 57,* 1060-1073.

American Psychological Association. (2003). Guidelines on multicultural education, training, research, practice, and organizational change for psychologists. *American Psychologist, 58,* 377-402.

American Psychological Association, Committee on Professional Practice and Standards. (1993). Record-keeping guidelines. *American Psychologist, 48,* 984-986.

American Psychological Association, Ethics Committee. (1995). Report of the Ethics Committee, 1994. *American Psychologist, 50,* 706-713

American Psychological Association, Ethics Committee. (1996). Report of the Ethics Committee, 1995. *American Psychologist, 51,* 1279-1286

American Psychological Association, Ethics Committee. (1997). Report of the Ethics Committee, 1996. *American Psychologist, 52,* 897-905.

American Psychological Association, Ethics Committee. (1998). Report of the Ethics Committee, 1997. *American Psychologist, 53,* 969-980.

American Psychological Association, Ethics Committee. (1999). Report of the Ethics Committee, 1998. *American Psychologist, 54,* 701-710.

American Psychological Association, Ethics Committee. (2000). Report of the Ethics Committee, 1999. *American Psychologist, 55,* 938-945.

American Psychological Association, Ethics Committee. (2001). Report of the Ethics Committee, 2000. *American Psychologist, 56,* 680-688.

American Psychological Association, Ethics Committee. (2002). Report of the Ethics Committee, 2001. *American Psychologist, 57,* 646-653.

American Psychological Association, Ethics Committee. (2003). Report of the Ethics Committee, 2002. *American Psychologist, 58,* 650-657.

American Psychological Association, Ethics Committee. (2004). Report of the Ethics Committee, 2003. *American Psychologist, 59,* 434-441.

American Psychological Association, Ethics Committee. (2005). Report of the Ethics Committee, 2004. *American Psychologist, 60,* 523-528.

Americans With Disabilities Act. Public Law 101-336. (1990). Available at http://www.usdoj.gov/crt/ada/adahom1.htm

Anderson, J., & Barret, B. (2001). *Ethics in HIV-related psychotherapy: Clinical decision making in complex cases.* Washington, DC: American Psychological Association.

Appelbaum, P. S. (1985). *Tarasoff* and the clinician: Problems in fulfilling the duty to protect. *American Journal of Psychiatry, 142,* 425-429.

Association of State and Provincial Psychology Boards. (2005). *ASPPB Code of Conduct.* Retrieved August 28, 2005, from http://www.asppb.org/publications/model/conductPrint.htm

Barnett, J., & Hillard, D. (2001). Psychologist distress and impairment: The availability, nature, and use of colleague assistance programs for psychologists. *Professional Psychology: Research and Practice, 32,* 205-210.

Barnett, J., & Neel, M. (2000). Must all psychologists study psychopharmacology? *Professional Psychology: Research and Practice, 31,* 619-627.

Beahrs, J., & Guthiel, T. (2001). Informed consent in psychotherapy. *American Journal of Psychiatry, 158,* 4-10.

Beauchamp, T., & Childress, J. (2001). *Principles of biomedical ethics* (5th ed.). New York: Oxford University Press.

Beck, A. T., Kovacs, M., & Weissman, A. (1979). Assessment of suicidal ideation: The Scale for Suicidal Ideation. *Journal of Consulting and Clinical Psychology, 47,* 343-352.

Beck, A. T., Weissman, A., Lester, D., & Trexler, L. (1974). The measurement of pessimism: The Hopelessness Scale. *Journal of Consulting and Clinical Psychology, 42,* 861-865.

Beckman, H. B., Markakis, K. M., Suchman, A. L., & Frankel, R. M. (1994). The doctor–patient relationship and malpractice. Lessons from plaintiff depositions. *Archives of Internal Medicine, 154,* 1365-1370.

Belar, C., Brown, R., Hersch, L., Hornyak, L., Rozensky, R., Sheridan, E., et al. (2001). Self-assessment in clinical health psychology: A model for ethical expansion of practice. *Professional Psychology: Research and Practice, 32,* 135-141.

Bellet, P., & Maloney, M. J. (1991). The importance of empathy as an interviewing skill in medicine. *Journal of the American Medical Association, 266,* 1831-1832.

Bender, E. (2005, May 20). Cost of malpractice suits requires more than money. *Psychiatric News, 40,* 25.

Bloom, B. (Ed.). (1956). *Taxonomy of educational objectives: The classification of educational goals.* New York: Longman, Green.

Bongar, B. (2002). *The suicidal patient: Clinical and legal standards of care* (2nd ed.). Washington, DC: American Psychological Association.

Borkovec, T., Echemendia, R., Ragusea, S., & Ruiz, M. (2001). The Pennsylvania Practice Research Network and future possibilities for clinically meaningful and scientifically rigorous psychotherapy effectiveness research. *Clinical Psychology: Science and Practice, 8,* 155-167.

Braaten, E., & Handelsman, M. (1997). Client preferences for informed consent information. *Ethics and Behavior, 7,* 311-328.

Brenner, E. (2003). Consumer-focused psychological assessment. *Professional Psychology: Research and Practice, 34,* 240-247.

Bricklin, P. (2001). Being ethical: More than obeying the law and avoiding harm. *Journal of Personality Assessment, 77,* 195-202.

Bricklin, P., Bennett, B., & Carroll, W. (2003). *Understanding licensing board disciplinary procedures.* Available from www.apait.org/resources/riskmanagement.

Brown, L. (2000). Feminist ethical considerations in forensic practice. In M. Brabeck (Ed.), *Practicing feminist ethics in psychology* (pp. 75-100). Washington, DC: American Psychological Association.

Buchwald, H., Avidor, Y., Braunwald, E., Jensen, M., Pories, W., Fahrbach, K., & Schoelles, K. (2004). Bariatric surgery: A systematic review and meta-analysis. *Journal of the American Medical Association, 292,* 1724-1737.

Burstin, H. R., Johnson, W. G., Lipsitz, S. R., & Brennan, T. A. (1993). Do the poor sue more? A case-control study of malpractice claims and socioeconomic status. *Journal of the American Medical Association, 270,* 1697-1701.

Busch, K., Fawcett, J., & Jacobs, D. (2003). Clinical correlates of inpatient suicide. *Journal of Clinical Psychiatry, 64,* 14-19.

Campanelli, R. (2005). Letter to Harcourt Publishing. Cited in Harcourt Assessment, Inc. *HIPAA Position Statement.* Retrieved August 17, 2005, from http://harcourtassessment.com/hai/images/pdf/legal/hipaa_position.pdf.

Caudill, O. B., & Pope, K. (1995). *Law and mental health professionals: California.* Washington, DC: American Psychological Association.

Chamberlain, J. (2004, November). No desire to fully retire. *Monitor on Psychology, 35,* 82-83.

Chemtob, C., Bauer, G., Hamada, R., Pelowski, S., & Muraoka, M. (1989). Patient suicide: Occupational hazard for psychologists and psychiatrists. *Professional Psychology: Research and Practice, 20,* 294-300.

Choudhry, N., Fletcher, R., & Soumerai, S. (2005). The relationship between clinical experience and quality of health care. *Annals of Internal Medicine, 142,* 260-273.

Clayton, S., & Bongar, B. (1994). The use of consultation in psychological practice: Ethical, legal, and clinical considerations. *Ethics & Behavior, 4,* 43-57.

Committee on Ethical Guidelines for Forensic Psychologists. (2006). Specialty guidelines for forensic psychologists. *Law and Human Behavior, 15,* 655-665.

Coryell, W., & Young, E. (2005). Clinical predictors of suicide in primary major depressive disorder. *Journal of Clinical Psychiatry, 66,* 412-417.

Coster, J., & Schwebel, M. (1997). Well-functioning in professional psychologists. *Professional Psychology: Research and Practice, 28,* 5-13.

Davis, D., O'Brien, M. A. T., Freemantle, N., Wolf, F., Mazmanian, P., & Taylor-Vaisey, A. (1999). Impact of formal continuing medical education. *Journal of the American Medical Association, 282,* 867-874.

Dlugos, R., & Friedlander, M. (2001). Passionately committed psychotherapists: A qualitative study of their experiences. *Professional Psychology: Research and Practice, 32,* 298-304.

Effective Listening Tops List of Skills Psychiatrists Need. (2000, August 4). *Psychiatric News, 35,* 8.

Elman, N., Illfelder-Kaye, J., & Robiner, W. (2005). Professional development: Training for professionalism as a foundation for competent practice in psychology. *Professional Psychology: Research and Practice, 36,* 367-375.

Epstein, R., & Hundert, E. (2002). Defining and assessing professional competence. *Journal of the American Medical Association, 287,* 226-235.

Etzioni, A. (1996). *The new golden rule: Community and morality in a democratic society.* New York: Basic Books.

Finn, S., & Tonsager, M. (1997). Information-gathering and therapeutic models of assessment: Complementary paradigms. *Psychological Assessment, 9,* 374-385.

Fischer, C. (2004). Individualized assessment moderates the impact of HIPAA Privacy Rules. *Journal of Personality Assessment, 82,* 35-38.

Fisher, C. (2002). Respecting and protecting mentally impaired persons in medical research. *Ethics & Behavior, 12,* 280-283.

Ginsburg, G., Albano, A. M., Findling, R., Kratochvil, C., & Walkup, J. (2005). Integrating cognitive behavior therapy and pharmacotherapy in the treatment of adolescent depression. *Cognitive and Behavioral Practice, 12,* 252-262.

Greenberg, I. (2003). Psychological aspects of bariatric surgery. *Nutrition in clinical practice, 18,* 124-130.

Greenberg, L., Gould, J., Gould-Saltman, D., & Stahl, P. (2003). Is the child's therapist part of the problem? What judges, attorneys, and mental health professionals need to know about court-related treatment for children. *Family Law Quarterly, 37,* 241-271.

Greenberg, S., & Shuman, D. (1997). Irreconcilable conflict between therapeutic and forensic roles. *Professional Psychology: Research and Practice, 28,* 50-57.

Guthiel, T., & Gabbard, G. (1998). Misuses and misunderstandings of boundary theory in clinical and regulatory settings. *American Journal of Psychiatry, 155,* 409-414.

Halpern, D. (2004, May). Hi yo' silver psychologists. *Monitor on Psychology, 35,* 5.

Handelsman, M. (1997). Colorado State Grievance Board sanctions. Cited in M. Handelsman. (2001). Learning to become ethical. In S. Walfish & A. K. Hess (Eds.), *Succeeding in graduate school: The career path for psychology students* (pp. 189-202). Mahwah, NJ: Erlbaum.

Handelsman, M., Knapp, S., & Gottlieb, M. (2002). Positive ethics. In C. R. Snyder & S. Lopez (Eds.), *Handbook of positive psychology* (pp. 731-744). New York: Oxford University Press.

Hansen, N. D., Pepitone-Arreola-Rockwell, F., & Greene, A. (2000). Multicultural competence: Criteria and case examples. *Professional Psychology: Research and Practice, 31,* 652-660 .

Harris, E. (2003, Winter). Resolving some areas of continuing confusion. *MassPsych: The Journal of the Massachusetts Psychological Association, 47,* 18-22, 29.

Harris, E. (2004, Spring/Summer). Some (relatively) simple risk management strategies. *MassPsych: The Journal of the Massachusetts Psychological Association, 48,* 27-28, 32.

Harway, M., & Hansen, M. (2004). *Spouse abuse: Assessing and treating battered women, batters, and their children* (2nd ed.). Sarasota, FL: Professional Resource Press.

Hays, J. R. (1990). Ten questions to ask an attorney before accepting a case. *The Texas Psychologist, 42*(3), 9-10.

Health Insurance Portability and Accountability Act. Public Law 104-191. (1996). Available at www.access.gpo.gov/nara/cfr/index.html

Hellman, I., Morrison, T., & Abramowitz, S. (1986). The stresses of psychotherapeutic work: A replication and extension. *Journal of Clinical Psychology, 42,* 197-205.

Hess, A. (1998). Accepting forensic case referrals: Ethical and professional considerations. *Professional Psychology: Research and Practice, 29,* 109-114.

Holloway, J. D. (2005, January). HIPAA: Safeguarding information. *Monitor on Psychology, 36,* 44.

Jacobson, J., Mulick, J., & Schwartz, A. (1995). A history of facilitated communications. *American Psychologist, 50,* 750-765.

Jaffee v. Redmond. 135 L. Ed. 2d 337 (1996).

Kalb, P. (1999). Health care fraud and abuse. *Journal of the American Medical Association, 282,* 1163-1168.

Karraker v. Rent-a-Center, 395 F. 3rd 786 (7th Cir. 2005).

Kessler, R., Berglund, P., Borges, G., Nock, M., & Wang, P. (2005). Trends in suicide ideation, plans, gestures, and attempts in the United States, 1990-1992 to 2001- 2003. *Journal of the American Medical Association, 293,* 2487-2495.

Kessler, R., Borges, G., & Walters, E. (1999). Prevalence of and risk factors for lifetime suicide attempts in the National Comorbidity Survey. *Archives of General Psychiatry, 56,* 617-626.

Kirkland, K., Kirkland, K. L., & Reaves, R. (2004). On the professional use of disciplinary data. *Professional Psychology: Research and Practice, 35,* 179-184.

Kitchener, K. S. (2000). *Foundations of ethical practice, research, and teaching in psychology.* Mahwah, NJ: Erlbaum.

Kleespies, P., & Dettmer, E. (2000). The stress of patient emergencies for the clinician: Incidence, impact, and means of coping. *Journal of Clinical Psychology, 56,* 1353-1369.

Kleespies, P., Penk, W., & Forsyth, J. (1993). The stress of patient suicidal behavior during clinical training: Incidence, impact, and recovery. *Professional Psychology: Research and Practice, 24,* 293-303.

Knapp, S. (2003, August). Could the Titanic disaster have been avoided? Or promoting patient welfare through a systems approach. *The Pennsylvania Psychologist, 63,* 4, 18, 36.

Knapp, S. (2005, May). Renewal fees for psychologists increase: Board cites rising costs of disciplinary actions. *The Pennsylvania Psychologist, 65,* 9-10.

Knapp, S., & Baturin, R. (2003, March). Child custody and custody-related evaluations and interventions: What every psychologist should know. *The Pennsylvania Psychologist, 63,* 3-4.

Knapp, S., & Keller, P. (2004a, January). Survey reveals stressful events for psychologists. *The Pennsylvania Psychologist, 64,* 6, 8.

Knapp, S., & Keller, P. (2004b, March). What enhances the professional skills of psychologists? *The Pennsylvania Psychologist, 64,* 11.

Knapp, S., & Lemoncelli, J. (2005), Treating children in high-conflict families. *The Pennsylvania Psychologist, 65,* 4.

Knapp, S., & Slattery, J. (2004). Professional boundaries in nontraditional settings. *Professional Psychology: Research and Practice, 35,* 553-558.

Knapp, S., Tepper, A., & Baturin, R. (2003, August). Practical considerations when responding to subpoenas and court orders. *The Pennsylvania Psychologist, 63,* 5, 16.

Knapp, S., & VandeCreek, L. (1987). *Privileged communications in the mental health professions.* New York: Van Nostrand Reinhold.

Knapp, S., & VandeCreek, L. (2003). *A guide to the 2002 revision of the American Psychological Association's ethics code.* Sarasota, FL: Professional Resource Press.

Knapp, S., & VandeCreek, L. (2004). A principle-based analysis of the American

Psychological Association's ethics code. *Psychotherapy: Theory, Research, Practice, Training, 41,* 247-254.

Knapp, S., & VandeCreek, L. (2005). *Practical ethics for psychologists: A positive approach.* Washington, DC: American Psychological Association.

Koocher, G. (2003). Ethical and legal issues in professional practice transitions. *Professional Psychology: Research and Practice, 34,* 383-387.

Krishnamurthy, R., VandeCreek, L., Kaslow, N., Tazeau, Y., Miville, M., Kerns, R., et al. (2004). Achieving competence in psychological assessment: Directions for education and training. *Journal of Clinical Psychology, 60,* 725-739.

Lam, A., & Sue, S. (2001). Client diversity. *Psychotherapy: Theory, Research, Practice, Training, 38,* 479-486.

Lasser, J., & Gottlieb, M. (2004). Treating patients distressed regarding their sexual orientation: Clinical and ethical alternatives. *Professional Psychology: Research and Practice, 35,* 194-200.

Lazarus, A. A. (1989). *Practice of multimodal therapy: Systematic, comprehensive, and effective psychotherapy.* Baltimore: Johns Hopkins University Press.

Lees-Haley, P., & Courtney, J. (2000). Disclosure of tests and raw test data to the courts: A need for reform. *Neuropsychology Review, 10,* 169-174.

Levant, R., Reed, G., Ragusea, S., DiCowden, M., Murphy, M., Sullivan, F., et al. (2001). Envisioning and accessing new roles for professional psychology. *Professional Psychology: Research and Practice, 32,* 79-87.

Levinson, W., Roter, D., Mullooly, J., Dull, V., & Frankel, R. (1997). Physician-patient communication: The relationship with malpractice claims among primary care physicians and surgeons. *Journal of the American Medical Association, 277,* 553-559.

Mahoney, M. (1997). Psychotherapists' personal problems and self-care patterns. *Professional Psychology: Research and Practice, 28,* 14-16.

Malony, H. N. (2000). The psychological evaluation of religious professionals. *Professional Psychology: Research and Practice, 31,* 521-525.

Manning, S. (2005). Dialectical behavior therapy of severe and chronic problems. In L. VandeCreek & T. Jackson (Eds.), *Innovations in clinical practice: Focus on adults* (pp. 97-114). Sarasota, FL: Professional Resource Press.

Mapes, B., & Knapp, S. (2005, December). Ethical and professional issues in assessing sexual offenders. *The Pennsylvania Psychologist, 64,* 3-4.

Maris, R. (1981). *Pathways to suicide: A survey of self-destructive behaviors.* Baltimore: Johns Hopkins University Press.

Monahan, J. (1981). *The clinical prediction of violent behavior.* Washington, DC: U. S. Government Printing Office .

Monahan, J., & Steadman, H. (1996). Violent storms and violent people: How meteorology can inform risk communication in mental health law. *American Psychologist, 51,* 931-938.

Montgomery, L., Cupit, B., & Wimberly, T. (1999). Complaints, malpractice, and risk management: Professional issues and personal experiences. *Professional Psychology: Research and Practice, 30,* 402-410.

Moreland, K., Eyde, L., Robertson, G., Primoff, E., & Most, R. (1995). Assessment of test user qualifications: A research-based measurement procedure. *American Psychologist, 50,* 14-23.

Newman, C. (2005). Reducing the risk of suicide in patients with bipolar disorders: Interventions and safeguards. *Cognitive and Behavioral Practice, 12,* 76-88.

Norko, M., & Baranoski, M. (2005). The state of contemporary risk assessment research. *Canadian Journal of Psychiatry, 50,* 18-26.

Oordt, M., Jobes, D., Rudd, M. D., Fonseca, V., Runyan, C., Stea, J., et al. (2005). Development of a clinical guide to enhance care for suicidal patients. *Professional Psychology: Research and Practice, 36,* 208-218.

Otto, R., & Heilbrun, K. (2002). The practice of forensic psychology: A look toward the future in light of the past. *American Psychologist, 57,* 5-18.

Pachankis, J., & Goldfried, M. (2004). Clinical issues in working with lesbian, gay, and bisexual clients. *Psychotherapy: Theory, Research, Practice, Training , 41,* 227-246.

Paris, J. (2002). Chronic suicidality among patients with borderline personality disorder. *Psychiatric Services, 53,* 738-742.

Paukert, A. (2005). An interview with Patricia Bricklin, Ph.D., Past President of Division 29. *Psychotherapy Bulletin, 40*(2), 12-15.

Peteet, J. (2004). *Doing the right thing: An approach to moral issues in mental health treatment.* Washington, DC: American Psychiatric Publishing.

Pomerantz, A., & Grice, J. (2001). Ethical beliefs of mental health professionals and undergraduates regarding therapist practices. *Journal of Clinical Psychology, 57,* 737-748.

Pope, K., & Brown, I. (1996). *Recovered memories of abuse: Assessment, therapy, forensics.* Washington, DC: American Psychological Association.

Pope, K., & Vasquez, M. (2005). *How to survive and thrive as a therapist: Information, ideas, and resources for psychologists in practice.* Washington, DC: American Psychological Association.

Ragusea, S. (2002). A professional living will for psychologists and other mental health professionals. In L. VandeCreek & T. Jackson (Eds.), *Innovations in clinical practice: A sourcebook* (Vol. 20, pp. 301-305). Sarasota, FL: Professional Resource Press.

Ragusea, A., & VandeCreek, L. (2003). Suggestions for the ethical practice of online psychotherapy. *Psychotherapy: Theory, Research, Practice, Training, 40,* 94-102.

Roberts, L.W. (2000). Evidence-based ethics and informed consent in mental illness research. *Archives of General Psychiatry, 57,* 540-542.

Ronnestad, M. H., & Orlinsky, D. (2005). Therapeutic work and professional development: Findings and practical implications of a long-term international study. *Psychotherapy Bulletin, 40*(2), 27-32 .

Rucker, A., Hite, B., & Hathaway, W. (2005, August 18). *Preliminary practice guidelines for interventions addressing religious/spiritual issues.* Poster session presented at the 113th Annual Convention of the American Psychological Association, Washington, DC.

Rudd, M. D., & Joiner, T. (1999). Assessment of suicidality in outpatient practice. In L. VandeCreek, & T. Jackson (Eds.), *Innovations in clinical practice: A sourcebook* (Vol. 17, pp. 101-117). Sarasota, FL: Professional Resource Press.

Rudd, M. D., Joiner, T., & Rajab, M. H. (1996). Relationships among suicide ideators, attempters, and multiple attempters in a young-adult sample. *Journal of Abnormal Psychology, 105,* 541-550.

Salinsky, J. (1997). Balint groups: History, aims and methods. Retrieved August 28, 2005, from http://familymed.musc.edu/balint/overview.html

Sanderson, C. (2002). Dialectical behavior therapy: A synthesis of acceptance and change in the treatment of borderline personality disorder. In L. VandeCreek & T. Jackson (Eds.), *Innovations in clinical practice: A sourcebook* (Vol. 20, pp. 23-39). Sarasota, FL: Professional Resource Press.

Schernhammer, E. (2005). Taking their own lives-The high rate of physician suicide. *New England Journal of Medicine, 352,* 2473-2476.

Schneider, M. S., Brown, L. S., & Glassgold, J. M. (2002). Implementing the resolution on appropriate therapeutic responses to sexual orientation: A guide for the perplexed. *Professional Psychology: Research and Practice, 33,* 265-276.

Simon, R. (1992). *Clinical psychiatry and the law* (2nd ed.). Washington, DC: American Psychiatric Press.

Simon, R. (2000). Taking the "sue" out of suicide: A forensic psychiatrist's perspective. *Psychiatric Annals, 30,* 399-407.

Steering Committee. (2001). Empirically supported therapy relationships: Conclusions and recommendations of the Division 29 Task Force. *Psychotherapy: Theory, Research, Practice, Training, 38,* 495-497.

Sternberg, R. (2003, March). Responsibility: One of the other three Rs. *Monitor on Psychology, 33,* 5.

Stuart, R. (2004). Twelve practical suggestions for achieving multicultural competence. *Professional Psychology: Research and Practice, 35,* 3-9.

Studdert, D., Mello, M., Sage, W., DesRoches, C., Peugh, J., Zapert, K., & Brennan, T. (2005). Defensive medicine among high-risk specialist physicians in a volatile malpractice environment. *Journal of the American Medical Association, 293,* 2609-2617.

Tarasoff v. Regents of the University of California et al., 551 P. 2d 334 (Cal. S. Ct. 1976).

Tryon, G., & Winograd, G. (2001). Goal consensus and collaboration. *Psychotherapy: Theory, Research, Practice, Training, 38,* 385-389.

Turner, S., DeMers, S., Fox, H. R., & Reed, G. (2001). APA's Guidelines for test user qualifications: An executive summary. *American Psychologist, 56,* 1099-1113.

U.S. Air Force. (n.d.). *Air Force guide for managing suicidal behavior.* Retrieved November 4, 2005, from http://afspp.afms.mil/idc/groups/public/documents/afms/ctb_016017.pdf

U.S. Department of Health and Human Services. (2002, August 14). Standards for Privacy of Individually Identifiable Health Information: Final Rule. *Federal Register, 67,* 53182-53277 .

U.S. Equal Employment Opportunity Commission & U.S. Department of Justice, Civil Rights Division. (2002, May). *Americans With Disabilities Act: Questions and answers.* Washington, DC: Author.

Valenstein, E. (1986). *Great and desperate cures: The rise and decline of psychosurgery and other radical treatments for mental illness.* New York: Basic Books.

VandeCreek, L., & Knapp, S. (2001). *Tarasoff and beyond: Legal and clinical considerations in the treatment of life endangering patients* (3rd ed.). Sarasota, FL: Professional Resource Press.

Van Horne, B. A. (2004). Psychology licensing board disciplinary actions: The realities. *Professional Psychology: Research and Practice, 35,* 170-178.

Woody, R. H. (1997). *Legally safe mental health practice: Psycholegal questions and answers.* Madison, CT: Psychosocial Press.

Wunsch, M. (2005). Guidelines for employment and practice building. In L. VandeCreek & T. Jackson (Eds.), *Innovations in clinical practice: Focus on adults* (pp. 135-152). Sarasota, FL: Professional Resource Press.

Yen, S., Pagano, M., Shea, M. T., Grilo, C., Gunderson, J., Skodol, A., et al. (2005). Recent life events preceding suicide attempts in a personality disorder sample: Findings from the collaborative longitudinal personality disorders study. *Journal of Consulting and Clinical Psychology, 73,* 99-105.

INDEX

APA Practice Organization (APAPO),
  58, 115, 125
APA record keeping guidelines, 46, 216
application, Bloom's taxonomy and,
  8, 9, 36, 44, 50
arbitration, 101
ASPPB. *See* Association of State and
  Provincial Psychology Boards
assertiveness, 41
assessment, 143–177
  diagnosis and, 144–145, 162
  DSM IV diagnosis, treatment plan,
    and suicide risk, 162
  management, treatment and, of
    patients at risk for suicide,
    155–171, 172, 173, 174, 177
  minister rehabilitation and, 149
  risk management and maximizing
    patient involvement in, 144
  sexual offenders risk, 149–152
  and testing for bariatric surgery,
    146, 148
assessment-based practices, retirement
  and, 215
Association for the Advancement of
  Psychology, 58
Association of State and Provincial
  Psychology Boards (ASPPB), 17,
  20, 21, 106
Association of State and Provincial
    Psychology Boards (ASPPB)
    Code of Conduct
  licensing boards and, 17
assurance behaviors, 57–58
attorneys, 98, 100, 110, 111, 112, 130,
  131, 132, 135, 137, 138–139,
  181, 183
  access to psychological test
    data/materials, 122, 123, 125
  cooperating with, 136
  forensic services when working
    for, 121
  mental health, 110
autonomy, patient, 32, 34, 164, 165, 193
  informed consent and, 82
avoidance behaviors, 58

B

Balint groups, 65
bariatric surgery assessment and

testing, 146, 148
barter for services, 205–206
BASIC ID, 55–56
Beahrs, J., 34
Beck Hopelessness Scale, 162
Belar, C., 69
beneficence, 32, 34, 58, 164, 193
Berglund, P., 159
billing issues, 38, 96, 204–207, 206
  collection agencies and, 207, 210
  community agency director,
    ethics and, 188, 190
  with couples' insurance, 204–205
  for forensic services, 137–138
  insurance and, 204–205, 207
  insurance companies and, 207
  managed care organizations
    and, 207
  nontherapeutic time demands
    and, 97
bipolar disorder (BPD), 167, 168
Bloom's Educational Taxonomy. *See*
  Bloom's taxonomy
Bloom's taxonomy, 6–9, 39, 58, 82,
  153, 169, 238
  analysis and, 8, 9, 36, 44, 50
  competence and, 62
  consultation and, 50
  documentation and, 43
  higher and lower levels of, 8–9
  informed consent and, 36, 93
  moral principles and, 32
  moving into new practice areas
    and, 70
  new risk management model
    and, 7–8
Bongar, B., 55
borderline personality disorder, 27,
  56. *See also* Cluster B personality
  disorders; personality disorder(s)
Borges, G., 159
boundaries
  context and, 78–80
  crossing by supervisee
    warned against, 183
  crossings v. boundary
    violations, 77, 87
  decisions and psychotherapy
    relationships, 80
  establishment with angry

Winograd, G., 34
wisdom, Sternberg on, 6
witnesses
    expert, 134, 139–140, 141
    fact, 134, 141
witness fee, 136–137
worst-case scenario, envisioning, 11, 28

Y

Young, E., 160

AUTHOR BIOGRAPHIES

Bruce E. Bennett, Ph.D.

Dr. Bennett, the Chief Executive Officer of the APA Insurance Trust, has served on the APA Council of Representatives and is a former member of the APA Board of Directors. He was instrumental in the drafting and passing the 1992 APA Ethics Code and served on the APA Committee to revise the Ethics Code in 2002. Dr. Bennett, a past president and Executive Director of the Illinois Psychological Association, maintained an active private practice in Illinois in addition to teaching courses on professional issues. His areas of expertise include professional liability and risk management, marketing and promotion of psychological services, and ethics. Dr. Bennett co-authored the APA monographs "Professional Liability and Risk Management" and "Ethics of Psychologists: A Commentary on the APA Ethics Code," and has served on committees of the APA, the American Bar Association, and the Illinois State Bar Association.

Patricia M. Bricklin, Ph.D.

Patricia M. Bricklin, Ph.D. is a Professor at Widener University, Chester, PA and partner in Bricklin Associates, an independent psychological practice. She is also Chair of the Pennsylvania State Board of Psychology and Consultant to the APA Insurance Trust. Dr. Bricklin focuses on ethics, legal and regulatory issues in professional practice and conducts classes, workshops and writes articles and books. Dr. Bricklin has also received national and state awards and reserved two honorary doctoral degrees for her work in these areas.

Eric Harris, J.D., Ed.D.

Dr. Harris, a licensed psychologist and attorney, is a Risk Management Consultant for the APA Insurance Trust, the legal counsel to the Massachusetts Psychological Association, and a faculty member at the Massachusetts School of Professional Psychology. Dr. Harris served on the APA Committee for the Advancement of Professional Practice (CAPP) and two terms on the APA Committee on Legal Issues. In the fifteen years before Dr. Harris became a consultant to APAIT, he conducted a part-time clinical psychology practice. Dr. Harris has written, consulted and lectured extensively on risk management, legal issues and on managed care.

Samuel Knapp, Ed.D.

Samuel Knapp, Ed.D., has been the Director of Professional Affairs for the Pennsylvania Psychological Association since 1986. His major interests include legal and ethical issues related to professional practice. Dr. Knapp has made numerous professional presentations and has written more than 100 peer reviewed articles and book chapters as well as several books.

Leon VandeCreek, Ph.D.

Leon VandeCreek earned his Ph.D. in clinical psychology from the University of South Dakota. He is currently a professor with the School of Professional Psychology at Wright State University. His professional interests are in professional issues and risk management, professional liability, and licensure. Dr. VandeCreek teaches doctoral courses in psychological assessment and ethics.

Jeffrey N. Younggren, Ph.D.

Jeffrey N. Younggren, a Fellow of the American Psychological Association, is a clinical and forensic psychologist who practices in Rolling Hills Estates, California. He is an associate clinical professor at the University of California, Los Angeles, School of Medicine and a Risk Management Consultant for the APA Insurance Trust. Dr. Younggren served as a member and chair of the Ethics Committees of the California Psychological Association and the American Psychological Association.